Routledge Revival

The Earth Sciences

Originally published in 1983, *The Earth Sciences: An Annotated Bibliography* is a compact and thematically organized guide that provides comprehensive access to themes and areas of study in the earth sciences. The bibliography is not exhaustive but provides a detailed and critical index to the most important literature in the field. The book's core focus is geology and examines the subject broadly, covering everything from glaciology, geomorphology, natural history and palaeontology, to oceanography, mapping, stratigraphy and evolution. The book provides detailed essays for each bibliographical chapter on the state of each field of research and the literature compiled for each bibliography will go as far back as around 1700 and contains a wide range of sources from across the world. This book will be of interest to academics and students of natural history, geology, and environmental sciences alike.

The Earth Sciences
An Annotated Bibliography

by Roy Porter

First published in 1983
by Garland Publishing, Inc.

This edition first published in 2019 by Routledge
2 Park Square, Milton Park, Abingdon, Oxon, OX14 4RN
and by Routledge
711 Third Avenue, New York, NY 10017

Routledge is an imprint of the Taylor & Francis Group, an informa business

© 1983 Roy Porter

All rights reserved. No part of this book may be reprinted or reproduced or utilised in any form or by any electronic, mechanical, or other means, now known or hereafter invented, including photocopying and recording, or in any information storage or retrieval system, without permission in writing from the publishers.

Publisher's Note
The publisher has gone to great lengths to ensure the quality of this reprint but points out that some imperfections in the original copies may be apparent.

Disclaimer
The publisher has made every effort to trace copyright holders and welcomes correspondence from those they have been unable to contact.

A Library of Congress record exists under LCCN: 81043367

ISBN 13: 978-0-367-35819-8 (hbk)
ISBN 13: 978-0-429-34211-0 (ebk)
ISBN 13: 978-0-367-35823-5 (pbk)

THE EARTH SCIENCES

BIBLIOGRAPHIES OF THE HISTORY
OF SCIENCE AND TECHNOLOGY
(Vol. 3)

GARLAND REFERENCE LIBRARY
OF THE HUMANITIES
(VOL. 315)

Volume 3

Bibliographies of the History of Science and Technology

Editors

Robert Multhauf
Smithsonian Institution, Washington, D.C.

Ellen Wells
Smithsonian Institution, Washington, D.C.

THE EARTH SCIENCES
An Annotated Bibliography

Roy Porter

GARLAND PUBLISHING, INC. • NEW YORK & LONDON
1983

© 1983 Roy Porter
All rights reserved

Library of Congress Cataloging in Publication Data
Porter, Roy, 1946–
  The earth sciences.
  (Bibliographies of the history of science and technology ; v. 3)
  (Garland reference library of the humanities ; v. 315)
  Includes index.
  1. Earth sciences—Bibliography. I. Title.
  II. Series. III. Series: Garland reference library of the humanities ; v. 315.
  Z6031.P67   1983   [QE26.2]   016.55   81-43367
  ISBN 0-8240-9267-8

Printed on acid-free, 250-year-life paper
Manufactured in the United States of America

TO JACK

GENERAL INTRODUCTION

This bibliography is one of a series designed to guide the reader into the history of science and technology. Anyone interested in any of the components of this vast subject area is part of our intended audience, not only the student, but also the scientist interested in the history of his own field (or faced with the necessity of writing an "historical introduction") and the historian, amateur or professional. The latter will not find the bibliographies "exhaustive," although in some fields he may find them the only existing bibliographies. He will in any case not find one of those endless lists in which the important is lumped with the trivial, but rather a "critical" bibliography, largely annotated, and indexed to lead the reader quickly to the most important (or only existing) literature.

Inasmuch as everyone treasures bibliographies, it is surprising how few there are in this field. Justly treasured are George Sarton's *Guide to the History of Science* (Waltham, Mass., 1952; 316 pp.), Eugene S. Ferguson's *Bibliography of the History of Technology* (Cambridge, Mass., 1968; 347 pp.), François Russo's *Histoire des Sciences et des Techniques. Bibliographie* (Paris, 2nd ed., 1969; 214 pp.), and Magda Whitrow's *ISIS Cumulative Bibliography. A bibliography of the history of science* (London, 1971–; 2131 pp. as of 1976). But all are limited, even the latter, by the virtual impossibility of doing justice to any particular field in a bibliography of limited size and almost unlimited subject matter.

For various reasons, mostly bad, the average scholar prefers adding to the literature, rather than sorting it out. The editors are indebted to the scholars represented in this series for their willingness to expend the time and effort required to pursue the latter objective. Our aim has been to establish a general framework which will give some uniformity to the series, but otherwise to leave the format and contents to the author/compiler. We have urged that introductions be used for essays on "the state of the field," and that selectivity be exercised to limit the length of each volume to the economically practical.

Since the historical literature ranges from very large (e.g., medicine) to very small (chemical technology), some bibliographies will be limited to the most important writings while others will include modest "contributions" and even primary sources. The problem is to give useful guidance into a particular field—or subfield—and its solution is largely left to the author/compiler.

In general, topical volumes (e.g., chemistry) will deal with the subject since about 1700, leaving earlier literature to area or chronological volumes (e.g., medieval science); but here, too, the volumes will vary according to the judgment of the author. The topics are international, with a few exceptions (Greece and Rome, Eastern Asia, the United States), but the literature covered depends, of course, on the linguistic equipment of the author and his access to "exotic" literatures.

Robert Multhauf
Ellen Wells

Smithsonian Institution
Washington, D.C.

CONTENTS

Introduction xi
Acknowledgments xix

1. Bibliography and Reference Works 3

2. General Histories
   A. Histories of Science 9
   B. Histories of Geology 10

3. Specialist Histories
   A. Geological Philosophies and Methods 19
   B. Stratigraphy, Structural Geology and Petrology 23
   C. Geomorphology 26
   D. Palaeontology 29
   E. Geology and Evolution 35
   F. Geology and Human Origins 37
   G. Earthquakes and Volcanoes 39
   H. Time and Historical Geology 40
   I. Mineralogy 43
   J. Glacial Geology 46
   K. Continental Drift and Plate Tectonics 48
   L. Mapping 50
   M. Practical Geology 53
   N. Chemical Geology 55

4. Cognate Sciences
   A. Geophysics 57
   B. Geography 58
   C. Oceanography 59
   D. Natural History 61
   E. Crystallography and Metallography 64

5. Studies by Area
   A. Britain   67
   B. United States   71
   C. Other, in Alphabetical Order by Country
      or Continent   76

6. Biographical Studies   85

7. Institutional Histories   147

8. The Social Dimension   157

9. Geology and Religion   161

10. Geology, Culture and the Arts   165

   Index   171

INTRODUCTION

The great geologists of the last century made history with their discovery of the secrets of the rocks, and they also wrote history. Some of these histories of geology—in the English language, the first few chapters of Charles Lyell's *Principles of Geology* (item 54) and Archibald Geikie's *Founders of Geology* (item 41) stand out—have proved lasting testaments of genius. They encompass a broad and confident vision of science's role in human destiny; they are geologically expert, they project a committed sense of the advancement of geology, they create a vivid feel for personality, and, not least, they are written in a graceful style which wears its learning easily and remains a joy to read.

Such masterpieces long exercised a hypnotic power, influential down to the present in the summary histories of geology still found at the beginning of geological textbooks. This has, however, proved a mixed blessing.

The great nineteenth-century geologist-historians had all the vices as well as the virtues of Victorian ("Whig") historians. Their accounts saw the history of the science essentially as the biographies of great men, comprising chronological pen portraits of the giants of geology. They saw the progress of their science arising out of jousts between heroes and villains, right and wrong doctrines, the true being based on Baconian empiricism, observation and fieldwork, the false being a tissue of speculation, polluted by metaphysics and theology. Fortunately, truth ultimately prevailed, and so the chronicle of geology could be penned as the unfolding pageant of progress leading up to the present, and beyond. Individual episodes and chapters in the history of geology formed moral vignettes: e.g., the life of William Smith showed the rewards of self-help, that of William Buckland the damage of unwisely mingling science and scripture. The history of the science, taken as a whole, was conscripted into the intellectual artillery of the geologist-historian in question, in Lyell's case, battling for Uniformitarianism, in Geikie's, for Plutonism.

Historical outlooks derived from these and other nineteenth-century syntheses such as Humboldt's (item 49), Whewell's (item 29) and Zittel's (item 74) continued to hold sway in the first half of this century, and the history of geology rather fell into the doldrums. This was partly because geology itself fell into the doldrums (history of geology being largely auxiliary to geology, conventional geology meant conventional history), and partly because the newly emerged professional historians of science tended to ignore the Earth sciences, concentrating their attentions on the spectacular intellectual transformations in the astrophysical sciences which occurred in the "Scientific Revolution" of the Early Modern period.

Since the Second World War, however, the study of the history of geology has been revitalized (due partly, over the last twenty years, to the ferment within geology itself, associated with Continental Drift, Plate Tectonics, the new "Catastrophism" and continuing debates over the mechanisms of biological evolution). Much of the credit for this must go to the enthusiasm, tireless activity and meticulous scholarship of geologists such as Joan and Victor Eyles, Hugh Torrens and John Challinor in Britain, and George White in America, who have quarried archives, built up libraries and rediscovered collections, publishing scores of biobibliographical studies, vastly consolidating our trustworthy knowledge of the lives and publications of hundreds of geologists, great and small. These labors have been augmented and capped by the publication of research guides, bibliographies and other scholarly aids, most recently and authoritatively W.A.S Sarjeant's five-volume *Geologists and the History of Geology* (item 20), which facilitate and expedite the work of student and scholar alike and have done much to lay the old mythological ghosts, errors and half truths which long haunted publications in this field.

Such studies have brought to attention archival riches, and, partly as a result, valuable works have appeared over the last generation tapping the resources of hitherto unused manuscript collections. These include a number of biographies on the grand

Introduction

scale, such as Leonard Wilson's account of Charles Lyell (item 587: only the first of a projected three volumes has yet appeared). Biographies of this kind are particularly welcome when their subjects are geologists who died within the last century, after the tradition of the lavish commemorative two-volume life and letters had become extinct. But there has also been a proliferation of archivally based, shorter, thematic studies, stimulated by the growth of doctoral research and appearing in the large number of newly founded journals in the history of science.

Above all, over the last thirty years the history of geology has become distanced from geology. So many of the issues which electrified and polarized geologists chronicling the history of their subject in the last century—the relation between Genesis and geology, between miracles and natural law, or the age of the Earth—can now be treated dispassionately, as objects of mere, but genuine, historical interest (though some controversial topics, such as the history of Catastrophism, still arouse passions). This is the more so as today many historians of geology are not geologists, with heresies to uncover and precedents to seek within their own discipline, but historians, who profess to be interested in the past for its own sake, wanting to find out how it really happened. The great transformation in the history of geology over the last generation has been the decline of canonizing and anathematizing history, of interest in who played on the winning side; and the corresponding rise of a historical approach concerned mainly with understanding the ideas and labors of past geologists on their own terms, recapturing the fine texture of the controversies they engaged in, reconstructing their outlooks, beliefs and scientific methodologies—in short, getting under their skin. Studies of this kind have revealed the richer affinities of geological ideas. Traditional historiography, for example, presented Uniformitarianism as simply scientific method applied to geology, whereas Catastrophism was science defiled with theology and ignorance; or saw Neptunism as an *a priori* theoretical prejudice, whereas Plutonism was an induction from fieldwork. New explorations of the wider intellectual horizons of geologists have revealed, however, that Uniformitarianism and Plutonism (to name but two "winning" doctrines) were themselves backed by philosophical, metaphysical and theological commitments. The writings of Gordon Davies (e.g., item 119) and Martin Rudwick (e.g., item 152), themselves geologists, have shown that the histories of geomorphology and palaeontology (and not just their *pre-histories*) must take into account the continuing role of wider intellectual beliefs.

Complementing this attempt to explore sympathetically the minds of individual geologists, there have been other major shifts of focus in the study of the growth of geology. One has been the renewed awareness—stimulated by the growth of "discipline history"—that geology as an organized, connected science called by that name is not yet two hundred years old. This has led to interest in the relationships between the sciences—in boundaries and bridges, diffusion, transmission and permeation, in cognitive dominion and imperialism—issuing, for instance, in studies of the rivalry between geologists and physicists in mid-Victorian times as to who would be the authority on the age of the Earth (185). But, more broadly, and stimulated by the environmentalist movements of the 1960s and 1970s, this awareness has helped show that geology is only one of many possible scientific approaches to the study of the Earth's crust, and has drawn attention back to the wider disciplinary matrices of natural history, natural theology and the natural philosophy of the terraqueous globe out of which it was constructed.

Another new perspective has been a shift toward a more socially focused history of geology. For some, this has meant investigating how material interests and everyday concerns shape scientific concepts (the social history of ideas): thus it has been suggested that G.P. Scrope, political economist as well as geologist, developed his particular ideas about geological time because of the way he thought about money (see item 641). But the impact of sociology has also nourished studies of the background, education and training of geologists, their ties and contacts, formal and informal, their research networks. There has of course been a long-standing tradition of celebratory official institutional history, accounts of societies, mining schools and national surveys, but this has been supplemented of late by more "Namierite" explorations of the internal dynamics and personal politics of these bodies (see, e.g., items 726, 741, 753).

Introduction

Much has been done, not least—as many of the works listed in Section 3A of this book, "Geological Philosophies and Methods," reveal—in bringing into the open for the first time the deep and genuine differences of opinion—methodological, ideological, historiographical—as to how the history of geology ought to be written, how far it should be about men or about movements, about facts or about theories, how far texts speak for themselves or need to have their meaning read into, or out of, them.

Much has been done; but more remains to be done. Perhaps surprisingly, even mainstream aspects of the practice of geology lack adequate connected synthetic treatment. There is no substantial history of geological mapping, no book examining the growth of visual representation in geology; there is not even a published history of the development of geological fieldwork. Mounds of field notebooks from the eighteenth and nineteenth centuries lie in archives waiting to be investigated. There is no history, even, of an institution so important as the Freiberg Mining Academy. While the history of geology in Britain, Germany and the United States is being eagerly researched, the story of the development of the science in such major centers as France and Italy lacks—with honorable exceptions—serious students (there is no modern history of French or Italian geology). Sadly also, few scholars today feel equipped to treat the history of geology on an international basis, or to undertake comparative studies of national traditions.

Certain periods remain neglected. Thematic treatments of geology since the 1870s are few and far between. If the early years of the nineteenth century were the heroic age of geology, and the middle third its golden age, the generations after the death of such figures as Humboldt, Von Buch, Lyell, Sedgwick and Murchison constitute a new dark age. Hardly any wide-ranging account exists of twentieth-century developments before the reviving fortunes of Continental Drift theory in the 1960s boosted by Plate Tectonics enlivens the story, posing the theoretical issue: does Plate Tectonics constitute a Kuhnian revolution in geology? (see Section 3K). Similarly, for Renaissance and seventeenth-century geology, we are still dependent (with the exception of certain scholarly articles, such as Roger's, item

62) on Adams's treatment (item 31), now almost fifty years old—a situation little likely to improve, as reading skills in Latin decline.

Away from the great tradition of charting advances in stratigraphy, palaeontology and geomorphology, the gaps loom even larger. Surprisingly, the relations between geology and the rise of industrialization remain little explored, despite Hall (item 45), and the key theme of the links between political and military imperialism, geological surveying and extractive industry in the Third World awaits a synthesizing historian (outside Europe and North America, there are to date few truly historical accounts of national geological surveys). And while the historical relations between geology and religion have been more coolly and therefore more fruitfully investigated of late, geology's connections with the visual arts, literature and aesthetics, and its general public standing, remain—despite noble exceptions such as Nicolson (item 799)—almost *terra incognita*. Geological prosopography—the study of collective biography—is another area where work has hardly begun. Major aspects of the social dimensions of geology—matters such as career structure, professionalization and remuneration—still await broad and, above all, comparative treatment.

But the last generation has seen important progress, not least in providing firm foundations of biographical data, bibliographical aids and works of reference to build on in the future. This present bibliography aims to be a brick in this foundation. It makes no pretence to completeness: the existence of W.A.S Sarjeant's encyclopedic five-volume bibliography, *Geologists and the History of Geology* (item 20), published in 1980, makes clear that the present book can be intended only as a practical working guide rather than as a definitive and exhaustive reference work. I have attempted to include those items which in my judgment will be of most use to the majority of English-speaking scholars and students interested in the mainstream of the history of geology. In my selection there is a bias toward the great age of the growth of geology, from about the mid-eighteenth century to the last third of the nineteenth; and toward the work of geologists of the chief Western languages (though both biases also reflect the state of the literature). I have doubtless omitted much through ignorance and inadvertence, but I have also followed a policy of

Introduction xvii

generally omitting items in languages which I do not read. Thus, I have essentially confined myself to works in English, French, German, Latin, Italian, and Spanish. I have provided descriptive and analytic comments on most entries, but have omitted these either when the title of a work is adequately self-explanatory or when, as in some cases, I have not had access to the item.

I have taken the history of geology in a broad sense, to include a wide range of scientific inquiries into the nature and history of the Earth. "Geology" as an organized discipline is but two hundred years old, and it is unwise and anachronistic to distinguish its history too rigidly from the development of cognate disciplines such as mineralogy, geography and crystallography. I have included brief sections on disciplines such as geophysics and natural history since their connections with geology were historically close and important. I have also included items exploring the social causes and consequences of geological inquiry (especially economic and applied geology). Historians of science have been taking the cultural milieu of the investigation of Nature more seriously over the last decades, and this is beginning to show in the scholarship in this field, as it always has shown in scholarly interest in the historical relations between geology and religion.

I have chosen not to list here standard histories of science in general, such as A.R. Hall's *The Scientific Revolution*, even when they include discussions of the development of geology. I have also omitted unpublished works such as Ph.D dissertations: these are already well indexed and abstracted in publications such as *Dissertation Abstracts International*. I have also not listed general bibliographical guides to the history of science, such as the *Dictionary of Scientific Biography* or the *Isis Cumulative Bibliography*, though obviously these should be consulted. The reader wanting an up-to-date guide to general histories of science, works of reference and bibliographical aids may be referred to P. Durbin (ed.), *A Guide to the Culture of Science, Technology and Medicine* (Free Press, New York, 1980); the *Dictionary of the History of Science*, ed. W.F. Bynum, E.J. Browne and Roy Porter (Macmillan, London, and Princeton University Press, Princeton, N.J., 1981) gives brief historical accounts of relevant scientific concepts.

In a compact and thematically organized guide such as this, it has not been thought necessary to provide detailed cross-referencing, and each item appears only once. Hence the reader, not finding references in a specific section, is advised to consult related sections (e.g., some entries on the history of geology in a particular nation appear under "5. Studies by Area," but further relevant items will be found under "7. Institutional Histories"). The Index provides comprehensive access (keyed to item number) to authors, to geologists mentioned, and to major departments and themes in the history of geology (e.g., Geosynclines, Stratigraphy).

Wellcome Institute for the
History of Medicine
London
June 1981

ACKNOWLEDGMENTS

The appearance of W.A.S. Sarjeant's *Geologists and the History of Geology* when this work was but partly under way immensely expedited the task of tracking down references. It is a magnificent work of scholarship and should be consulted by anyone seriously interested in the fine texture of the history of geology. I gratefully acknowledge my debts to it. Friends and colleagues too numerous to name also contributed many helpful suggestions for entries. Verna Cole, Rosemary Jenkins and Tracy Saul performed wonders in the arduous task of typing the manuscript, and I wish to thank Frieda Houser in particular for taking on her shoulders so much of the business of organizing the completion of this work and compiling much of the index.

June 1981

VIEW OF THE TEMPLE OF SERAPIS AT PUZZUOLI, IN 1836.

The Temple of Serapis at Puzzuoli in 1836 from Charles Lyell, *Principles of Geology*, Frontispiece to ninth edition, London, 1853.

The evidence of changing water lines on the pillars of the temple was used by Lyell to demonstrate shifts in the relative levels of land and sea.

Graphic depiction of the stages of the Earth from Creation to Parousia from T. Burnet, *The Theory of the Earth*, 2nd edition, London, R. Norton for W. Kettilby, 1691, Frontispiece.

Burnet's theory postulated seven separate stages for the Earth, from its initial creation (top right) as matter in motion to its final destiny as a star. The Earth was currently in mid-course.

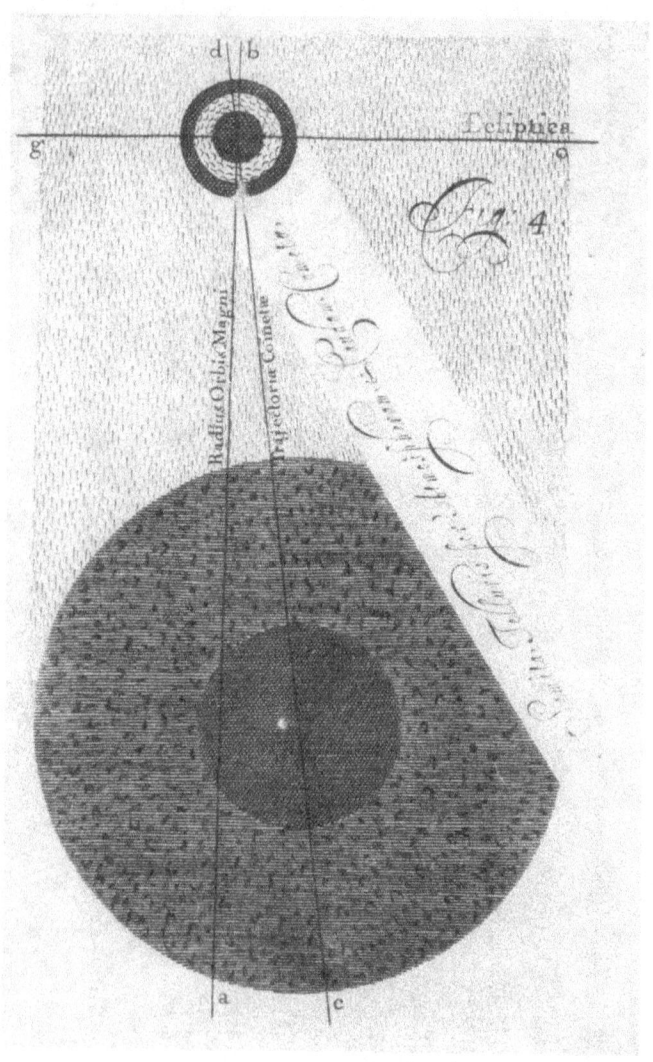

The explanation of Noah's Deluge from W. Whiston, *New Theory of the Earth*, London, 1696, Fig. 4.

Whiston sought to demonstrate that Noah's Flood was actually the immersion of the Earth in the tail of a comet which had passed nearby.

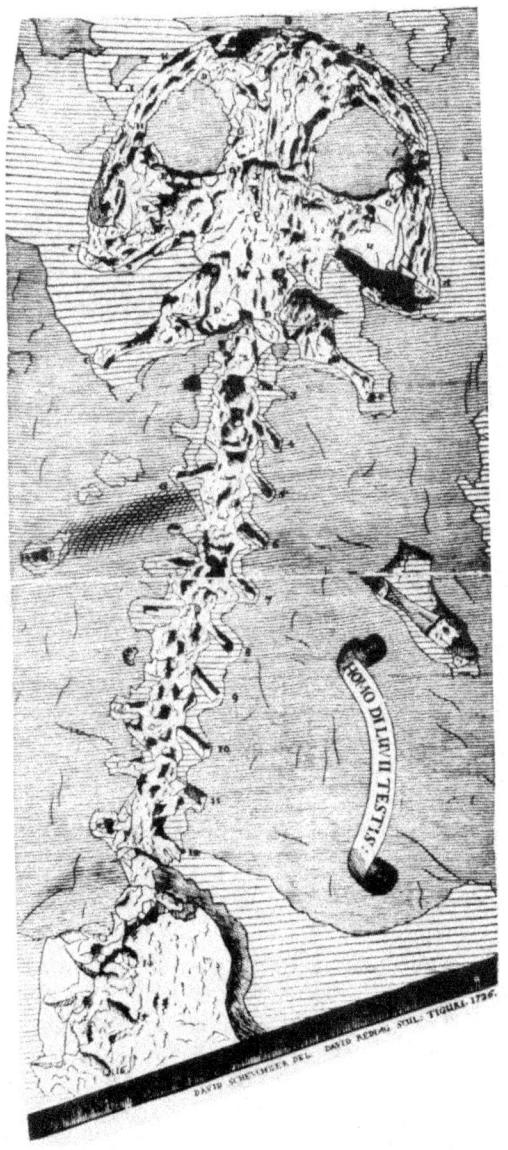

"Homo diluvii testis" from C. J. Schneer, ed., *Toward a History of Geology*, Cambridge, Mass., 1969, p. 192.

J. J. Scheuchzer claimed in his *Physica sacra* (1731) that these were the fossil remains of a man who had been drowned in Noah's Flood. Later investigators identified the fossil as a giant salamander.

"Awful changes" reproduced from R. J. Chorley et al., *The History of the Study of Landforms*, vol. I, London, Methuen, 1964, p. 104, Fig. 22.

A cartoon by Henry de la Beche lampooning the Lyellian doctrine of the eventual repetition of all geological conditions. The captions read (top) "Man only found in a fossil state—Reappearance of Ichthyosauri"; " 'A change came o'er the spirit of my dream'—Byron"; (bottom) "A lecture— 'You will at once perceive,' continued Professor Ichthyosaurus, 'that the skull before us belonged to some of the lower order of animals the teeth are very insignificant the power of the jaws trifling and altogether it seems wonderful how the creature could have procured food.' "

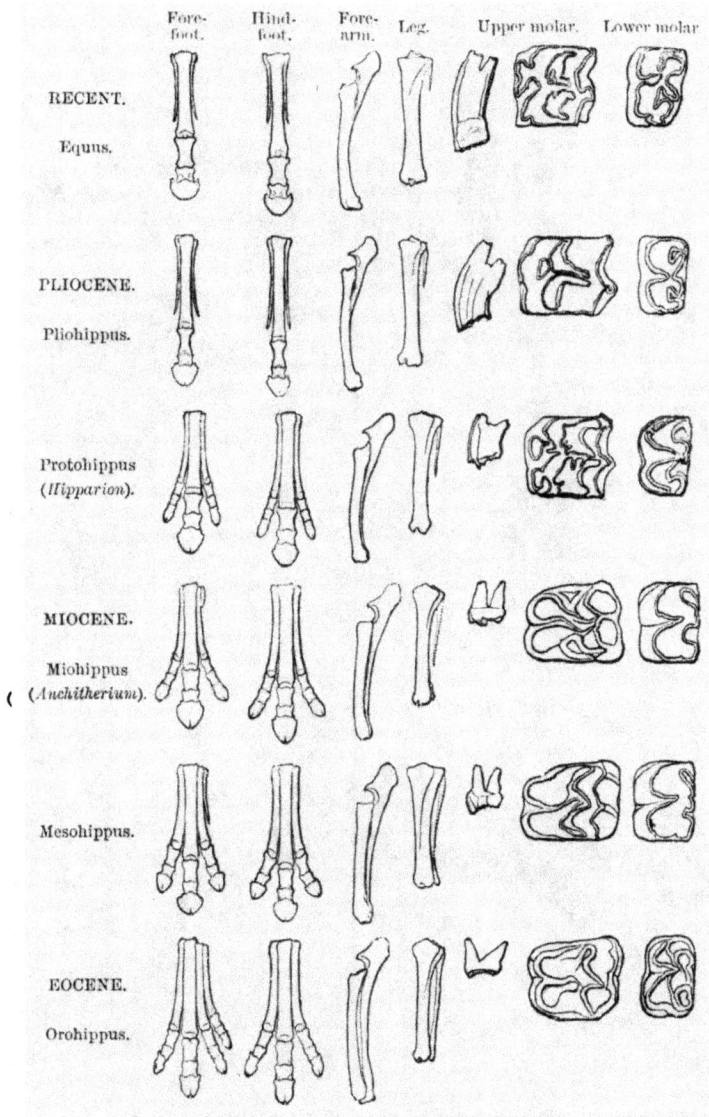

Fig. 33.—Geological development of the horse tribe (Eohippus since discovered).

Geological development of the horse tribe from A. R. Wallace, *Darwinism*, London, 1889, Fig. 33, p. 388.

Extensive fossil finds in America in the latter part of the nineteenth century permitted the historical reconstruction of the horse to be seen as strong evidence in favour of biological evolution.

The Megatherium from W. Buckland, *Bridgewater Treatise: Geology and Mineralogy Considered with Relation to Natural Theology*, 2 vols, London, 1836, Fig. I facing p. 110.

The megatherium (i.e., "huge beast") was one of the early extinct quadrupeds to be reconstructed by Georges Cuvier. He demonstrated it to be related to the sloths although it was rhinoceros-sized.

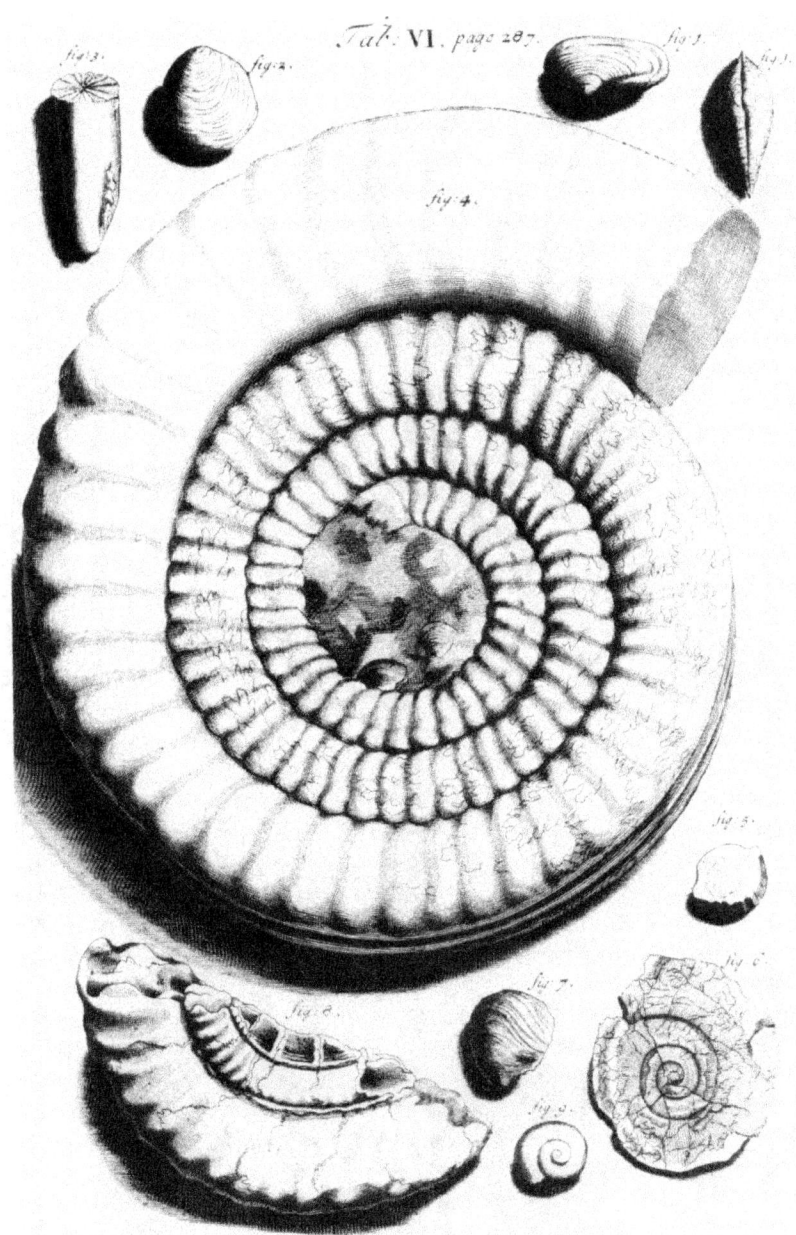

Ammonites and other fossils from *The Posthumous Works of Robert Hooke* (London, 1705).

Hooke was a leading late seventeenth-century advocate of the view that fossils were genuine organic remains. The broken and fractured nature of many specimens appeared to him confirmatory evidence.

Duria Antiquior, or Ancient Dorsetshire, from P. J. McCartney, *Henry de la Beche: Observations on an Observer*, Cardiff, National Museum of Wales, 1977, p. 45.
De la Beche's attempt to reconstruct the fauna and flora of the Liassic period.

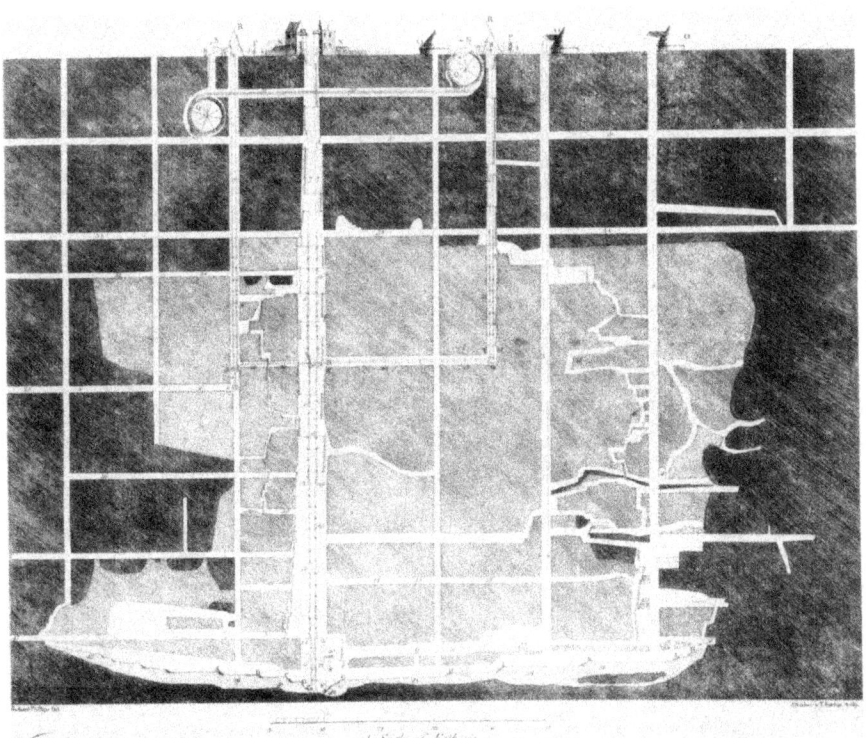

Bullen Garden Mine from William Pryce, *Mineralogia Cornubiensis*, London, 1778, plate IV, facing p. 172.

An example of an eighteenth-century Cornish metal mine section. Note the water wheel for drainage at Q, and the "fire engines" (i.e., Newcomen steam pumps) at N.

Columns of hexagonal basalt from R. E. Raspe, *An Introduction to the Natural History of the Terrestrial Sphere*, trans by A. N. Iversen and A. V. Carozzi, New York, Hafner, 1970, p. xlii, Fig. 5, originally published in 1763.

Raspe was a pioneer of the "vulcanist" position, which argued for the igneous origin of basaltic formations and their association in the Earth's history with volcanic activity.

Terrace canyons of the Colorado River reproduced from R. J. Chorley et al., *The History of the Study of Landforms*, vol. I, London, Methuen, 1964, p. 526, Fig. 108.
   A classic illustration of fluvial erosion, from J. W. Powell's "Exploration of the Colorado River of the West," Washington, 1875.

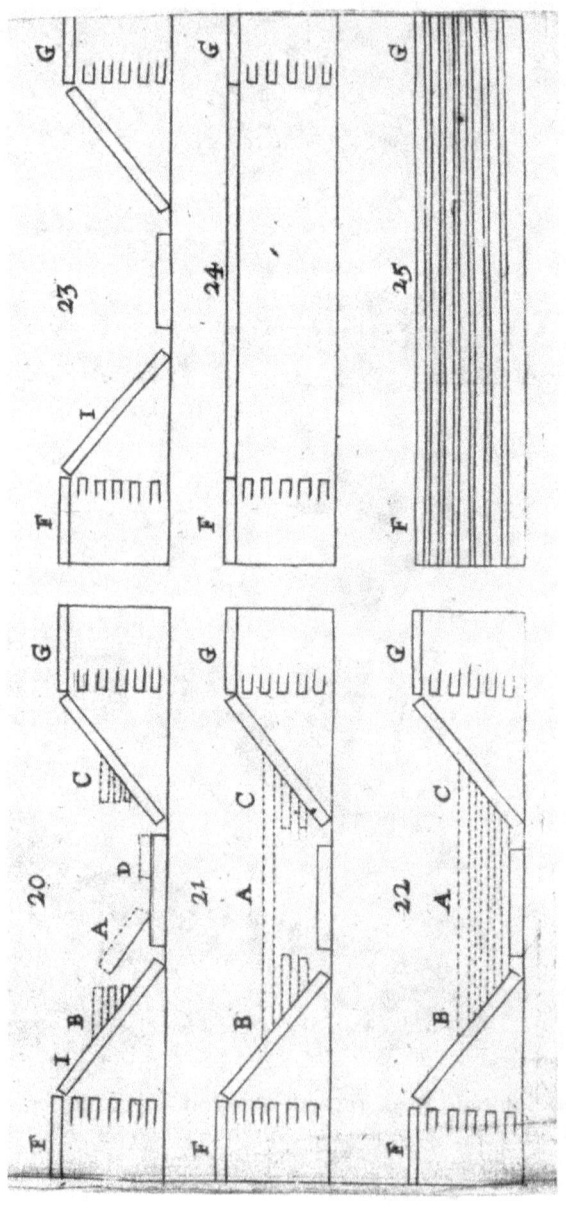

The formation of fossil-bearing strata from N. Steno, *The Prodromus to a Dissertation Concerning Solids Naturally Contained Within Solids*. London, J. Winter, 1671, Figs. 20–25. Steno believed that the order of the strata had been laid down over time, sedimented out of an aqueous fluid and embodying organic remains. Occasional crustal collapses account for diversities of topography.

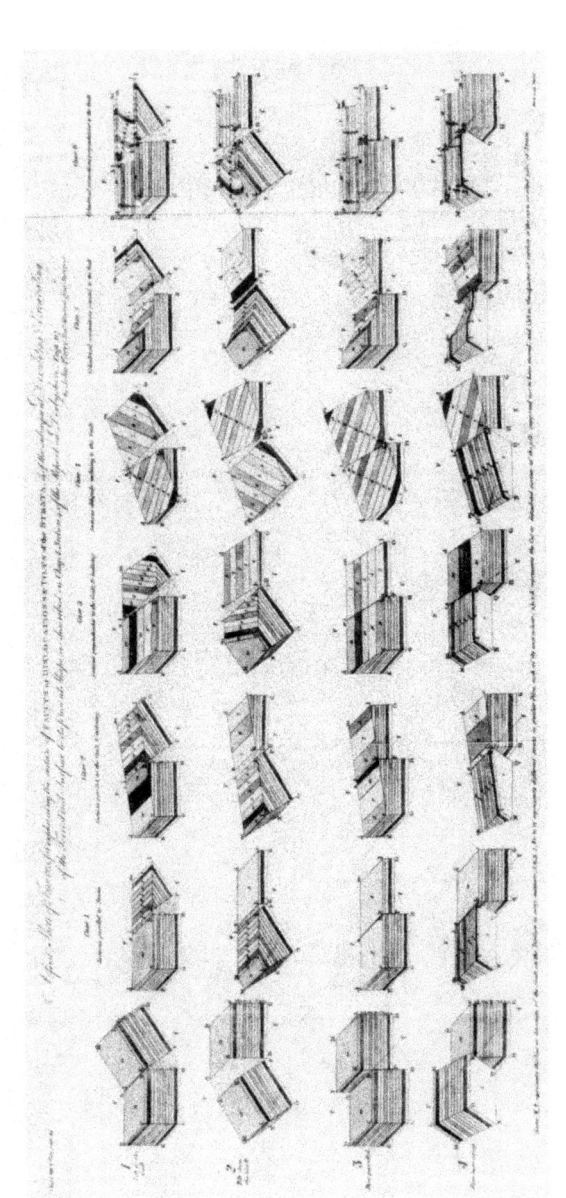

Block diagrams illustrating faulting from J. Farey, *General view of the agriculture and minerals of Derbyshire*, 3 vols, London, 1811–1815, vol. II, Plate III facing p. 113.

Farey's were amongst the earliest three-dimensional geometrical structural diagrams, illustrating the varieties of faulting, folding, dislocation, and tilting.

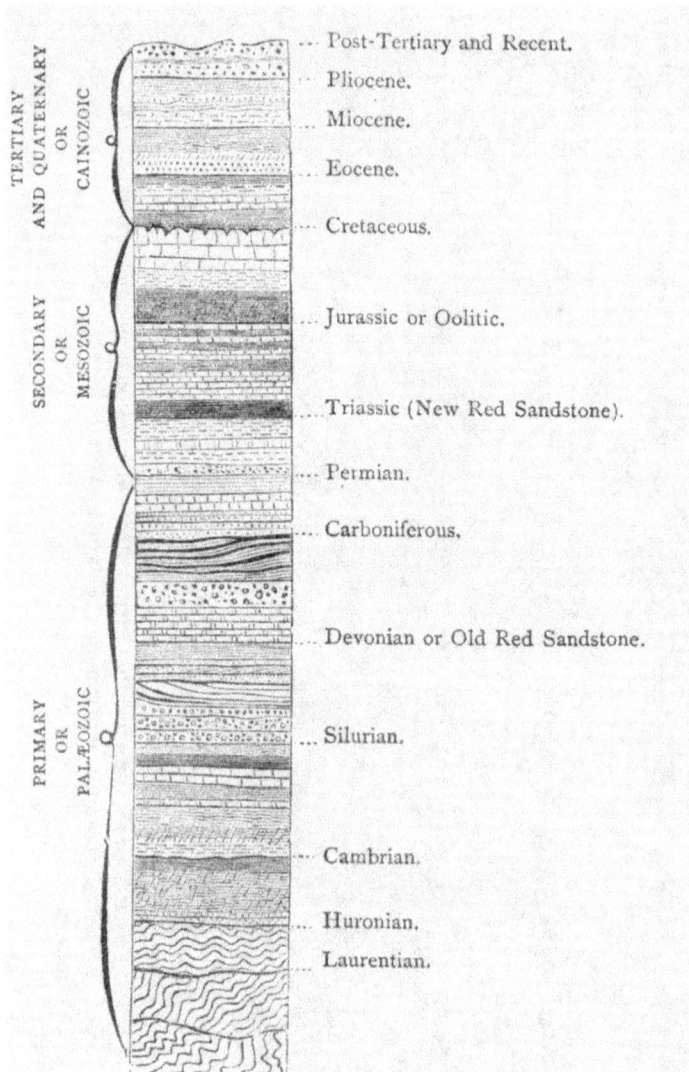

Fig. 1.—Ideal Section of the Crust of the Earth.

Ideal section of the crust of the earth from T. H. Huxley, *American Addresses*, London, 1888, Fig. I, p. 15. Nineteenth century developments in stratigraphy and in visual geological representation made idealized strata sections of this kind one of the most common forms of geological illustration.

THE EARTH SCIENCES

1. BIBLIOGRAPHY AND REFERENCE WORKS

Includes bibliographies, works of reference, source books, collections of essays and historiographical surveys.

1. AGASSIZ, Louis J.R. *Bibliographia Zoologiae et Geologiae. A General Catalogue of All Books, Tracts and Memoirs on Zoology and Geology.* Edited by H.E. STRICKLAND and Sir William JARDINE. 4 vols. London: Ray Society, 1848-1854, pp. 506; 492; 657; 604. Reprinted Folkestone, Kent: Dawson, 1967-1968.

   Still a major guide to writings in zoology and geology up to the first third of the nineteenth century, listed by author.

2. ALBRITTON, Claude C., Jr., ed. *The Fabric of Geology.* Reading, Mass., and London: Addison-Wesley Publishing Co., 1963, pp. x+372.

   Essays by various authors mainly on the philosophy of geology but including some detailed discussion of James Hutton and G.K. Gilbert. Contains a valuable bibliography of the philosophy of geology.

3. ALBRITTON, Claude C., Jr. "Second Bibliography and Index for the Philosophy of Geology." *Journal for the Graduate Research Center, Dallas, Texas*, 33, no. 2 (1964), 73-114.

   A follow-up to the bibliography printed in the above item. A third appears in the same journal, 35 (1966), 55-87.

4. ARKELL, William J., and TOMKEIEFF, Sergei I. *English Rock Terms Chiefly as Used by Miners and Quarrymen.* University of Durham Publications. Oxford: University Press, 1953, pp. xx+138.

   An alphabetical dictionary of English vernacular rock terms.

5. BASSETT, Douglas A. "History of Geology." Pp. 400-436 in WOOD, D.N., ed. *Use of Earth Sciences Literature*. London: Butterworths, 1973, pp. x+458.

    The most useful short, discursive and critical introduction to works in the history of geology, arranged by topics and nations.

6. BRIDSON, Gavin, and HARVEY, Anthony P. "A Checklist of Natural History Bibliographies and Bibliographical Scholarship, 1966-1970." *Journal of the Society for the Bibliography of Natural History*, 5 (1971), 428-467.

    Material relating to the history and bibliography of the Earth sciences appears on pp. 447-454.

7. BRIDSON, G., and HARVEY, A.P. "A Checklist of Natural History Bibliographies and Bibliographical Scholarship 1970-1971." *Journal of the Society for the Bibliography of Natural History*, 6 (1973), 263-292.

    Listing of material from 1970 and 1971 relating to the history and bibliography of geology appears on pp. 280-284.

8. CLOUD, Preston E., ed. *Adventures in Earth History, Being a Volume of Significant Writings from Original Sources, on Cosmology, Geology, Climatology, Oceanography, Organic Evolution, and Related Topics of Interest to Students of Earth History, from the Time of Nicolaus Steno to the Present*. San Francisco, Calif.: Freeman, 1971, pp. xv+992.

    Short extracts, in English, from leading geologists, thematically arranged around such topics as "Ordering Principles in Earth History," "Origin of the Universe, Solar System and Planets" and "Antiquity of the Earth." Generous in its extracts from twentieth-century material. Each section contains a linking explanatory commentary.

9. EYLES, Victor A. "The History of Geology." *History of Science*, 5 (1966), 77-86.

    Lists scholarly aids available for study of the early history of geology, and comments on the wide range of primary sources hitherto untapped.

10. FREEMAN, R.B. *British Natural History Books, 1495-1900: A Handlist*. Folkestone, Kent: Dawson Books, 1980, pp. 438.

Especially valuable for listings of books sometimes omitted in academic bibliographies, e.g., children's books and picture books. Contains a good subject index and chronological list.

11. JORDANOVA, L.J., and PORTER, Roy S., eds. *Images of the Earth: Essays in the History of the Environmental Sciences*. British Society for the History of Science Monographs, 1, Chalfont St Giles, England: British Society for the History of Science, 1979, pp. xx+282.

    Essays by various authors (listed separately in this volume) looking at some of the wider contexts of the development of the Earth sciences. The introduction surveys recent developments in the historiography of the Earth sciences.

12. LA ROCQUE, Aurele. "Milestones in the History of Geology: A Chronological List of Important Events in the Development of Geology." *Journal of Geological Education*, 22 (1974), 195-203.

13. MATHER, K.F., ed. *Source-Book in Geology, 1900-1950*. Cambridge, Mass.: Harvard University Press; London: Oxford University Press, 1967, pp. 435.

    Brief extracts (generally about five pages each) in English from the writings of geologists from Leonardo da Vinci to the beginning of the twentieth century, arranged by author, with brief biographical introductions. The most wide-ranging source book.

14. MEISEL, Max. *A Bibliography of American Natural History. The Pioneer Century, 1769-1865. The Role Played by the Scientific Societies: Scientific Journals: Natural History Museum and Botanic Gardens: State Geological and Natural History Surveys: Federal Exploring Expeditions in the Rise and Progress of American Botany, Geology, Mineralogy, Palaeontology and Zoology*. 3 vols. Vol. 1: *An Annotated Bibliography of the Publications Relating to the History, Biography and Bibliography of American Natural History and its Institutions, during Colonial Times and the Pioneer Century, which have been Published up to 1924 with a Classified Subject and Geographical Index: and a Bibliography of Biographies*. Vol. 2: *The Institutions Founded or Organized between 1845 and 1865. Bibliography of Books. Chronological Tables. Index of Authors and Institutions.*

Addenda to Volume I. Vol. 3: *The Institutions which have contributed to the Rise and Progress of American Natural History, which were Founded or Organized between 1769 and 1844*. Brooklyn, N.Y.: Premier Publishing, 1924-1929, pp. 244; 741; 749.

Vol. 2 is particularly useful for historians of geology as it offers thorough bibliographical accounts of the work of state geological surveys and of local naturalists' societies. Includes some critical discussion.

15. PORTER, R. "The Terraqueous Globe." Pp. 285-326 in ROUSSEAU, G.S., and PORTER, Roy, eds. *The Ferment of Knowledge: Studies in the Historiography of Eighteenth Century Science*. Cambridge: Cambridge University Press, 1980, pp. xii+500.

   A critical survey of scholarship published during the last twenty-five years on the history of the Earth sciences during the Enlightenment.

16. PORTER, Roy, and POULTON, K. "Research in British Geology 1660-1800: A Survey and Thematic Bibliography." *Annals of Science*, 34 (1977), 33-42.

   Discusses developments in the historiography of geology in the decade since Rappaport's and Eyles's articles, and offers a topically arranged bibliography of 119 items.

17. PORTER, R., and POULTON, K. "Geology in Britain 1660-1800: A Selective Biographical Bibliography." *Journal of the Society for the Bibliography of Natural History*, 9 (1978), 74-84.

   Lists biographical materials for some of the major British geologists.

18. RAPPAPORT, R. "Problems and Sources in the History of Geology, 1749-1810." *History of Science*, 3 (1964), 60-78.

   Emphasizes the need for adequate study of Hutton and Werner and the need for thematic monographs on the question of the time-scale, geological dynamics, classification, palaeontology and cartography.

19. ROBERTS, G. *An Etymological and Explanatory Dictionary of the Terms and Language of Geology*. London: Longman, 1839, pp. xii+183.

   A useful handbook.

Bibliography and Reference Works

20. SARJEANT, W.A.S. *Geologists and the History of Geology: An International Bibliography from the Origins to 1978*. 5 vols. New York: Arno Press; London: Macmillan, 1980, pp. 4526.

    By far the most comprehensive bibliography of the history of geology ever assembled. Particularly strong on the biographies of geologists over the last two centuries, and very thoroughly indexed; somewhat less complete on the wider cultural and intellectual aspects of the science.

21. SCHMIDT, Peter. "Zur Kenntnis der für die Geschichte und Philosophie der Geowissenschaften wichtigen Materialien in Bibliotheken, Archiven, Museum und ähnlichen Einrichtungen der D.D.R." *Zeitschrift für Geologischen Wissenschaft*, 5 (1977), 493-513.

    Helpful discussion of materials for the history of geology available in the D.D.R.

22. SCHNEER, Cecil J., ed. *Toward a History of Geology*. Cambridge, Mass., and London: M.I.T. Press, 1969, pp. vi+469.

    Essays by various authors (separately listed in this volume) examining particular features of the development of geology from the Renaissance to the late nineteenth century.

23. SCHRÖDER, Wilfried. "Why Research into the History of Geosciences?" *EOS. Transactions, American Geophysical Union*, 62 (1981), 521-522.

    Discusses the value to the development of research in the geophysical sciences of a historical understanding of past movements.

24. WELLS, J.W., and WHITE, G.W. "Biographies of Geologists." *Ohio Journal of Science*, 58 (1958), 285-298.

    List of 210 biographies of geologists, mainly book-length works.

25. WHITE, George W. *Annotated Bibliography for the History of Geology*. Urbana, Ill.: The Author, 1964, pp. 34.

    This is reprinted in the author's collection of essays, *Essays on History of Geology* (New York: Arno Press, 1978), which collects essays, articles, bibliographies, reviews and memorials which appeared over the past twenty-five years. The "Annotated Bibliography of Books for the History of Geology" is particularly valuable.

26. WHITE, James F., ed. *Study of the Earth: Readings in Geological Science*. Englewood Cliffs, N.J.: Prentice-Hall, 1962, pp. 408.

    Brief extracts from geological writings from James Hutton onwards on such topics as "The Law of Uniformity and Geologic Time," "The Earth Model--Problems and Implications" and "Crystal Features and Processes."

2. GENERAL HISTORIES

A. Histories of Science

The following general accounts of the nature and history of science give special prominence to the special nature of thinking in the Earth sciences.

27. GILLISPIE, Charles C. *The Edge of Objectivity; an Essay in the History of Scientific Ideas*. Princeton, N.J.: Princeton University Press, 1960, pp. 562.

The most stimulating single-volume general history of the emergence of scientific thinking, arguing that geological science emerged through the abandonment of anthropomorphic ideas of time and creation. This notion is particularly associated with the Uniformitarianism of James Hutton (1726-1797) and Charles Lyell (1797-1875).

28. PANTIN, C.F.A. *The Relations Between the Sciences*. Cambridge: University Press, 1968, pp. x+206.

A semi-philosophical, semi-historical attempt at a classification of the sciences, suggesting that the natural history sciences, geology included, should be seen as "extended sciences" because they deal with phenomena explicable only in terms of the unique conjunction of many different natural forces.

29. WHEWELL, Reverend William. *History of the Inductive Sciences, from the Earliest to the Present Times*. 3 vols. London: Parker, 1837, pp. xxxvi+437; vii+535; vii+624.

This magisterial general history of science includes an important account of the geological debates leading up to and surrounding Lyell's *Principles of Geology* (1830). Whewell's labelling of "Uniformitarians" and

"Catastrophists" is overly rigid but has exercised great influence among historians of geology.

30. WHEWELL, W. *The Philosophy of the Inductive Sciences.* 2 vols. London: J. Parker, 1840, pp. cxx+523; iv+586.

   A classic formulation of the philosophy of geological science, arguing that Huttonian and Lyellian Uniformitarianism is inapplicable, having been improperly introduced by way of false analogy with the physical sciences. The correct philosophy is "palaetiological"-- i.e., the geological sciences are necessarily sciences of origins and development.

B. Histories of Geology

Includes works dealing with general aspects of the history of geology in more than one country or covering more than one century.

31. ADAMS, Frank D. *The Birth and Development of the Geological Sciences.* Baltimore, Md.: Williams and Wilkins, 1938, pp. 506. Reprinted New York: Dover Books, 1954.

   Examines the rise of knowledge about the Earth, rocks, strata, minerals, volcanoes, earthquakes, etc., from antiquity chiefly to about the end of the eighteenth century, with copious translations from original sources. Particularly strong on presenting the views of Medieval and Renaissance naturalists. Though dated in its interpretations, it remains the fullest and most detailed account in English.

32. ARCHIAC, Adolphe d'. *Histoire des progrès de la géologie de 1834 à 1845.* 8 vols. Paris: Société Géologique de France, 1847-1860, pp. xxvii+679; 1100; 624; 600; 619; 731; 714; 680.

   Scrupulous survey of developments in geology, thematically arranged. Vol. 1 deals with cosmogony and geophysics, vol. 2 with quaternary and diluvian geology, vol. 3 with the tertiary and with igneous rocks, vols. 4 and 5 with the Cretacean, vols. 6 and 7 with the Jurassic, and vol. 8 with the Triassic.

33. BAILEY, E.B. "A Hundred Years of Geology, 1851-1951." *Advancement of Science,* 9 (1952), 9-18.

Compact and wide-ranging survey of developments from 1851 to 1951, emphasizing the potential of Continental Drift theory for transforming geology, and the need to improve techniques of ocean surveying.

34. BERINGER, C. *Geschichte der Geologie und des Geologischen Weltbildes*. Stuttgart: Enke-Verlag, 1954, pp. vii+158.

    The best short interpretative account of the history of the Earth sciences; particularly valuable for its balanced assessment of the work of geologists of different nationalities.

35. BLACKER, C., and LOEWE, M., eds. *Ancient Cosmologies*. London: Allen and Unwin, 1975, pp. 270.

    Studies on the cosmogonies of the world's great civilizations, the section on Jewish cosmology being especially valuable as background to the biblically-based theories of the Earth that flourished in the seventeenth and eighteenth centuries and focused on such issues as Creation, the Flood and the Abyss.

36. BROMEHEAD, C.E.N. "Geology in Embryo (up to 1600 A.D.)." *Proceedings of the Geological Association*, 56 (1945), 89-134.

    Contains useful detailed discussions of figures such as Adelard of Bath, Pliny and Pausanias and concentrates chiefly on the views of Greek and Roman naturalists.

37. CAILLEUX, André. *Histoire de la géologie*. "Que Sais-Je" series, no. 962. Paris: Presses Universitaires de France, 1961, pp. 126.

    Strong on the relations between geology and other sciences and on the national and cultural contexts within which geology has developed. Covers the period from antiquity to the present.

38. COLLIER, Katherine B. *Cosmogonies of Our Fathers. Some Theories of the Seventeenth and the Eighteenth Centuries*. Studies in History, Economics and Public Law, ed. by the Faculty of Political Science of Columbia University, no. 402. New York: Columbia University Press; London: P.S. King & Son Ltd., 1934, pp. 500.

    Extensive resumés and discussion of the chief theories of the origins, nature and destiny of the globe, from the tradition of Scriptural exegesis to the emergence of recognizably modern geology in the age of Werner and Hutton. Focuses chiefly on the interface between scientific ideas and religious beliefs.

39. EYLES, Victor A. "The Extent of Geological Knowledge in the Eighteenth Century, and the Methods by Which It Was Diffused." Pp. 159-183 in SCHNEER, C.J., ed. *Toward a History of Geology*. Cambridge, Mass., and London: M.I.T. Press, 1969, pp. vi+469.

    Well-researched and thoroughly documented account of the centers of geological investigations and teaching, giving much attention to practical geology and mineralogy and mining schools. Important information on geological publishing, particularly in scientific periodicals, and on geological translators and translations. Also examines the development of stratigraphical approaches through the emergence of fieldwork.

40. FENTON, Carroll L., and FENTON, Mildred A. *The Story of the Great Geologists*. Garden City, N.Y.: Doubleday, Doran, 1945, pp. xvi+301.

    Revised and enlarged as *Giants of Geology*. Garden City, N.Y.: Doubleday, 1952, pp. xvi+333.

41. GEIKIE, Archibald. *The Founders of Geology*. London: Macmillan; New York: The Macmillan Co., 1901, pp. x+297. Reprinted New York: Dover Publications, 1962, pp. xi+486.

    Attractive biographically-based chapters on the great geologists, their fieldwork and discoveries, since antiquity. Argues that the success of geology from the eighteenth century resulted from the emancipation of systematic observation from religious authority and mere speculation. Despite its biases (pro-Uniformitarian, pro-Plutonist), still very readable and informative.

42. GLACKEN, C.J. *Traces on the Rhodian Shore*. Berkeley: University of California Press, 1967, pp. xxviii+763.

    Wide-ranging survey of the development of ideas about the environment in Classical and Christian culture up to the end of the eighteenth century, stressing the background in natural theology and ideas of the relationship between the physical environment and flora and fauna.

43. GREENE, John C. *The Death of Adam: Evolution and Its Impact on Western Thought.* Ames: Iowa State University Press, 1959, pp. 382.

   Traces the conflict from the seventeenth century of two competing world-outlooks, the "static," associated with a cosmogony of "creationism" and a natural theology of adaptation and design, and the "dynamic," which sees natural order as emergent over time as the product of natural forces. Argues that geology was part of the dynamic outlook which eventually triumphed in Darwinian evolutionism.

44. GUNTAU, Martin. "The Emergence of Geology as a Scientific Discipline." *History of Science,* 16 (1978), 280-290.

   Poses the question why a distinctively "geological" discipline arose toward the end of the eighteenth century out of previous, largely natural history-based investigations of the Earth. Emphasizes the importance in this of the practical needs of industry for more scientific techniques of mineral prospecting, and of the secularization of views of Nature associated with the Enlightenment.

45. HALL, D.H. *History of the Earth Sciences during the Scientific and Industrial Revolutions with Special Emphasis on the Physical Geosciences.* Amsterdam, Oxford and New York: Elsevier, 1976, pp. xi+297.

   An ambitious attempt to show that the emergence of the modern Earth sciences was intimately associated with the rise of the Western capitalist economy and its imperialist civilization. Welcome for setting geology in context of other Earth sciences, such as geophysics and seismology. Based entirely on secondary sources, so some of its more sweeping connections must be viewed with caution.

46. HAWKES, Leonard. "Some Aspects of the Progress of Geology in the Last Fifty Years; I and II." *Geological Society of London, Quarterly Journal,* 113 (1957), 309-321; (1958), 395-410.

   The first part argues that twentieth-century geological developments have confirmed the applicability of Lyellian Uniformitarianism. The second discusses developments in ideas about the internal structure and forces of the globe; treats Continental Drift theory with some skepticism.

47. HOFFMAN, Friedrich. *Geschichte der Geognosie, und Schilderung der Vulkanischen Erscheihungen. Vorlesungen Gehalten an der Universität zu Berlin in den Jahren*

1834 und 1835. Berlin: Nicolaischen Buchhandlung, 1838, pp. ix+596.

A survey of the history of geology is followed by an extensive description of volcanic features, theories of vulcanism and observations on leading scientists in that field.

48. HÖLDER, Helmut. *Geologie und Paläontologie in Texten und ihrer Geschichte*. Orbis Academicus Series, Freiburg and München: Verlag Karl Alber, 1960, pp. xvii+566.

    A massive compilation of primary sources arranged by topics, with extensive quotations.

49. HUMBOLDT, A. Von. *Cosmos*. Trans. A. Pritchard. 3 vols. London: Bohn, 1845-1848, pp. 742 (vols. 1 and 2 continuously paginated); 289.

    Vol. 2 contains an extended psychologically focused historical account of man's changing perception of his physical environment, viewed as a product of his changing actual relationship to the globe as a result of the spread of civilization. Important insights into the idea of the sacredness of the Earth and the growth of the idea of the uniformity of Nature. Originally published as *Kosmos. Entwurf einer physischen Weltbeschreibung* (Stuttgart, 1845-1848).

50. KEFERSTEIN, Christian. *Geschichte und Literatur der Geognosie. Ein Versuch*. Halle, 1840, pp. xiv+281.

    Brief early history of geology.

51. KELLY, Sister Suzanne. "Theories of the Earth in Renaissance Cosmologies." Pp. 214-225 in SCHNEER, C.J., ed. *Toward a History of Geology*. Cambridge, Mass., and London: M.I.T. Press, 1969, pp. vi+469.

    Examines theories of the Earth in the Renaissance, especially the ideas of Paracelsus.

52. LAUNAY, Louis A.A. de. *La Science géologique. Ses Méthodes. Ses Resultats. Ses Problèmes. Son Histoire*. Paris: Librairie Armand Colin, 1905, pp. 750.

    The first ninety-two pages give a summary history of geology.

53. LENOBLE, Robert. *La Géologie au milieu de XVIIe siècle*. Les Conférences du Palais de la Découverte, Series D. no. 27. Paris: Université de Paris, 1954, pp. 36.

Histories of Geology

54. LYELL, Charles. *Principles of Geology, or the Modern Changes of the Earth and Its Inhabitants Considered as Illustrative of Geology*. 3 vols. London: Murray, 1830-1833, pp. xv+511; xii+330; xxxi+398+109.

    Lyell's polemical introductory historical chapters in the first volume, clearing the way and setting the scene for his arguments for Uniformitarianism, are still worth reading for their cultural sweep and gracious style, though Lyell's judgments, particularly on "Scriptural geologists" and on Werner, are unfair and ahistorical.

55. MARGERIE, Emmanuel de. *Critique et géologie: Contribution à l'histoire des sciences de la terre (1882-1947)*. 4 vols. Paris: Colin, 1943-1948, pp. lxix+2107.

    A personal history of geology over the last century, the first volume being largely personal, the second concerning the oceans, the third dealing with the geology of Spain and France, and the last with the Jura of France and Switzerland.

56. MOORE, R. *The Earth We Live On*. London: Jonathan Cape, 1957, pp. 348.

    A popular history of geology, biographically organized, taking the story from the mid-eighteenth century (Guettard, Desmarest, Hutton) up to the present day. Well illustrated.

57. MORELLO, Nicoletta. *La Macchina della Terra*. Turin: Loescher Editore, 1979, pp. 231.

    Extracts from the main theorists of the Earth from the seventeenth century onwards with brief accompanying commentary.

58. NORTH, F.J. "From Giraldus Cambrensis to the Geological Map: The Evolution of a Science." *Transactions of the Cardiff Naturalists Society*, 64 (1933), 20-97.

    Wide-ranging discussion of the history of geology in Britain, with generous quotations from primary sources, paying special attention to investigators of South Wales.

59. PESCHEL, Oscar. *Geschichte der Erdkunde bis auf Alexander von Humboldt und Carl Ritter*. Geologie (pp. 615-630). Munich: Cotta, 1865, pp. xx+706. Reprinted in facsimile, Amsterdam: Meridian Publishing Co., 1961.

    A history of exploration and geographical ideas, the later chapters paying some attention to geology.

60. PORTER, Roy. "Man and the Earth." Pp. 288-309 in HALLAM, A., ed. *Planet Earth*. Oxford: Elsevier, 1977, pp. 320.

    A brief history of the Earth sciences emphasizing the play of broad social, cultural, religious and economic factors in their formation, and particularly examining the science of geology over the last two centuries. Accompanied by short biographies of some seventy leading geologists.

61. RAMSAY, Andrew C. *Passages from the History of Geology: Being an Introductory Lecture at University College, London, in Continuation of the Inaugural Lecture of 1848*. London: Taylor, Walton and Maberly, 1849, pp. 37.

    A derivative account, drawing heavily upon the historical chapters in Lyell's *Principles of Geology*.

62. ROGER, J. "La Théorie de la terre au XVIIe siècle." *Revue d'Histoire des Sciences*, 26 (1973-1974), 23-48.

    Emphasizes that theories of the Earth from the seventeenth to the nineteenth centuries should be seen not primarily as an overture to geology, but as an intellectual and scientific genre in their own right. Particularly examines Descartes and Thomas Burnet.

63. SARTON, George. "La Synthèse géologique de 1775 à 1918." *Isis*, 11 (1919), 357-394.

    Pays particular attention to the synthesis of Eduard Suess at the end of the nineteenth century.

64. TATON, R. *Histoire générale des sciences*. 4 vols. Paris: Presses Universitaires de France, 1957-1964, pp. viii+625; vii+800; viii+775; viii+1080. English trans. as *A General History of the Sciences*. London: Thames and Hudson, 1964.

    Contains surveys of the history of the Earth sciences since the Renaissance by P. Delaunay, R. Furon, J. Orcel and P. Tardi.

65. TAYLOR, E.G.R. "The English Worldmakers of the Seventeenth Century and Their Influence on the Earth Sciences." *Geographical Review*, 38 (1948), 104-112.

    Analyzes the theories of the Earth of Burnet, Robinson and Ray, assessing the influence on them of the "New Science," particularly Descartes.

Histories of Geology

66. TAYLOR, Kenneth L. "Geology in 1776: Some Notes on the Character of an Incipient Science." Pp. 75-90 in SCHNEER, C.J., ed. *Two Hundred Years of Geology in America. Proceedings of the New Hampshire Bicentennial Conference on the History of Geology.* Hanover, N.H.: University Press of New England, 1979, pp. xvi+385.

    Valuable discussion of the conceptual shifts involved in the emergence of specifically *geological* Earth science toward the end of the eighteenth century, stressing the importance of the new idea of development or history.

67. THOMAS, H.H. "The Rise of Geology and Its Influence on Contemporary Thought." *Annals of Science*, 5 (1947), 325-341.

    A brief chronological account from the late seventeenth century to the time of Lyell.

68. TIKHOMIROV, Vladimir V. "On the Most Important Factors in the Development of Geology during the First Half of the 19th Century." *Actes du XIe Congrès International d'Histoire des Sciences* [1965], 4 (1968), 161-165.

    Divides the history of geology into four stages: (a) origins in the eighteenth century; (b) the heroic period of the early nineteenth century, with the formulation of Uniformitarianism and the development of palaeontology; (c) the second half of the nineteenth century, with the growth of microscopic techniques and the application of the idea of evolution; (d) the modern period, marked by the theory of geosynclines.

69. VOGELSANG, H. *Philosophie der Geologie und mikroskopische Gesteinsstudien.* Bonn: Cohen, 1867, pp. 229.

    The first section surveys geology in its relations to its principles and to other sciences, the second gives a biographical history of the science from Agricola to Bischof, and the third assesses the state of modern geology, particularly examining petrology and petrography.

70. WAGENBRETH, Otfried. "Die Entwicklung des geologischen Weltbildes in den letzten 200 Jahren." *Forschungen und Fortschritte. Korrespondenzblatt* (Nachrichtenblatt) *der deutschen Wissenschaft und Technik*, 41 (1967), 365-371.

71. WILSON, L.G. "Geology on the Eve of Charles Lyell's First Visit to America, 1841." *Proceedings of the American Philosophical Society*, 124 (1980), 168-202.

   Argues that there was a profound gulf in the 1830s between Lyellian Uniformitarianism and his opponents, who clung to notions of catastrophic interventions during the course of Earth history and a much briefer time-scale. Sees Catastrophism as being ultimately religiously motivated.

72. WOODWARD, Horace B. *History of Geology.* London: Watts, 1911, pp. 154.

   A brief and derivative account.

73. ZIGNO, Achille De. *Della Geologia e Suoi Progressi Prima del Secolo XIX.* Padua: Sicca, 1853, pp. 75.

74. ZITTEL, Karl A. von. *Geschichte der Geologie und Paläontologie bis Ende des 19. Jahrhunderts.* Geschichte der Wissenschaften in Deutschland, Neuere Zeit, vol 23. Munich and Leipzig: Oldenbourg, 1899, pp. xi+868. English ed. *History of Geology and Palaeontology to the end of the 19th Century.* Trans. by M.O. Gordon. London: Walter Scott, 1901, pp. xvi+562.

   Valuable to the English-speaking reader particularly for its very detailed accounts of eighteenth- and nineteenth-century German mineralogy, stratigraphy, petrology and palaeontology. The English edition is slightly abridged and lacks most of the documentation of the original.

3. SPECIALIST HISTORIES

A. Geological Philosophies and Methods

75. ADAMS, Frank D. "Earliest Use of the Term Geology."
    Bulletin of the Geological Society of America, 43
    (1932), 121-123.

    Examines isolated uses of the word before its growing popularity in the last decades of the eighteenth century. See Dean below (item 83).

76. ALBRITTON, Claude C., Jr., ed. *Uniformity and Simplicity. A Symposium on the Principle of the Uniformity of Nature*. Geological Society of America, special paper, No. 89. New York: Geological Society of America, 1967, pp. 99.

    Contains historical discussion as to the variety of interpretations of the meaning of the "uniformity of nature" implied within Lyellian Uniformitarianism.

77. ALBRITTON, Claude C., Jr., ed. *Philosophy of Geohistory: 1785-1970*. Benchmark Papers in Geology. Stroudsburg, Pa.: Dowden, Hutchinson and Ross, 1975, pp. xiii+386.

    Reprints major discussions of the philosophy of geology from James Hutton onwards, and accounts by historians such as R. Hooykaas and S. Toulmin.

78. BARTHOLOMEW, Michael. "The Non-Progress of Non-Progression: Two Responses to Lyell's Doctrine." *The British Journal for the History of Science*, 9 (1976), 166-174.

    Examines Murchison's responses to Lyell's belief that the fossil record showed no evidence of organic progress, and Darwin's more sympathetic acceptance of the negative evidence of the fossil record.

79. BÜLOW, Karl von. "Der Weg des Aktualismus in England, Frankreich und Deutschland." *Bericht der geologischen Gesellschaft der D.D.R.*, 5 (1960), 160-174.

   Sees Actualism in two ways: as a hypothesis about the steady-state condition of the Earth, and as a working methodological hypothesis for geologists--that one should proceed from known causes. The latter interpretation is the one currently favored by geologists.

80. CANNON, W.F. "The Uniformitarian-Catastrophist Debate." *Isis*, 51 (1960), 38-55.

   Traces discussions about the methodology of geology and the pattern of Earth history mainly among British geologists in the 1830s and 1840s following in the wake of Charles Lyell's *Principles of geology* (1830-1833). Points out the practical, rather than theoretical, nature of most geologists' concerns, and that the debate was made an issue of principle by the philosopher of science William Whewell, who coined the terms "Uniformitarian" and "Catastrophist."

81. CANNON, W.F. "The Impact of Uniformitarianism. Two Letters from John Herschel to Charles Lyell, 1836-1837." *Proceedings of the American Philosophical Society*, 115 (1961), 301-314.

   Herschel's letters acknowledge that Lyell's Uniformitarianism slots into the movement within the philosophy and methodology of science for naturalistically subsuming more events under natural law, but pose the question as to whether the origin of species--as well as their extinction--should be drawn within this explanatory framework.

82. CANNON, W.F. "Charles Lyell, Radical Actualism and Theory." *The British Journal for the History of Science*, 9 (1976), 104-120.

   Argues for the presence of deeply Actualistic tendencies in geologists usually thought of as Catastrophists, such as William Buckland.

83. DEAN, D.R. "The Word 'Geology.'" *Annals of Science*, 36 (1979), 35-43.

   This fullest history of the word, with many new examples, helps to document the emergence of the modern science.

84. GUNTAU, Martin. "Bermerkungen zum Determinismus in der Geologie." *Wissenschaftliche Zeitschrift der Humboldt-Universität Berlin. Math.-naturwissenschaft. Reihe,* 12 (1963), 431-434; 14 (1965), 667-672.

85. GUNTAU, MARTIN. "Der Actualismus in den geologischen Wissenschaften. Versuch einer philosophischen Analyse der Auffassungen zum Aktualismus in der Geschichter der geologischen Wissenschaften." *Freiberger Forschungsheft,* D55 (1967), 1-94.

86. GUNTAU, Martin. "Actualism in the History of the Geological Sciences." *Acts of the XIe International Congress for the History of Science* [1965], 4 (1968), 226-230.

   Discusses the attitudes of geologists, mainly during the twentieth century, to Lyellian Actualism. A shorter, English version of the above item.

87. GUNTAU, Martin. "Zu den Begriffe Aktualismus und Gesetz in den geologischen Wissenschaften." *Zeitschrift für geologischen Wissenschaften,* 5 (1977), 933-935.

   Discusses the meaning of Actualism and natural law in the geology of Von Hoff and Lyell.

88. HOOYKAAS, Reijer. "The Parallel Between the History of the Earth and the History of the Animal World." *Archives Internationales d'Histoire des Sciences,* 10 (1957), 3-18.

   Investigates the concept of the history of life and the history of the Earth as found in Cuvier, Lamarck, Geoffroy St. Hilaire and Robert Chambers, showing how it was Catastrophists who were the champions of change in the organic world.

89. HOOYKAAS, Reijer. *Natural Law and Divine Miracle: A Historical-Critical Study of the Principle of Uniformity in Geology, Biology, and Theology.* Leiden: Brill, 1959, pp. 237.

   A major attempt to define and explain outlooks and methods in geology, biology and theology. "Uniformitarianism" is belief in absolute uniformity of the laws of nature in degree and intensity, at all times and in all places. "Actualism" is belief that the same laws of nature have always operated, but at varying levels, changing over time. "Catastrophism" is the view that accepts that currently operating laws of nature do not adequately explain events, which are occasionally caused by forces beyond them. Most historical examples are taken from nineteenth-century geology and biology.

90. HOOYKAAS, Reijer. "Geological Uniformitarianism and Evolution." *Archives Internationales d'Histoire des Sciences*, 19, nos. 74-75, (1966), 3-19.

   Disputes Huxley's view that "consistent uniformitarianism postulates evolution as much in the organic as in the inorganic world," arguing greater parallels between Catastrophic and evolutionary views of the history of life.

91. HOOYKAAS, Reijer. "Catastrophism in Geology, Its Scientific Character in Relation to Actualism and Uniformitarianism." *Medeeling Koninklÿke Nederlandse Akademische Wetenschappelÿke Afdeeling voor Letterkunde*, 33 (1970).

   Argues that despite the views of most modern geologists and historians there is nothing inherently unscientific about the belief that Earth history has been punctuated by great revolutions, beyond the regular operations of Nature; and that the Catastrophist geologists of the early nineteenth century were just as scientific as their opponents. Catastrophism is not necessarily in the service of religious orthodoxy, and Uniformitarianism can itself be dogmatic.

92. RUDWICK, M.J.S. "A Critique of Uniformitarian Geology. A Letter from W.D. Conybeare to Charles Lyell, 1841." *Proceedings of the American Philosophical Society*, 111 (1967), 272-287.

   Conybeare's letter exposes some of the rhetoric in Lyell's campaign against "Catastrophism" and pinpoints difficulties in Lyell's theory--e.g., his denial of progression in the fossil record and the ambiguities of his idea of absolute uniformity.

93. RUDWICK, M.J.S. "Uniformity and Progression: Reflections on the Structure of Geological Theory in the Age of Lyell." Pp. 209-227 in ROLLER, D., ed. *Perspectives in the History of Science and Technology*. Norman: University of Oklahoma Press, 1971, pp. 308.

   Attempts to differentiate among implications and meanings of "uniformity" and "progress" as applied to methods and philosophies in the history of geology. Stresses that Catastrophism was not necessarily religiously motivated, and that belief in the uniformity of Nature can either be a heuristic device or a metaphysical commitment to a steady-state universe.

94. RUSE, M. "Charles Lyell and the Philosophers of Science." *The British Journal for the History of Science*, 9 (1976), 121-131.

    Examines John Herschel's sympathies with Lyell's naturalism and Whewell's hostility to Lyell's notion that geology was a cyclical science on the model of astronomy.

95A. SCHRÖDER, W. *Disziplingeschichte als wissenschaftliche Selbstreflexion der historischen Wissenschaftsforschung.* Frankfurt-am-Main: Verlag Peter D. Lang, 1981, pp. 85.

    Includes case studies of Hermann Fritz, Emil Wiechert, Alfred Wegener, V. Bjerknes, etc., to illustrate problems of scientific disciplines in the light of the philosophies of science of Kuhn, Popper and Lakatos.

95B. WATZNAUER, A. "Das geologische Weltbild G.C. FÜCHSELS (1722-1773), J.G. LEHMANNS (1719-1767) und C.E.A. v. HOFFS (1771-1837) und seine Nachwirkung bis zur Gegenwart." *Zeitschrift für geologische Wissenschaften*, 8 (1980), 63-72.

    Argues that the writings of Füchsel, Lehmann and Von Hoff illustrate the Enlightenment embracing of empiricism and rejection of *a prioristic* reasoning.

96. WOLLGAST, S. "Gedanken zur Aufklärungszeit--Zur Ideengeschichte der Zeit." *Zeitschrift für geologische Wissenschaften*, 8 (1980), 5-24.

    Discusses the natural philosophical background to Enlightenment geology.

B. Stratigraphy, Structural Geology and Petrology

97. BARRELL, Joseph. "A Century of Geology. The Growth of Knowledge of Earth Structure." Pp. 153-192 in DANA, Edward S., et al. *A Century of Science in America with Special Reference to the American Journal of Science, 1818-1918.* New Haven, Conn.: Yale University Press; London: Oxford University Press, 1918, pp. xii+ 458.

Surveys the rise and decline of the metamorphic theory of granite in America, the Neptunist-Plutonist controversy and the unravelling of Appalachian structures, leading to the theory of geosynclines and geoanticlines.

98. BASCOM, F. *Fifty Years of Progress in Petrography and Petrology, 1876-1926*. Johns Hopkins University Studies in Geology, no. 8. Baltimore, Md.: Johns Hopkins University Press, 1927.

99. BASSETT, Michael G. "100 Years of Ordovician Geology." *Episodes: Geological Newsletter, International Union of Geological Sciences*, no. 2 (July 1979), 18-21.

   Summary account of the introduction and gradual acceptance of Lapworth's term "Ordovician," with an emphasis on the role of international congresses in the late nineteenth century.

100. CROOK, Thomas. *History of the Theory of Ore Deposits: with a Chapter on the Rise of Petrology*. London: T. Murby; New York: Van Nostrand, 1933, pp. 163.

   Biographically based, with successive chapters examining ideas from Agricola, through to Van Hise, Kemp, Lindgren, Goodchild, Morrow, Campbell and Spurs. The final chapter briefly examines the growth of petrology.

101. CROSS, Whitman. "The Development of Systematic Petrography in the Nineteenth Century." *Journal of Geology*, 10 (1902), 331-376; 451-499.

   Largely biographically organized, emphasizing the contributions of Naumann, von Cotta, Senft, Blum, Roth, Scheere, Zirkel and Richthofen, and the microscopical work of Lasaulx, Rosenbusch, Fogué and Levy. Stresses the gradualness of the evolution of petrographic ideas.

102. FISCHER, W. *Gesteins- und Lagerstättenbildung im Wandel der wissenschaftlichen Auschauung*. Stuttgart: Schwizerbart, 1961, pp. xiii+592.

   Important introductory survey to the history of petrology.

103. GINSBURG, Robert N., ed. *Evolving Concepts in Sedimentology*. Johns Hopkins University Studies in Geology, no. 21. Baltimore, Md., and London: Johns Hopkins University Press, 1973, pp. ix+191.

Seven essays surveying twentieth-century developments in sedimentology, particularly in America.

104. HERITSCH, Franz. *The Nappe Theory in the Alps (Alpine Tectonics, 1905-1928)*. London: Methuen, 1929, pp. xxx+ 228.

    Mainly an account of researches carried out at the beginning of the twentieth century, but the first chapter includes a brief survey of earlier theories of Alpine Tectonics.

105. LOEWINSON-LESSING, F.Y. *A Historical Survey of Petrology*. Trans. S.I. TOMKEIEFF. Edinburgh: Oliver and Boyd, 1954, pp. x+112.

    Concentrates on the emergence of petrology as a separate science in the last third of the nineteenth century in the work of Credner, Naumann, Zirkel, Rosenbusch, Fouqué, Kalkowsky, Teall and Roth.

106. PIRSSON, Louis V. "The Rise of Petrology as a Science." Pp. 248-267 in DANA, Edward S., et al. *A Century of Science in America with Special Reference to the American Journal of Science, 1818-1918*. New Haven, Conn.: Yale University Press; London: Oxford University Press, 1918, pp. xii+458.

    America's role in the early development of petrology was limited.

107. READ, Herbert Harold. *The Granite Controversy*. London: Thomas Murby, 1957, pp. xix+430.

    Collected essays and addresses evaluating the Huttonian igneous theory of granite and the Wernerian aqueous theory, and investigating applications of these theories to modern geology.

108. SIGSBY, Robert J. "A Brief History of the Petrographic Microscope." *The Compass*, 43 (1966), 94-103.

109. TEALL, J.J. Harris. "The Evolution of Petrological Ideas. [Sedimentary Rocks: Crystalline Schists and Metamorphic Rocks]." *Quarterly Journal of the Geological Society of London*, 58 (1902), lxiii-lxxviii.

    Examines theories of the origin and nature of sedimentary and metamorphic rocks with particular emphasis on the work of Bischof and Walther.

110. TOMKEIEFF, S.I. "The Classification of Igneous Rocks: An Historical Approach." *Geological Magazine*, 76 (1939), 41-48.

    An account of petrological classification in the nineteenth century from Pinkerton to Vogelsang, emphasizing the value of grain size as a criterion for arrangement.

111. TOMKEIEFF, Sergei I. "Unconformity--An Historical Study." *Proceedings of the Geological Association*, 73 (1962), 383-417.

    Shows that several early geologists such as Steno, Strachey and Guettard were aware of unconformity, but that James Hutton was the first to see its significance for Earth history.

C. Geomorphology

112. BISWAS, Asit K. *History of Hydrology*. Amsterdam and London: North-Holland Publishing Co., 1970, pp. x+336.

    A detailed, biographically based survey of the various aspects of the scientific study of surface water, with extensive attention to the role of instruments and experiments in advancing knowledge. Chapters particularly relevant to the history of geology survey controversy on the origin of rivers, the salinity of the sea and the question of the existence of a central abyss.

113. CHALLINOR, John. "A Brief Review of Some Aspects of Geomorphology in England and Wales." *Mercian Geologist*, 6 (1978), 283-290.

    Challenges the applicability of Davisian geomorphology to certain aspects of the British Isles, using historical data.

114. CHORLEY, R.J., DUNN, A.J., and BECKINSALE, R.P. *The History of the Study of Landforms, or the Development of Geomorphology*. Vol. 1: *Geomorphology Before Davis*. London: Methuen, 1964, pp. xvi+678.

    A biographically arranged history, starting toward the end of the eighteenth century and taking developments through to the end of the nineteenth, stressing particularly the role of Huttonian Uniformitarianism in advancing the science. Strongest on British and American science.

115. CHORLEY, R.J., DUNN, A.J., and BECKINSALE, R.P. *The History of the Study of Landforms, or the Development of Geomorphology*. Vol. 2: *The Life and Work of William Morris Davis*. London: Methuen, 1973, pp. xxii+874.

    A full biography tracing the life and emphasizing the achievements of the founder of modern geomorphology.

116. DAVIES, Gordon L. "The Concept of Denudation in Seventeenth-Century England." *Journal of the History of Ideas*, 27 (1966), 278-284.

    Discusses the many viewpoints--factual, religious, aesthetic, philosophical--which reinforced belief that the Earth was continually decaying, in old age, nearing extinction and seriously malfunctioning. This outlook stimulated important insights into geomorphological forces at work.

117. DAVIES, G.L. "Early British Geomorphology 1578-1705." *Geographical Journal*, 132 (1966), 252-262.

    Examines accounts in early natural histories, travelers' reports, etc., of rivers changing course, coastal erosion, underground rivers, etc.--within the intellectual framework of belief that the Earth was in decay and nearing its end.

118. DAVIES, Gordon L. "The Eighteenth-Century Denudation Dilemma and the Huttonian Theory of the Earth." *Annals of Science*, 22 (1966), 129-138.

    The dilemma was that eighteenth-century philosophical and religious outlooks denied that the Earth's surface had undergone great change, since this would have implied disorder and imperfection. Huttonian geology solved the dilemma by showing that it was gradual natural change which preserved order and prevented decay.

119. DAVIES, G.L. *The Earth in Decay. A History of British Geomorphology, 1578-1878*. London: Macdonald Technical and Scientific; New York: American Elsevier Publishing Company Incorporated, 1969, pp. xvi+390.

A major examination of changing attitudes to land forms in the light both of fieldwork evidence and of religious, philosophical and aesthetic attitudes. Argues in particular that "modern" notions of the enormous extent of denudation could not develop until the eighteenth century's natural theology of design and adaptation had been abandoned. An important section examines controversies over glaciation and Ice Ages.

120. DOTT, R.H., Jr. "The Geosyncline--First Major Geological Concept 'Made in America.'" Pp. 239-264 in SCHNEER, C.J., ed. *Two Hundred Years of Geology in America. Proceedings of the New Hampshire Bicentennial Conference on the History of Geology.* Hanover, N.H.: University Press of New England, 1979, pp. xvi+385.

Shows that it was the special challenge of the American landscape which led to James Hall's dictum, "The greater the accumulation, the higher the mountain range."

121. JORDANOVA, L.J. "Earth Science and Environmental Medicine: The Synthesis of the Late Enlightenment." Pp. 119-114 in JORDANOVA, L.J., and PORTER, Roy, eds. *Images of the Earth*. Chalfont St Giles, Bucks: The British Society for the History of Science, 1979, pp. xx+282.

Examines the relations between knowledge of the Earth and questions of the understanding of Man, life, disease, health and hygiene particularly among the *Idéologues* in France at the turn of the nineteenth century.

122. KING, Cuchlaine A., ed. *Landforms and Geomorphology: Concepts and History*. Benchmark papers in geology, 28. Stroudsburg, Pa.: Dowden, Hutchinson, & Ross, 1976, pp. xv+404.

A series of extracts from the major geomorphological writings, past and present.

123. MIDDLETON, W.E. Knowles. *A History of the Theories of Rain and Other Forms of Precipitation*. London: Oldbourne, 1966, pp. viii+223.

Of interest in context of geomorphological theories of the hydrological cycle. Deals with several meteorologists, e.g., J.A. De Luc, who were also prominent as geologists.

124. PAGE, L.E. "Diluvialism and Its Critics in Great Britain in the Early Nineteenth Century." Pp. 257-271 in SCHNEER, C.J., ed. *Toward a History of Geology*. Cambridge, Mass., and London: M.I.T. Press, 1969, pp. vi+469.

    Repudiates the view that all Neptunists were merely religious apologists, emphasizing that there were many different forms of diluvial theory, of varying degrees of scientific credibility. Concentrates on William Buckland and John Fleming.

125. TAYLOR, E.G.R. "The Origin of Continents and Oceans: A Seventeenth Century Controversy." *Geographical Journal*, 116 (1950), 193-198.

    Examines seventeenth-century theories of the Earth in the light of widespread assumptions that the Earth was in decay. Special attention is given to the work of Thomas Burnet.

126. TUAN, Yi-fu. *The Hydrologic Cycle and the Wisdom of God. A Theme in Geoteleology*. University of Toronto Department of Geography Research Publication, no. 1. Toronto: University of Toronto Press, 1968, pp. xiv+160.

    The natural theology of order, design and adaptation predominant in the eighteenth century encouraged a notion of the terrestrial economy as a self-contained, self-recycling system. This permitted understanding of the role of mountains, volcanoes and earthquakes in forming the landscape and new theories of the origin of rivers.

127. WEGMANN, E. "Changing Ideas about Moving Shorelines." Pp. 386-414 in SCHNEER, C.J., ed. *Toward a History of Geology*. Cambridge, Mass., and London: M.I.T. Press, 1969, pp. vi+469.

    Surveys the eighteenth- and nineteenth-century controversy concerning the question of the changing sea-level of the Baltic, examining mythological as well as scientific elements.

D. Palaeontology

128. ANDREWS, H. *The Fossil Hunters. In Search of Ancient Plants*. Ithaca, N.Y., and London: Cornell University Press, 1980, pp. 422.

A history of palaeobotany starting chiefly with the work of Brongniart and Sternberg, and including important surveys of recent developments in the science in Scandinavia, the United States, the Soviet Union, France, Britain and Germany.

129. BLAKE, John F. "History of the Restoration of Extinct Animals." *Proceedings of the Geological Association*, 5 (1877), 91-103.

    Examines progress over the previous twenty-five years in the understanding of graptolites, trilobites, belemnites, ammonites and cephalopods.

130. BOWLER, Peter J. *Fossils and Progress: Paleontology and the Idea of Progressive Evolution in the 19th Century.* New York: Science History Publications, 1976, pp. viii+191.

    Examines rival attempts to understand the pattern of life history, against a geological background, in the light of the extensive fossil discoveries of the 1820-1840 period. Shows that most palaeontologists argued for a "progressive," though nonevolutionary, development of life over geological time, despite the considerable ambiguities of and gaps in the fossil record.

131. BULMAN, Oliver M.B. "Recent Developments and Trends in Paleontology." *Advancement of Science*, 16 (1959), 33-42.

    Stresses the degree to which modern palaeontological advances depend on technical innovations in photography, grinding apparatus and microscopes, and discusses palaeontology's contribution to the species concept.

132. COLBERT, Edwin H. *Men and Dinosaurs: The Search in Field and Laboratory.* New York: E.P. Dutton and Company, 1968, pp. xviii+283.

    Emphasizes the personal aspects of the development of the study of extinct saurians, concentrating on the biographies of naturalists from William Buckland and Gideon Mantell to recent inquiries. Interested primarily in the North American context.

133. COX, Leonard R. "British Palaeontology: A Retrospect and Survey." *Proceedings of the Geological Association*, 67 (1956), 208-220.

A brief survey underlining the importance of the work of Hooke in relating fossils to Earth history, and of the natural historians of the late seventeenth century, such as Ray and Plot, in beginning a regional classification of English fossils.

134. DELAIR, Justin B. "A History of the Early Discoveries of Liassic Ichthyosaurs in Dorset and Somerset (1779-1835)." *Proceedings of the Dorset Natural History and Archaeological Society*, 90 (1969), 115-127.

    Examines the early history of random finds by amateur naturalists such as the Rev. Peter Hawker, before examining the better-known contributions of Mary Anning, De la Beche, and Everard Home.

135. DELAIR, J.B., and SARJEANT, W.A.S. "The Earliest Discoveries of Dinosaurs." *Isis*, 66 (1975), 5-25.

    The authors list and describe observations on fossil dinosaurs from the seventeenth to the mid-nineteenth century, with particular emphasis on Buckland and Mantell.

136. DESMOND, Adrian J. *The Hot-Blooded Dinosaurs: A Revolution in Palaeontology*. London: Blond & Briggs, 1975, pp. 238.

    A narrative history of the discovery and reconstruction of extinct giant vertebrates from the pioneering comparative anatomy of Georges Cuvier, through the impact of Darwinian theory, to present speculations as to the cause of their cataclysmic extinction.

137. EDWARDS, W.N. *The Early History of Palaeontology*. London: British Museum (Natural History), 1967, pp. 68.

    A short and mainly derivative treatment, but with some interesting illustrations.

138. FURON, Raymond. *La Paléontologie. La Science des fossiles, son histoire, ses enseignements, ses curiosités*. 2nd ed. Paris: Payot, 1951, pp. 287.

    Includes a brief review of the history of palaeontology down to the present.

139. GERSTNER, Patsy A. "Vertebrate Paleontology, an Early Nineteenth-Century Transatlantic Science." *Journal of the History of Biology*, 3 (1970), 137-148.

Investigates mutual influences of America and Europe on early nineteenth-century palaeontology with special emphasis on Richard Harlan.

140. GOTHAN, Walther. *Die Probleme der Paläobotanik und ihre geschichtliche Entwicklung.* Probleme der Wissenschaften in Vergangenheit und Gegenwart, no. 10. Berlin: Wissenschaftliches Editions Gesellschaft, 1948.

141. GREGORY, Joseph T. "North American Vertebrate Paleontology, 1776-1976." Pp. 305-335 in SCHNEER, C.J., ed. *Two Hundred Years of Geology in America. Proceedings of the New Hampshire Bicentennial Conference on the History of Geology.* Hanover, N.H.: University Press of New England, 1979, pp. xvi+385.

Correctly stresses the immensè importance of American finds and research for the international development of the science.

142A. HOWARD, Robert V. *The Dawnseekers: The First History of American Paleontology.* Foreword by Gilbert F. Stucker. New York and London: Harcourt Brace Jovanovich, 1975, pp. xiii+314.

A comprehensive narrative which gives due prominence to eighteenth-century inquiries and also to the recent work of palaeontologists such as George Gaylord Simpson. Concerned more with American exploration than with the history of palaeontology *per se*.

142B. HOWE, S.R., SHARPE, T., and TORRENS, H.S. *Ichthyosaurs. A History of Fossil "Sea-dragons."* Cardiff: National Museum of Wales, 1981.

143. JUST, Theodor K. "Fifty Years of Paleobotany 1906-56." Pp. 590-605 in STEERE, William C. *Fifty Years of Botany: Golden Jubilee Volume of the Botanical Society of America.* New York: McGraw-Hill, 1958.

144. LANHAM, Url. *The Bone Hunters.* New York and London: Columbia University Press, 1973, pp. x+285.

A narrative history of the development of the search for fossils in the United States in the nineteenth century, concentrating on Othniel Charles Marsh and Edward Drinker Cope but also chronicling the achievements of free-lance bone-hunters.

145. LULL, Richard S. "On the Development of Vertebrate
Paleontology." Pp. 217-247 in DANA, Edward S., et al.
A Century of Science in America, with Special Reference to the American Journal of Science 1818-1918.
New Haven, Conn.: Yale University Press; London:
Oxford University Press, 1918, pp. xii+458.

Emphasizes the contributions of Cope, Marsh and Osborn
not just to American vertebrate palaeontology but to
the international development of evolutionary theory.

146. NELSON, Clifford M. "Ammonites: Ammon's Horns into
Cephalopods." *Journal of the Society for the Bibliography of Natural History*, 5 (1968), 1-18.

History of the recognition of ammonites and of their
organic origin. The extensive and detailed historical
references are also valuable for subjects other than
cephalopods.

147. OAKLEY, Kenneth P. "Folklore of Fossils." *Antiquity*,
39 (1965), 9-16, 117-125.

Examines the magical and medicinal lore traditionally
associated with fossils, and popular myths about their
origin and nature, paying particular attention to
crinoids and belemnites.

148. OSTROM, John H., and McINTOSH, John S. *Marsh's Dinosaurs: The Collections from Como Bluff.* New Haven, Conn.,
and London: Yale University Press, 1966, pp. xiv+388.

Reproductions from Marsh's drawings from his finds
at the great Jurassic dinosaur and mammal quarries,
with a historical introduction.

149. PLATE, Robert. *The Dinosaur Hunters--Othniel C. Marsh
and Edward D. Cope.* New York: David McKay Co., 1964,
pp. 281.

150. ROLFE, W.D. Ian. "Fossils." Pp. 32-38 in CHALMERS-HUNT,
J.M., ed. *Natural History Auctions 1700-1972: A
Register of Sales in the British Isles.* London:
Sotheby Parke Bernet, 1976, pp. xii+189.

Lists sales of fossil collections in Britain.

151. RUDWICK, M.J.S. "Problems in the Recognition of Fossils
as Organic Remains." *Proceedings of the 10th International Congress of the History of Science*, 8 (1962-1963), 85-87.

Explains the metaphysical and technical grounds on which it was commonly believed in the Early Modern period that bone-like and shell-like objects found embedded within rock were not organic remains but *lapides sui generis*.

152. RUDWICK, M.J.S. *The Meaning of Fossils. Episodes in the History of Palaeontology*. London: Macdonald; New York: American Elsevier, 1972, pp. 287.

    A history of palaeontology from the Renaissance into the present century, stressing the enormous, and sometimes revolutionary, conceptual shifts that have occurred in the understanding of fossil objects, above all the belief, first common in the late seventeenth century, that they were indeed animal remains, and the later acceptance that many were the remains of species now extinct.

153. RUDWICK, M.J.S. "Lyell's Dream of a Statistical Palaeontology." *Palaeontology*, 21 (1978), 22-44.

    Examines the intellectual background to Lyell's introduction in 1833 of the terms "Eocene," "Miocene," and "Pliocene" as part of his analysis of Cainozoic Earth history.

154. RUDWICK, M.J.S. "History of Paleontology Before Darwin." Pp. 375-384 in FAIRBRIDGE, R.W., and JABLONSKI, D., eds. *The Encyclopedia of Palaeontology*. Stroudsburg, Pa.: Dowden, Hutchinson and Ross, 1979.

    An account of the development of the interpretation of fossils from the sixteenth century.

155. SIMPSON, George G. "Beginnings of Vertebrate Paleontology in North America." *American Philosophical Society Proceedings*, 86 (1942), 130-135.

    Traces development from the bone finds of Longueuil and Croghan in the eighteenth century down to the mid-nineteenth century, with appendices dealing with the activities and collection of the American Philosophical Society.

156. STUBBLEFIELD, Sir James. "Relationship of Paleontology to Stratigraphy." *Advancement of Science*, 11 (1954), 149-159.

A synoptic survey, emphasizing the contributions that palaeontology has made to stratigraphy, through examination of the work of William Smith, Georges Cuvier and Charles Lyell. Also shows palaeontology's role in the development of geological mapping.

157. VISSER, R.P.W. "Dutch Palaeontologists of the 18th Century." *Janus*, 62 (1975), 125-149.

    Discusses the work of naturalists such as Camper, Drouin and Ranouw, explores contemporary debate on the nature of fossils and gives an account of fossil collections, some of them still surviving.

158. WEAVER, C.E. "Invertebrate Paleontology and Historical Geology from 1850 to 1950." In *A Century of Progress in the Natural Sciences 1853-1953*. California Academy of Sciences, San Francisco, 1955, pp. 807.

159. WENDT, H. *Before the Deluge: The Story of Palaeontology.* London: Gollancz, 1968, pp. xii+419.

    A well-researched popular history of palaeontology from the time of Steno stressing the religious context of early ideas, and placing due emphasis upon the variety of complex philosophical frameworks of thought within which fossil remains were successively interpreted. Gives due weight to French and German explorations.

E. Geology and Evolution

160. BARTHOLOMEW, M.J. "Lyell and Evolution: An Account of Lyell's Response to the Prospect of an Evolutionary Ancestry for Man." *The British Journal for the History of Science*, 6 (1973), 261-303.

    Shows that one element of Lyell's assertion of Uniformitarian geology from the 1830s was his fierce anti-evolutionism, particularly for man's origins. Lyell was deeply concerned in the 1850s at the prospect of Darwin's using his own geological outlook as the basis of evolutionary theory. Lyell's subsequent acceptance of evolutionism was unwilling and partial, as he wished to preserve a spiritual-religious view of the dignity of man.

161. BOURDIER, Franck. "Geoffroy Saint-Hilaire Versus Cuvier: The Campaign for Paleontological Evolution (1825-1936)." Pp. 36-61 in SCHNEER, Cecil J., ed. *Toward a History of Geology*. Cambridge, Mass., and London: M.I.T. Press, 1969, pp. vi+469.

   Charts the controversy between Geoffroy St Hilaire (who supported a saltatory evolution interpretation of the fossil record) and Cuvier, who was a catastrophist and special creationist, and argues that Cuvier was successful in blackening Geoffroy's scientific reputation.

162. BURKHARDT, Richard W., Jr. *The Spirit of System: Lamarck and Evolutionary Biology*. Cambridge, Mass.: Harvard University Press, 1977, pp. xii+286.

   Establishes that evolutionism was only one aspect--perhaps not a very important one--of Lamarck's perspective on the relation between life and the terraqueous globe. Shows how Lamarck's geological views--with their emphasis upon slow change over an extended time-scale--fit in with his vision of an active and all-embracing monistic Nature.

163. CORSI, Pietro. "The Importance of French Transformist Ideas for the Second Volume of Lyell's *Principles of Geology*." *The British Journal for the History of Science*, 11 (1978), 221-244.

   Analyzes the extended discussion of French evolutionary ideas--particularly Lamarck's--in Lyell's *Principles of Geology*. Lyell marshalled strong factual arguments against them, but also was emotionally committed to a view of the special creation of man, and wished to utilize the assumption of species fixity to establish a palaeontological basis for the division of geological time into epochs.

164. EISELEY, Loren C. *Darwin's Century: Evolution and the Men Who Discovered It*. London: Gollancz, 1959, pp. xvii+378.

   Well-written and popular account of the various strands of scientific development in geology, embryology, ecology and comparative anatomy, all which were to make Darwin's evolutionary synthesis possible.

165. GOULD, S.J. *Ontogeny and Phylogeny*. Cambridge, Mass.: Harvard University Press, 1977, pp. ix+501.

Explores the history of the idea that there is a relationship between the development of an individual and the evolutionary history of his lineage, showing the role of the idea in the interpretation of fossil evidence in the nineteenth century.

F. Geology and Human Origins

166. BOYLAN, P.J. "The Controversy of the Moulin-Quignon Jaw: The Role of Hugh Falconer." Pp. 171-199 in JORDANOVA, L.J., and PORTER, Roy, eds. *Images of the Earth*. Chalfont St Giles, Bucks: The British Society for the History of Science, 1979, pp. xx+282.

Examines national rivalries between the British and the French as a factor in the controversy as to the authenticity of Boucher de Perthes's claimed fossil human remains in the 1860s.

167. DANIEL, Glyn. *The Origins and Growth of Archaeology*. New York: Thomas Y. Crowell Co., 1967, pp. 298.

Traces from Early Modern times the gradual shift from seeking man's past in written documents to examining artifacts (and then seeking to discover them); and from an antiquarian approach to a properly historical scientific archaeology. Shows that the notion of "prehistory" did not emerge until into the nineteenth century, allowing a much extended view of the timescale for man's history.

168. ELLIOT SMITH, Sir Grafton. *The Search for Man's Ancestors*. The Forum Series, no. 16. London: Watts, 1931, pp. viii+56.

169. GRUBER, H.E. *Darwin on Man: A Psychological Study of Scientific Creativity Together with Darwin's Early and Unpublished Notebooks*. London: Wildwood House, 1974, pp. xxv+495.

Geological as well as biological and natural history notebooks are examined to suggest that the pattern of Darwin's intellectual creativity was one of numerous successive partial insights, rather than a single "blinding flash."

170. GRUBER, Jacob W. "The Neanderthal Controversy: Nineteenth-Century Version." *Scientific Monthly*, 67 (1948), 436-439.

    Brief discussion of reactions to finds of fossil man from the end of the eighteenth century to Boucher de Perthes.

171. LEAKEY, Louis S.B., and GOODALL, Vanne M. *Unveiling Man's Origins: Ten Decades of Thought about Human Evolution.* Cambridge, Mass.: Schenkman Publishing Co., 1969, pp. xvii+220.

    A brief narrative dealing with discoveries of fossil man since the 1860s.

172. LYON, John. "The Search for Fossil Man: Cinq Personnages à la recherche du temps perdu." *Isis*, 61 (1970), 68-84.

    Discusses the attitudes of leading geologists--such as Cuvier, Buckland, McEnery, Journal and de Serres--to the issue of the likelihood of finding fossil evidence of "prehistoric" man.

173. SENET, André. *L'Homme à la recherche de ses ancêtres.* Paris: Librairie Plon, 1954, pp. xii+274.

    A narrative and semi-popular history of palaeontology focusing on the search for human remains from the time of Boucher de Perthes.

174. YOUNG, R.M. "The Historiographic and Ideological Contexts of the Nineteenth Century Debate on Man's Place in Nature." Pp. 344-438 in YOUNG, R.M., and TEICH, M., eds. *Changing Perspectives in the History of Science. Essays in Honour of Joseph Needham.* London: Heinemann, 1973, pp. xxi+488.

    Places the nineteenth-century debate concerning the scientific evidence for man's place in Nature within the wider contexts of Victorian and current values--philosophical, religious, moral and political--questioning the autonomy of the scientific controversies.

G. Earthquakes and Volcanoes

175. BEER, Sir Gavin de. "The Volcanoes of Auvergne." *Annals of Science*, 18 (1962), 49-62.

    Analyzes the significance of geological investigation of these extinct volcanoes from the mid-eighteenth century for the development of Vulcanism and Plutonism and ideas of the activity of the Earth.

176. CAROZZI, Albert V. "Rudolf Erich Raspe and the Basalt Controversy." *Studies in Romanticism*, 8 (1969), 235-250.

    Raspe was a pioneer Vulcanist, showing the connection between basalt and volcanic activity in the past and arguing for the igneous origin of basalts and similar rock forms.

177. CAROZZI, A.V. "Robert Hooke, Rudolf Erich Raspe, and the Concept of Earthquakes." *Isis*, 61 (1970), 85-91.

    Shows that both Hooke and Raspe believed that earthquakes had both played a more important role in Earth history than commonly imagined, and frequently had a constructive rather than a destructive effect. Raspe was the chief rediscoverer and popularizer of Hooke's geological thought in the eighteenth century.

178. DAVISON, C. *A History of British Earthquakes*. Cambridge: Cambridge University Press, 1924, pp. xviii+416.

    Contains a brief historical introduction examining accounts and interpretations of British earthquakes of earlier centuries.

179. DAVISON, Charles. *The Founders of Seismology*. Cambridge: University Press, 1927, pp. xiv+240.

    Mainly biographical in focus, tracing the analysis of seismic activity from John Michell, through Italian pioneers such as Bertelli, Mercalli and Tacchini, to John Milne and Fusakichi Omori.

180. ELLENBERGER, F. "Précisions nouvelles sur la découverte des volcans de France." *Histoire et Nature*, 12/13 (1978), 3-42.

A contextual study of the discovery by Guettard in 1751 of extinct volcanoes in central France, examining previous geological investigation of the area.

181. GÜTH, D., GERMANN, D., and STELZNER, J. *Zur Geschichte der Forschungseinrichtung für Seismologie in Jena von 1899-1969.* Potsdam, 1974.

182. SCHMIDT, P. "Gedanken zum Umbruch in der europaischen Seismologie während des 18. Jahrhunderts." *Zeitschrift für Geologische Wissenschaften*, 8 (1980), 189-206.

    Investigates the development of seismology in the eighteenth century, paying attention to both philosophical and technical developments.

183. STOKES, Evelyn. "Volcanic Studies by Members of the Royal Society of London 1665-1780." *Earth Science Journal*, 5 (1971), 46-70.

    Biographically based sketches from the time of Hooke to Sir William Hamilton. Indicates the importance of the *Philosophical Transactions* as a repository for information.

H. Time and Historical Geology

184A. ALBRITTON, Claude C., Jr. *The Abyss of Time: Changing Conceptions of the Earth's Antiquity after the Sixteenth Century.* San Francisco, Calif.: Freeman, Cooper and Co., 1980, pp. 251.

    A history of the concept of geological time, presented through a series of cameo sketches of the leading contributors, paying special attention to Hooke, Burnet, Benoit de Maillet, Buffon, Hutton and William Smith, and culminating in a discussion of the role of quantitative analysis of radioactive materials in dating geological epochs.

184B. BURCHFIELD, J.D. "Darwin and the Dilemma of Geological Time." *Isis*, 65 (1974), 301-321.

    The author discusses the embarrassment caused by Darwin's naive calculations of the time taken to denude the Weald, in the context of the post-*Origin* debates as to whether the globe was old enough to allow evolutionary change to have been as gradual as Darwin stipulated.

185. BURCHFIELD, Joe D. *Lord Kelvin and the Age of the Earth*. New York: Science History Publishing, 1975, pp. xii+260.

Examines the arguments used by Kelvin and his supporters to show that thermodynamics would not grant to Uniformitarian geologists the enormous amounts of time their emphasis upon gradual causation required. Kelvin's opposition was dictated partly by his religious hostility to Darwinian evolutionism, and partly by his sense of the scientific superiority of physics over the less rigorous discipline of geology.

186. DEAN, D.R. "The Age of the Earth Controversy: Beginnings to Hutton." *Annals of Science*, 38 (1981), 435-456.

Major controversies about the age of the Earth from antiquity to the eighteenth century show us that Hutton was by no means the first thinker to insist upon the immensity of geological time.

187. EICHER, Don L. *Geologic Time*. Englewood Cliffs, N.J.: Prentice-Hall, 1968, pp. 149.

The first chapter is a brisk history of ideas about the age of the Earth, from the Medieval myths through Hutton, down to estimates based on modern ideas of radioactivity.

188. HABER, Francis C. *The Age of the World. Moses to Darwin*. Baltimore, Md.: The Johns Hopkins University Press, 1959, pp. xi+303.

Examines the gradual shift from the assumption of a short time-scale of some few thousands of years to modern geological time which accompanied the abandonment of the scientific authority of the Bible and the discovery of the immense thickness and successive deposition of the strata. Stresses the role of Enlightenment thinkers in developing speculative evolutionary theories of the Earth.

189. MEYER, H. *The Age of the World*. Allentown, Pa.: Muhlenberg College, 1951, pp. 133.

Investigates the humanistic and scholarly traditions of determining the age of the Earth through comparative and philological approaches toward written authorities in the sixteenth and seventeenth centuries.

190. OLDROYD, D.R. "Historicism and the Rise of Historical Geology." *History of Science*, 17 (1979), 191-213; 227-257.

   Examines the emergence of a specifically historical approach to the science of the Earth in the late eighteenth and early nineteenth centuries in the light of the "historicist" movement in general culture. Contains a sympathetic discussion of the constructive role of Wernerian geology.

191. PORTER, R. "The History of Time." Pp. 5-44 in GRANT, J., ed. *The Book of Time*. Newton Abbot: David and Charles, 1980, pp. 320.

   A popular account of the development of ideas of geological time and the history of the Earth and life from within a broad cultural context.

192. ROSSI, P. *I Segni del Tempo*. Milan: Feltrinelli, 1979, pp. 346.

   An exploration of the growing importance of historical thinking, evolutionary explorations and the lengthening of the historical time-scale in European thought in the seventeenth and eighteenth centuries. Contains a section on theories of the Earth seen within a wide cultural context.

193. RUDWICK, M.J.S. "Lyell on Etna, and the Antiquity of the Earth." Pp. 288-304 in SCHNEER, C.J., ed. *Toward a History of Geology*. Cambridge, Mass., and London: M.I.T. Press, 1969, pp. vi+469.

   Emphasizes that Lyell's notion of the immense age of the Earth, developed partly as a result of his exploration of Etna, formed part of a complex philosophical system of Uniformitarianism.

194. SCHNEER, C. "The Rise of Historical Geology in the Seventeenth Century." *Isis*, 45 (1954), 256-268.

   Argues that the seventeenth-century development of geology has two main roots: (a) antiquarian interest in digging up and interpreting human remains and (b) the imperative in the Scientific Revolution to put knowledge--in this case of time past--onto a natural footing.

195. SCHOLL, D.W. "The History of Stratigraphy and the Development of the Geologic Time Scale." *The Compass*, 34 (1957), 278-285.

196. TASCH, Paul. "A Quantitative Estimate of Geological Time by Lyell." *Isis*, 66 (1975), 406.

 Discusses some of Lyell's private computations of geological time.

197. TOULMIN, Stephen, and GOODFIELD, June. *The Discovery of Time*. New York: Harper & Row, 1965, pp. 280.

 Sees the development of the idea of geological time in the context of the rise of notions of human history from the Renaissance onward. Places biological evolutionism in its relation to Lyellian time.

198. TUVESON, E.L. *Millennium and Utopia*. Berkeley: University of California Press, 1949. Reprinted Gloucester, Mass.: Peter Smith, 1962.

 Stresses the role of Christian eschatology, especially Millennialist thinking, in developing that sense of Nature evolving over time which became so central to the geological world-picture.

I. Mineralogy

199. ALBURY, W.R., and OLDROYD, D.R. "From Renaissance Mineral Studies to Historical Geology, in the Light of Michel Foucault's 'The Order of Things.'" *The British Journal for the History of Science*, 10 (1977), 187-215.

 Argues that Foucault's belief that there was a fundamental shift in European thought at the end of the eighteenth century from an essentially static outlook which stressed "order" to a genetic outlook which stressed history and change can be extended to the development of the Earth sciences as well, particularly with regard to the emergence of historical geology in the work of Werner and Hutton.

200. BURKE, John G. "Mineral Classification in the Early Nineteenth Century." Pp. 62-77 in SCHNEER, C.J., ed. *Toward a History of Geology*. Cambridge, Mass., and London: M.I.T. Press, 1969, pp. vi+469.

Investigates differences of opinion between Haüy, Berzelius and Dufrénoy as to whether mineral classification should have a physical or a chemical basis.

201. CAMPBELL SMITH, W. "Early Mineralogy in Great Britain and Ireland." *Bulletin of the British Museum (Natural History)*. Historical Series, 6 (1978), 49-74.

    Investigates the mineralogical inquiries of naturalists such as John Woodward, J.R. Forster and Mendes da Costa, leading up to the more important work of Kirwan and Jameson.

202. EMBREY, Peter G. "Minerals." Pp. 39-44 in CHALMERS-HUNT, J.M., ed. *Natural History Auctions, 1700-1972. A Register of Sales in the British Isles*. London: Sotheby Parke Bernet, 1976, pp. x+189.

    Lists sales of mineral collections in Britain.

203A. FORD, William E. "The Growth of Mineralogy from 1818 to 1918." Pp. 268-283 in DANA, Edward S., et al. *A Century of Science in America, with Special Reference to the American Journal of Science, 1818-1918*. New Haven, Conn.: Yale University Press; London: Oxford University Press, 1918, pp. xii+458.

    Stresses the importance of Silliman, Cleaveland and Dana in developing interest in the science in the United States, and assesses the later eminence of S.L. Penfield.

203B. GREENE, John C., and BURKE, John G. "The Science of Minerals in the Age of Jefferson." *Transactions of the American Philosophical Society*, 68, pt. 4 (1978).

    Investigates the European background of mineralogy toward the end of the eighteenth century, examines mineralogy in early Philadelphia and New York, and then discusses the work of Cleaveland and Silliman in the early years of the nineteenth century.

204. GROTH, P. *Entwicklungsgeschichte der mineralogischen Wissenschaften*. Berlin: Springer, 1926, pp. vi+262.

    Chiefly a history of crystallography with excerpts from major primary texts and extensive references, but also includes a survey particularly of modern developments in mineralogy.

Mineralogy

205. GUNTAU, M. "Die Entwicklung der Vorstellungen von der Mineralogie in der Wissenschaftsgeschichte." *Geologie*, 18 (1969), 526-537.

Shows how various kinds of investigation of the Earth were understood within terms of mineralogy up to the end of the eighteenth century, and investigates the role of Werner as a systematizer of mineralogy.

206. HOOYKAAS, Reijer. "The Species Concept in 18th Century Mineralogy." *Archives Internationales d'Histoire des Sciences*, nos. 18-19 (1952), 45-55.

Examines the attempts of eighteenth-century mineralogists to order the mineral kingdom within a classification similar to that employed by Linnaeus for the animal and vegetable kingdoms.

207A. KOBELL, Franz von. *Geschichte der Mineralogie von 1650-1850*. Geschichte der Wissenschaften in Deutschland. München: Merhoff's-Verlag, 1863, pp. iv+204.

Very thorough, particularly on German mineralogy, and pays welcome attention to the history of nomenclature and classification.

207B. MULTHAUF, Robert P. *Neptune's Gift: A History of Common Salt*. Baltimore, Md., and London: The Johns Hopkins University Press, 1978, pp. xviii+325.

Includes a discussion of salt geology.

208. OLDROYD, D.R. "Some Phlogistic Mineralogical Schemes Illustrative of the Evolution of the Concept of 'Earth' in the Seventeenth and Eighteenth Centuries." *Annals of Science*, 31 (1974), 269-306.

Discusses mineralogists such as J.J. Becher and J.F. Henckel to illustrate the physico-chemical ideas underlying the notion of mineral composition.

209. OLDROYD, D.R. "Mechanical Mineralogy." *Ambix*, 21 (1974), 157-178.

Examines attempts within the corpuscularian philosophy of the seventeenth and eighteenth centuries to account for mineral structure, and atomistic theories of the Earth.

210. OLDROYD, D.R. "Mineralogy and the 'Chemical Revolution.'" *Centaurus*, 1 (1975), 54-71.

    Assesses the impact of Lavoisierian chemistry on mineral classification.

211. ORCEL, Jean. *Les Sciences minéralogiques au XIXe siècle. (Minéralogie, cristallographie, lithologie.)* Les Conférences du Palais de la Découverte, ser. D, no. 92. Paris: Université de Paris, 1962, pp. 39.

    Largely biographically organized account of key developments.

212. ORCEL, Jean. "Considérations générales sur les rapports entre la minéralogie et les autres sciences." *Bulletin de la Société Française de Minéralogie et de Cristallographie*, 77 (1954), 45-69.

213. ORCEL, Jean. "Essai sur le concept d'espèce et les classifications en mineralogie et petrographie. Aperçu historique et philosophique." *Revue Roumaine de Geologie, Geophysique et Geographie*, 10 (1966), 3-39.

    Examines chemical, physical, atomic and other criteria for mineral classification using historical examples chiefly from the eighteenth century.

J. Glacial Geology

214. BREMNER, A. "Glacial and Post-Glacial Geology." *Transactions of the Edinburgh Geological Society*, 13 (1935), 260-270.

    On the work of members of the Edinburgh Geological Society which contributed to the acceptance of the land-ice theory.

215. DAVIES, G.L. "Early Discoverers. XXVI. Another Forgotten Pioneer of the Glacial Theory: James Hutton." *Journal of Glaciology*, 7 (1968), 115-116.

    Claims that Playfair's theory of erratic boulders was really Hutton's.

216. FRÄNGSMYR, Tore. *Upptackten av Istiden: Studier i den Moderna Geolognins Framvaxt.* (The Discovery of the

Ice Age.) Lychnos-Bibliotek, 29. Stockholm: Almqvist & Wiksell, 1976, pp. 188.

Pays particular attention to the role of Swedish scientists in the development of theories of the former extent of glaciation, especially Berzelius and Joroll. Emphasizes how the establishment of the theory of Ice Ages runs counter to a positivistic account of the history of geology in which Lyellian Uniformitarianism is praised.

217. GARWOOD, E. "Speculation and Research in Alpine Glaciology: An Historical Review." *Quarterly Journal of the Geological Society of London*, 88 (1932), xciii-cxviii.

    Considers the history of glaciology in four periods (before 1840; 1840-1862; 1862-1899; after 1900) with a postscript on the role of ice in the formation of Alpine scenery.

218. HANSEN, Bert. "The Early History of Glacial Theory in British Geology." *Journal of Glaciology*, 9 (1970), 135-141.

    Examines the mixed response in Britain to Agassiz's notion of an Ice Age, stressing Buckland's sympathetic response, and Lyell's initial opposition, supporting the earlier Drift theory.

219. HARRIS, A.W. "The Glacial Theory: Some of Its Beginnings." *Proceedings of the Liverpool Geological Society*, 85 (1944-1947), 47-51.

    Synoptic account of the pre-Agassiz period and of the introduction of the glacial theory to Britain.

220. NORTH, F.J. "Centenary of the Glacial Theory." *Proceedings of the Geological Association*, 54 (1943), 1-28.

    Well-documented account of shifting views of the effects of floods and glaciation from seventeenth-century theories of Noah's Flood to Karl Schimper's *Die Erdzeit*.

221. PATTEN, Donald W. *The Biblical Flood and the Ice Epoch: A Study in Scientific History*. Seattle, Wash.: Pacific Meridian Publishing Co., 1966.

222. ROWLINSON, J.S. "The Theory of Glaciers." *Notes and Records of the Royal Society of London*, 26 (1971), 189-204.

On the controversy between J. Tyndall and J.D. Forbes over the way glaciers move. Forbes proposed that they flowed as if a viscous fluid, Tyndall thought they operated according to a system of fracture and regelation. The modern view is nearer to Forbes's than to Tyndall's.

223. RUDWICK, M.J.S. "The Glacial Theory." *History of Science*, 8 (1969), 136-157.

   Emphasizes the methodological and philosophical difficulties which glacial theory from Charpentier to Agassiz presented both to Progressionist and especially to Uniformitarian geologists, with its assumption of sudden, disruptive refrigeration.

224. SCHULZ, Werner. "Die Entwicklung zur Inlandeistheorie im südlichen Ostseeraum. Zum einhundertjährigen Bestehen der Inlandeistheorie." *Zeitschrift für geologische Wissenschaft*, 3 (1975), 1023-1035.

225. SEYLAZ, L. "Early Discoverers. XV. A Forgotten Pioneer of the Glacial Theory: John Playfair." *Journal of Glaciology*, 4 (1962), 124-126.

   Describes Playfair's deduction that erratic boulders of the Jura had been transported by ice.

K. Continental Drift and Plate Tectonics

226. CAROZZI, Albert V. "New Historical Data on the Origin of the Theory of Continental Drift." *Bulletin of the Geological Society of America*, 81 (1970), 283-285.

   Argues that--contrary to common assumption--Francis Bacon and François Placet should not be viewed as forerunners of Continental Drift theory. A. Snider (1858) is the first writer who should be so regarded.

227. FRANKEL, Henry. "Arthur Holmes and Continental Drift." *The British Journal for the History of Science*, 11 (1978), 130-150.

   Examines Holmes's attempts to deal with some of the objections to Wegener's theory, especially his "convection current hypothesis."

228. FRANKEL, Henry. "Why Drift Theory Was Accepted with the Confirmation of Harry Hess's Concept of Sea Floor Spreading." Pp. 337-356 in SCHNEER, C.J., ed. *Two Hundred Years of Geology in America. Proceedings of the New Hampshire Bicentennial Conference on the History of Geology*. Hanover, N.H.: University Press of New England, 1979, pp. xvi+385.

Argues that the synthesizing power of Hess's sea-floor-spreading hypothesis was not sufficient to win assent to Drift theory. Rather, Drift theory came in with the corroboration of the Vine-Matthews hypothesis and the Wilson transform-fault hypothesis.

229. HALLAM, A. "Alfred Wegener and the Hypothesis of Continental Drift." *Scientific American*, 232 (2) (1975), 88-97.

Suggests that Wegener was able to propose his revolutionary hypothesis partly because he wasn't an orthodox mainstream geologist. Primarily a meteorologist, Wegener believed that the lateral motion of continents was possible since they floated on a substratum of viscous dense material and were moved by forces set up by the Earth's rotation.

230. HALLAM, Anthony. *A Revolution in the Earth Sciences. From Continental Drift to Plate Tectonics*. Oxford: Clarendon Press, 1973, pp. 127.

Argues that Wegener's championing of the theory of Continental Drift won but indifferent support until the physical hypothesis of plate tectonics gave it explanatory support. Hallam views the swift and remarkable success of plate tectonics in the light of T.S. Kuhn's notion that scientific revolutions occur through paradigm switches.

231. KITTS, David B. "Continental Drift and Scientific Revolution." *Bulletin of the American Association of Petroleum Geologists*, 58 (1974), 2490-2496.

Denies the applicability of Kuhn's notion of "scientific revolution" to the acceptance of the theory of Continental Drift, arguing rather that it constitutes an episode in the evolution of geological theory.

232. LAUDAN, Rachel. "The Recent Revolution in Geology and Kuhn's Theory of Scientific Change." Pp. 284-296 in

GUTTING, G., ed. *Paradigms and Revolutions: Applications of Appraisals of Thomas Kuhn's Philosophy of Science.* Notre Dame, Ind.: University of Notre Dame Press, 1980.

Discusses the applicability of Kuhn's notion of paradigm and scientific revolution to the development of plate tectonics, criticizing in detail Kitts's account (see item 231).

233. MARVIN, Ursula B. *Continental Drift: The Evolution of a Concept.* Washington, D.C.: Smithsonian Institution Press, 1973, pp. 239.

Early chapters survey theories of migrating continents and oceans advanced from the eighteenth century. After an assessment of Wegener's work, the author asks why Drift theory was so neglected until the 1960s, and examines its recent dramatic acceptance.

234. RUPKE, Nicolaas A. "Continental Drift Before 1900." *Nature*, 227 (1970), 349-350.

Argues that the so-called precursors of the theory of Continental Drift, such as Francis Bacon, had no clear theory. Their ideas were Catastrophic, unlike modern Drift theory.

L. Mapping

235. BAGROW, L. *History of Cartography.* Trans. D.L. Paiseley. London: C.A. Watts, 1964, pp. 310.

A world-wide and well-illustrated survey of the development of cartographic techniques (paying less attention to the growth of surveying as such). Discusses the growth of physical geography and cartography in the sixteenth and seventeenth centuries as important background to the rise of geological mapping in the eighteenth century.

236. BROWN, L.A. *The Story of Maps.* London: Cresset, 1951, pp. xx+396.

A history of cartography, chiefly up to the Early Modern period, examining the Classical geography of Ptolemy and stressing the intimate relations between

Mapping   51

  map-making and navigation, and relevance to the history
  of geology for tracing the growth of physical knowledge
  of the oceans.

237. CAILLEUX, André. "The Geological Map of North America
  (1752) of J.E. Guettard." Pp. 43-52 in SCHNEER, C.J.,
  ed. *Two Hundred Years of Geology in America. Proceedings of the New Hampshire Bicentennial Conference on the History of Geology.* Hanover, N.H.: University
  Press of New England, 1979, pp. xvi+385.

  Reproduces and discusses the earliest geological map
  of America, produced by Guettard (who had not visited
  America).

238. EYLES, V.A. "Mineralogical Maps as Forerunners of Modern
  Geological Maps." *Cartographic Journal*, 9 (1972),
  133-135.

  Traces the development of geological cartography
  from the eighteenth-century practice of marking the
  location of mineral deposits on topographic maps through
  to the development of the present-day geological map
  showing the distribution of geological formations. By
  the opening of the nineteenth century the geological
  map had largely superseded the mineralogical map,
  although some characteristics of the latter persisted
  into that century.

239. IRELAND, H.A. "History of the Development of Geologic
  Maps." *Bulletin of the Geological Society of America*,
  54 (1943), 1227-1280.

  Covers the development of mapping in Europe, Asia,
  Australia, New Zealand and the Americas, and world maps.
  Contains a useful list of references and bibliography.
  Interesting on the effects of such technological changes
  as the introduction of chromolithography.

240. JUDD, John W. "The Earliest Geological Maps of Scotland
  and Ireland." *Geological Magazine*, 35 (1898), 145-
  149.

  Examines John MacCulloch's work in Scotland and Richard
  Griffith's in Ireland.

241. LEIGHTON, Henry. "One Hundred Years of New York State
  Geologic Maps 1809-1909." *Bulletin of the New York
  State Museum*, 133 (1910), 115-155.

242. NORTH, F.J. *Geological Maps; Their History and Development, with Special Reference to Wales.* Cardiff: National Museum of Wales and Press Board of the University of Wales, 1928, pp. vi+134.

   The first section examines the development of geological maps in Britain from Martin Lister's first proposals late in the seventeenth century; the second section discusses the development of the mapping of Wales in the nineteenth century; and the third lists geological maps of Wales.

243. RAPPAPORT, Rhoda. "The Geological Atlas of Guettard, Lavoisier, and Monnet: Conflicting Views of the Nature of Geology." Pp. 272-287 in SCHNEER, C.J., ed. *Toward a History of Geology.* Cambridge, Mass., and London: M.I.T. Press, 1969, pp. vi+469.

   The Atlas did not contain geological maps as they came to be standardized in the nineteenth century, but rather a map of France containing extensive mineral spot symbols.

244. RUDWICK, Martin J.S. "The Emergence of a Visual Language for Geological Science, 1760-1840." *History of Science,* 14 (1976), 149-195.

   Argues that the visual language of geology (maps, columns, cross sections, etc.) is a very complex and highly artificial language of signs and conventions. Traces its development into classic mid-nineteenth-century forms and analyzes its relationship to more naturalistic traditions of landscape representation.

245. WELLS, John W. "Notes on the Earliest Geological Maps of the United States 1756-1832." *Journal of the Washington Academy of Science,* 49 (1959), 198-204.

   Traces American geological mapping from Guettard's map of 1756 (which located earths and minerals by spot symbols) up to the work of Maclure.

246. WHITE, G. "William Maclure's Maps of the Geology of the United States." *Journal of the Society for the Bibliography of Natural History,* 8 (1977), 266-269.

   Examines the pioneering maps attached to the various versions of Maclure's important *Geology of the United States,* first published in 1809.

M. Practical Geology

247. BARRETT, Sir W., and BESTERMAN, T. *The Divining Rod: An Experimental and Psychological Investigation.* London: Methuen, 1926, pp. xxiii+336.

    An inquiry into the scientific status of dowsing, with extensive use of historical materials.

248. BENTZ, Alfred. "Die Entwicklung der Erdölgeologie." *Zeitschrift der deutschen geologischen Gesellschaft*, 100 (1948), 188-197.

249. BROWN, Bahngrell W. "Origin of Petroleum Geology." *Bulletin of the American Association of Petroleum Geologists*, 56 (1972), 566-568.

    Argues that the first clear statement of the principle of structural control for petroleum migration is traceable to T. Sterry Hunt, not I.C. White as is often claimed. Argues the importance of Hunt in nineteenth-century geology.

250. DeGOLYER, Everette L. *The Development of the Art of Prospecting with Special Reference to the American Petroleum Industry.* Cyrus Fogg Brackett Lecture. Princeton, N.J.: Princeton University Press, 1939.

251. DeGOLYER, Everette L. "Notes on the Early History of Applied Geophysics in the Petroleum Industry." *Journal of the Society of Petroleum Geophysicists*, 6 (1935), 1-10.

252. DeGOLYER, Everette L. *The Development of the Art of Prospecting. With Special Reference to the American Petroleum Industry.* Princeton, N.J.: Princeton University (Guild of Brackett Lectures), 1940.

253. DICKEY, Parke A. "100 Years of Oil Geology." *GeoTimes*, 3, no. 6 (1959), 6-9, 24-25; no. 7, 6-7, 24-25.

254. GUNTAU, M. "Kriterien für die Herausbildung der Lagerstättenlehie als Wissenschaft im 19. Jahrhundert." *Geologie*, 20 (1971), 348-360.

    An investigation of the development of economic geology in German-speaking lands from the sixteenth to the nineteenth centuries.

255. JORDAN, William M. "Geology and the Industrial-Transportation Revolution in Early to Mid-Nineteenth Century Pennsylvania." Pp. 91-103 in SCHNEER, C.J., ed. *Two Hundred Years of Geology in America. Proceedings of the New Hampshire Bicentennial Conference on the History of Geology*. Hanover, N.H.: University Press of New England, 1979, pp. xvi+385.

   Stresses the important utilitarian stimuli for the development of East Coast geomorphology.

256. LEGGET, R.F. "Geology in the Service of Man." Pp. 242-261 in ALBRITTON, C., Jr., ed. *The Fabric of Geology*. Stanford, Calif.: Freeman, Cooper, 1963, pp. x+372.

   Broad chronological discussion of the relations of geological knowledge to practical application, focusing on surveying activities in the nineteenth century.

257. OWEN, Edgar W. "Remarks on the History of American Petroleum Geology." *Journal of the Washington Academy of Science*, 49 (1959), 256-260.

258. OWEN, Edgar W. "Trek of the Oil Finders: A History of Exploration for Petroleum." *Memoirs of the American Association of Petroleum Geologists*, 6 (1975), pp. 1647.

   Shows the powerful interconnections in America after 1859 between the economics of petroleum prospecting and the interests of major geologists such as Newberry, Winchell, Hunt and Andrews. The emphasis is on the United States but sections deal also with the Middle East, the Soviet Union, Africa and the North Sea.

259. PARSONS, A.B., ed. *Seventy-five Years of Progress in the Mineral Industry, 1871-1946. Including the Proceedings of the Seventy-Fifth Anniversary of the American Institute of Mining and Metallurgical Engineers, and World Conference on Mineral Resources ... 1947*. New York: American Institute of Mining and Metallurgical Engineers, 1947, pp. xii+817.

   Explores the development of economic geology in the United States, and gives a full history of the American Institute of Mining and Metallurgical Engineers.

260. PORTER, R. "The Industrial Revolution and the Rise of the Science of Geology." Pp. 320-343 in TEICH, M., and YOUNG, R.M., eds. *Changing Perspectives in the*

History of Science. Essays in Honour of Joseph Needham.
London: Heinemann, 1973, pp. xxi+488.

Argues that the connections between the English Industrial Revolution and the new science of geology were less close than might have been the case. This resulted from the *laissez-faire* nature of British capitalism, suspicious of interference and outside expertise, and snobbery among geologists who wanted their science to be "pure" rather than "applied."

261. SMITH, C.S. "Porcelain and Plutonism." Pp. 317-338 in SCHNEER, C.J., ed. *Toward a History of Geology.* Cambridge, Mass., and London: M.I.T. Press, 1969, pp. vi+469.

    Investigates the relations between the development of the china and porcelain ceramics industries in eighteenth-century Europe and the attempts of Huttonian geologists to demonstrate the igneous origin of basaltic rocks.

262. VOGT, E.Z., and HYMAN, R. *Water Witching U.S.A.* Chicago: University of Chicago Press, 1959, pp. xii+248.

    A history of American dowsing.

263. WÄCHTLER, E., ed. *Geologie und Industrielle Revolution.* Freiberg: Bergakademie, 1979.

    Essays on the relations between geological science and industrialization by M. Guntau, R. Porter and E. Wächtler.

N. Chemical Geology

264. BROCK, W.H. "Chemical Geology or Geological Chemistry?" Pp. 147-170 in JORDANOVA, L.J., and PORTER, Roy, eds. *Images of the Earth.* Chalfont St Giles, Bucks: The British Society for the History of Science, 1979, pp. xx+282.

    Investigates the interface between geology and chemistry in the mid-nineteenth century by focusing on the controversy between Sterry Hunt (who argued for the primacy of chemical knowledge in formulating a theory of the interior of the Earth) and David Forbes,

who asserted the sovereignty of geological facts.
Geologists resisted being dictated to by chemists.

265. DONOVAN, Arthur. "James Hutton, Joseph Black, and the Chemical Theory of Heat" (Abstract). Pp. 357-358 in SCHNEER, C.J., ed. *Two Hundred Years of Geology in America. Proceedings of the New Hampshire Bicentennial Conference on the History of Geology*. Hanover, N.H.: University Press of New England, 1979, pp. xvi+385.

    Places Hutton's theory of geological heat in the context of Joseph Black's chemistry.

266. MANTEN, A.A. "Historical Foundations of Chemical Geology and Geochemistry." *Chemical Geology*, 1 (1966), 5-31.

267. VINOGRADOV, A.P. "Half a Century of Geochemistry." *Geochemistry International*, 4 (1969), 1027-1029.

4. COGNATE SCIENCES

A. Geophysics

268. BRUSH, Stephen G. "Nineteenth-Century Debates About the Inside of the Earth: Solid, Liquid or Gas?" *Annals of Science*, 36 (1979), 225-254.

    Analyzes William Hopkins's astronomical objections, and William Thomson's physical objections, to geologists' belief that the Earth had a molten core beneath a thin crust.

269. BURKE, John G. "The Earth's Central Heat: From Fourier to Kelvin." *Actes du VIIIe Congrès International d'Histoire des Sciences* [1971], (1974), 91-96.

    Discusses the similarities and contrasts between geologists' and physicists' conceptions of the Earth's interior and its thermal gradient in the age of Lyellian Uniformitarianism.

270. GILLMOR, C. Stewart. "The Place of the Geophysical Sciences in 19th-Century Natural Philosophy." *Eos*, 56 (1975), 4-7.

271. HARRADON, H.D. "Some Early Contributions to the History of Geomagnetism I-VI." *Terrestrial Magnetism and Atmospheric Electricity*, 48 (1943), 3-17, 79-92, 127-130, 197-202.

    Brief accounts of significant works from the time of Peter Peregrinus (thirteenth century) onward.

272. LAWRENCE, Philip. "Heaven and Earth--The Relation of the Nebular Hypothesis to Geology." Pp. 253-281 in YOURGRAU, Wolfgang, and BRECK, Allen D., eds. *Cosmology, History and Theology*. New York: Plenum, 1977, pp. 409.

Considers the geological implications of the work chiefly of Laplace for the notion of an evolving yet also cooling Earth.

273. MITCHELL, A.C. "Chapters in the History of Terrestrial Magnetism. I. On the Directive Property of a Magnet in the Earth's Field and the Origin of the Nautical Compass." *Terrestrial Magnetism and Atmospheric Electricity*, 37 (1932), 105-146; 42 (1937), 241-280; 44 (1939), 77-80.

    Discusses Classical examples, and the Early Modern period, and investigates Chinese magnetic ideas in some depth.

B. Geography

274. ALTENGARTEN, James S., and MOLYNEAUX, Gary Anderson. *The History, Philosophy, and Methodology of Geography: A Bibliography Selected for Education and Research.* Monticello, Ill.: Council of Planning Librarians, 1976, pp. 56.

275. BROC, Numa. *La Géographie des philosophes: Géographes et voyageurs au XVIIIe siècle.* Paris: Ophrys, 1975, pp. 595.

    Suggests a complex dialectic in which the junction of preconceived philosophical ideas with the findings of travelers was responsible for new eighteenth-century thinking on such topics as the global relation of land and sea, mountains and valleys, and the existence of an undiscovered Southern Continent. Usefully shows how much of the globe was still virtually *terra incognita* during the Enlightenment period.

276. DICKINSON, R.E. *The Makers of Modern Geography.* London: Routledge and Kegan Paul, 1969, pp. xiv+305.

    Examines the development of physical geography in the hands of Ritter, Humboldt, Richthofen and Penck.

277. FENNEMAN, Nevin M. "The Rise of Physiography." *Bulletin of the Geological Society of America*, 50 (1939), 349-359.

Surveys the study of physical geography from the time of the Ancients, concentrating on its late nineteenth-century development in the work of Penck, Gilbert and Davis.

278. FREEMAN, T.W. *A Hundred Years of Geography*. London: Gerald Duckworth, 1961, pp. 335. Reprinted with revisions, 1965.

 A history of geography over the last century, emphasizing the evolution of the science and academic discipline.

279. HETTNER, Alfred. *Die Geographie. Ihre Geschichte, ihr Wesen und ihre Methoden*. Breslau: Hirt, 1927, pp. viii+463.

 A wide-ranging history, strong on Classical sources and stressing the interrelations of geography with cultural shifts.

280. STODDART, D.R. "'That Victorian Science': Huxley's *Physiography* and Its Impact on Geography." *Transactions of the Institute of British Geographers*, 66 (1975), 17-40.

 Describes the impact of Huxley's *Physiography* on the way the Earth's physical features were studied in Britain. Its popularity and the subject's ultimate decline resulted from the educational changes of 1870-1880. Physiography's role as an Earth science was taken over by geomorphology.

C. Oceanography

281. BURSTYN, Harold L., and SCHLEE, Susan B. "The Study of Ocean Currents in America Before 1930." Pp. 145-155 in SCHNEER, C.J., ed. *Two Hundred Years of Geology in America. Proceedings of the New Hampshire Bicentennial Conference on the History of Geology*. Hanover, N.H.: University Press of New England, 1979, pp. xvi+ 385.

 Examines both the investigations of private individuals and federal-backed surveys, paying special attention to studies of ice.

282. DEACON, M. *Scientists and the Sea 1650-1900: A Study of Marine Science*. London: Academic Press, 1971, pp. xvi+445.

   Gives considerable attention to investigations of geological interest from the time of Hooke and Halley through to Murray's *Challenger* expedition.

283. DEACON, Margaret B., ed. *Oceanography: Concepts and History*. Benchmark Papers in Geology, 35. Stroudsburg, Pa.: Dowden, Hutchinson and Ross, 1978, pp. xvii+394.

   Extracts from primary writings on ocean science of the last three centuries.

284. HERDMAN, W.A. *Founders of Oceanography and Their Work: An Introduction to the Science of the Sea*. London: Edward Arnold & Company, 1923, pp. 340.

   Concentrates on the period from the mid-nineteenth century, focusing on the work of Edward Forbes, Louis and Alexander Agassiz and Sir John Murray.

285. IDYLL, C.P., ed. *Exploring the Ocean: A History of Oceanography*. New York: Crowell, 1970, pp. viii+280.

   A popular account focusing mainly on the last two centuries. Chapter 4 discusses geophysical themes such as the relations between the continents and the oceans and the theory of the tides and the currents.

286. LADD, H.S., and GUNTER, G. "The Development of Marine Paleoecology." *Geological Society of America, Memoirs*, 67 (1957), 67-74.

   Summary of the work of the great names in marine palaeoecology.

287. MENARD, William H. "Very Like a Spear." Pp. 19-20 in SCHNEER, C.J., ed. *Two Hundred Years of Geology in America. Proceedings of the New Hampshire Bicentennial Conference on the History of Geology*. Hanover, N.H.: University Press of New England, 1979, pp. xvi+385.

   A personal account of the transformation of marine geology in the light of plate tectonics over the last twenty years.

288. MILLS, E.L. "Edward Forbes, John Gwyn Jeffreys and British Dredging Before the *Challenger* Expedition." *Journal of the Society for the Bibliography of Natural History*, 8 (1978), 507-536.

   Assessing the contributions to marine biology of two little-known naturalists from 1830 to 1860.

289. THEODORIDES, J. "Les Débuts de la biologie marine en France: H. Ardouin et H. Milne-Edwards 1826-1829." *Congrès International d'Histoire d'Oceanographie* (Monaco), spec. no. 2 (1968), 417-437.

D. Natural History

290. ADAMS, A. *The Eternal Quest: The Story of the Great Naturalists*. London: Constable; New York: Putnam's, 1970, pp. 509.

   Includes discussions of Buffon, Cuvier, Lyell and Darwin.

291. BYNUM, W.F. "The Great Chain of Being after Forty Years." *History of Science*, 13 (1975), 1-28.

   Assesses Lovejoy's book (item 300) and argues that one factor in the late eighteenth-century demise of the idea was the growing recognition of extinction (from increased knowledge of the fossil record), and hence the acceptance of "gaps" in Nature.

292. DANCE, S. Peter. *Shell Collecting: An Illustrated History*. London: Faber & Faber, 1966, pp. 344.

   Deals with fossil conchology, and with debates about the use of fossil shells as evidence of Earth history from the eighteenth century. Important accounts of the major shell and fossil collections.

293. DAUDIN, H. *Etudes d'histoire des sciences naturelles*. 2 vols. Vol. 1: *Cuvier et Lamarck*. Vol. 2: *Les Classes zoologiques et l'idée de série animale, 1790-1830*. Paris: Alcan, 1926, pp. 460; 338.

   Touches upon the place of fossils and the possibility of extinction in the work of naturalists operating within the assumptions of the Great Chain of Being.

294. FOUCAULT, M. *The Order of Things*. London: Tavistock, 1970, pp. xxxv+387.

   Argues a sharp epistemological break with Cuvier at the beginning of the nineteenth century, permitting study of the Earth and of fossils to become for the first time truly historical, and thereby distinguishing geology and palaeontology from the earlier (and "static") science of natural history.

295. GLASS, H.B., TEMKIN, O., and STRAUS, W.L., eds. *Forerunners of Darwin*. Baltimore, Md.: The Johns Hopkins University Press, 1959, pp. xx+471.

   A collection of essays mainly on the history of biology but also containing discussions of the emergence of ideas of geological time and the relationships between biological and geological evolutionism.

296. GOULD, S.J. *Ever Since Darwin: Reflections in Natural History*. Harmondsworth, Middlesex: Penguin, 1980, pp. 285.

   Includes valuable essays on Thomas Burnet's theory of the Earth, the Catastrophist geology of Velikovsky, and the Uniformitarian-Catastrophist debate.

297. GUYENOT, E. *Les Sciences de la vie aux XVIIe et XVIIIe siècle*. Paris: Michel, 1957, pp. 462.

   Mainly deals with French naturalists and the emergence of zoology and physiology, but contains discussions of some issues of importance in the history of geology, e.g., the nature of coral.

298. HOENIGER, F.D., and HOENIGER, J.F.M. *The Growth of Natural History in Stuart England from Gerard to the Royal Society*. Charlottesville: University Press of Virginia for the Folger Shakespeare Library, 1969, pp. 60.

   Of interest to the historian of geology because of its discussion of county natural histories, and encyclopedic traditions, both of which included accounts of minerals and fossils, and of the Baconian impulse toward systematic observation.

299. LEPENIES, W. *Das Ende der Naturgeschichte*. Munich: Hanser Verlag, 1976, pp. 277.

Examines the shift from the largely atemporal orientation of the natural history sciences toward the end of the eighteenth century to the later emphasis on history and the developments of which geology is an instance.

300. LOVEJOY, A.O. *The Great Chain of Being*. Cambridge, Mass.: Harvard University Press, 1936, pp. x+376.

    Details the metaphysical foundations for the notion of the three kingdoms of Nature, upon which much pre-1800 mineralogy and understanding of fossils was based.

301. MORNET, D. *Les Sciences de la nature en France, au XVIIIe siècle. Un Chapitre de l'histoire des idées*. Paris: Colin, 1911, pp. x+291.

    Classic discussion of the natural history sciences in their public dimension: their popularization, connections with the arts and literature and uses in the context of religious piety and popular morality. Includes an important account of library holdings of natural history books.

302. NORDENSKIÖLD, Erik. *The History of Biology: A Survey*. New York: Tudor Publishing Co., 1928, pp. x+630.

    Explores the role of geology in the development of *Naturphilosophie* and evolutionary theory, and contains biographical sections on major geologists.

303. RITTERBUSH, P. *Overtures to Biology: The Speculations of Eighteenth Century Biologists*. New Haven, Conn.: Yale University Press, 1964, pp. ix+287.

    Discusses eighteenth-century accounts of the nature of life. Of relevance for its accounts of Erasmus Darwin, Lamarck, John Hunter and Humphry Davy in relation to ideas of cosmic energy and activity.

304. SACHS, Julius von. *Geschichte der Botanik vom 16. Jahrhundert bis 1860*. Geschichte der Wissenschaften in Deutschland, Neuere Zeit, vol. XV. Munich: Oldenbourg, 1875. English trans. by H.E.F. Garnsey. Oxford: Clarendon Press, 1890, pp. 865.

    The discussions of seventeenth- and eighteenth-century botanists occasionally touch on the issues of fossil plants.

E. Crystallography and Metallography

305. AITCHESON, L. *A History of Metals*. 2 vols. London: Macdonald and Evans, 1960, pp. 198.

    The first volume takes the development of the theory of metals (focusing on element theory and alchemy) and its practical applications up to the Scientific Revolution. A chapter in vol. 2 is devoted to the imperialist explorations for metals in the nineteenth century, in America, India and Australia in particular.

306. BURKE, John G. *Origins of the Science of Crystals*. Berkeley and Los Angeles: University of California Press, 1966, pp. 198.

    Examines changing concepts from the magical theories, and explanations in terms of Aristotelian elements, common in the sixteenth and seventeenth centuries, through the mechanical philosophy's emphasis on corpuscles and the renewed eighteenth-century interest in chemical explanations. Ends with a discussion of Haüy's more geometrical ideas.

307. Item deleted.

308. HOOYKAAS, Reijer. *La Naissance de la cristallographie en France au XVIIIe siècle*. Paris: Université de Paris, 1953.

    Focuses on the work of Romé de l'Isle.

309. METZGER, H. *La Genèse de la science des cristaux*. Paris: Blanchard, 1969, pp. 248.

    Discusses the analysis of crystal structure and growth mainly within the chemical theories and corpuscular philosophy of the eighteenth century.

310. SCHNEER, Cecil J., ed. *Crystal Form and Structure*. Benchmark Papers in Geology, 34. Stroudsburg, Pa.: Dowden, Hutchinson & Ross, 1977, pp. xiii+388.

    Extracts from primary writings in the history of crystallography over the last three centuries, with linking commentary.

311. SMITH, C.S. *A History of Metallography*. Chicago: University of Chicago Press, 1960, pp. xxi+291.

Crystallography and Metallography

A well-illustrated account both of the deployment and of the science of metals in the major civilizations. Microscopic studies of metal structure are particularly examined, with a chapter devoted to the work of Sorby.

5. STUDIES BY AREA

A. Britain

312. BASSETT, Douglas A. *A Source-Book of Geological, Geomorphological and Soil Maps for Wales and the Welsh Borders (1800-1966)*. Cardiff: National Museum of Wales, 1967, pp. x+239.

    Lists geological papers of historical importance and gives a guide to the secondary historiographical literature.

313. CHALLINOR, John. *The History of British Geology: A Bibliographical Study*. Newton Abbot: David and Charles, 1971, pp. 224.

    Some eighty brief sections survey the major themes of British geology, and appendices give accounts of secondary literature, an index of authors and an index of place names.

314. CHALLINOR, John. "The Early Progress of British Geology. I. From Leland to Woodward, 1538-1718." *Annals of Science*, 9 (1953), 124-153.

315. CHALLINOR, John. "The Early Progress of British Geology. II. From Strachey to Michell, 1719-1788." *Annals of Science*, 10 (1954), 1-9.

316. CHALLINOR, John. "The Early Progress of British Geology. III. From Hutton to Playfair, 1788-1802." *Annals of Science*, 10 (1954), 107-148.

317. CHALLINOR, John. "The Progress of British Geology during the Early Part of the Nineteenth Century." *Annals of Science*, 26 (1970), 177-234.

A series of informative articles giving brief biographical details about the major British geologists, bibliographical listings of their work, and some discussion of their ideas, accompanied by copious extracts from their published writings.

318. CHALLINOR, J. "From Whitehurst's 'Inquiry' to Farey's 'Derbyshire,' a Chapter in the History of English Geology." *Transactions of the North Staffordshire Field Club*, 81 (1947), 52-88.

    Developments in geological investigations in Derbyshire in the late eighteenth and early nineteenth centuries.

319. Item deleted.

320. CHALLINOR, John. "North Staffordshire Geology, 1811-1948: The Progress of Research and a Short Guide to the Literature." *Transactions of the North Staffordshire Field Club*, 83 (1948-51), 1-26; 84 (1949-50), 27-48; 85 (1950-51), 49-64.

321. CHALLINOR, John. "Geological Research in Cardiganshire, 1842-1949." *Ceredigion. Journal of the Cardiganshire Antiquarian Society*, 1 (1951), 144-176.

322. CHALLINOR, John. "Literature Relating to the Geology, Mineralogy and Palaeontology of North Staffordshire." *Transactions of the North Staffordshire Field Club*, 80 (1946), 1-4.

323. DAVIES, Gordon L. "From Flood and Fire to Rivers and Ice--Three Hundred Years of Irish Geomorphology." *Irish Geography*, 5 (1964), 1-16.

    A survey of geomorphology in Ireland emphasizing the work of Kirwan, William Hamilton, Jukes and Kinahan.

324. EYLES, Victor A. "Scientific Activity in the Bristol Region in the Past." Pp. 123-143 in *British Association for the Advancement of Science. Bristol and Its Adjoining Counties*. Bristol: Arrowsmith, 1955.

    Discusses the work of early geologists such as Catcott, and the pioneer studies of Buckland and Conybeare.

325. FITTON, William H. "Notes on the History of English Geology." *Philosophical Magazine*, 1 (1832-1833), 147-160, 268-275, 442-450; 2 (1833-1834), 37-57.

Of historical importance chiefly for its stress on the key role of William Smith in the development of British stratigraphy and palaeontology.

326. FLETT, John S. "Pioneers of British Geology." *Journal of the Proceedings of the Royal Society New South Wales*, 73 (1939), 41-66.

 Traces British geology from the rivalry of the Wernerians and Huttonians down to the time of Sedgwick and Murchison.

327. GEIKIE, Archibald. *The First Century of Geology in Britain: Being Two Presidential Addresses to the Geological Society of London, 26th September 1907 and 21st February 1908*. London: The Geological Society, 1908, pp. 1-25+xliii+cxxv.

 An account of nineteenth-century British geology, stressing the role of members of the Geological Society of London, and in particular the Society's role in the promotion of the empirical descriptive geology of the British Isles and its mapping.

328. GEIKIE, A. "The Scottish School of Geology." Inaugural Lecture, Edinburgh, 1871. Reprinted in *Geological Sketches at Home and Abroad*. London: Macmillan, 1882, pp. x+382.

 The Scottish School is above all James Hutton and his followers, John Playfair and Sir James Hall. Argues that Hutton was the father of British geology because of his abandonment of religious dogma and armchair speculation in favor of empirical fieldwork, and admires Hutton's perception of the extent of denudation and the active powers of the Earth.

329. HOLLAND, Sir Thomas H. "Geology in Edinburgh at the Beginning of the Nineteenth Century." Address delivered at the Celebration of the Centenary of the Edinburgh Geological Society. *Transactions of the Edinburgh Geological Society*, 13 (1935), 202-209.

 Surveys Scottish geology from the time of Hutton, taking in the Edinburgh Geological Society and the Wernerian Natural History Society, and the importance of the British Association meeting in 1834.

330. NORTH, F.J. "From the Geological Map to the Geological Survey." *Transactions of the Cardiff Naturalists Society*, 65 (1934), 41-115.

   Survey of pioneer geology in Glamorgan in the work of Greenough, Buckland, Dillwyn, Conybeare and De la Beche.

331. NORTH, F.J. "Further Chapters in the History of Geology in South Wales; Sir H.T. De la Beche and the Geological Survey." *Transactions of the Cardiff Naturalists Society*, 67 (1934), 31-103.

   Focuses mainly on the history of the Geological Survey in South Wales, concentrating on the work of De la Beche, William Logan and Andrew Ramsay.

332. PORTER, Roy. *The Making of Geology. Earth Science in Britain 1660-1815*. Cambridge: Cambridge University Press, 1977, pp. xi+288.

   Attempts to show the transformation from a variety of approaches to investigation and understanding of the Earth to the specific and new science of *geology* as it emerged in Britain during the eighteenth century, paying attention to the broad social and cultural contexts.

333. RAISTRICK, Arthur. *Yorkshire Maps and Mapmakers*. Clapham: The Dalesman Publications Co., 1969, pp. 68.

   A chapter on geological and enclosure maps traces developments from Martin Lister's proposal of the 1680s through to the mapping of William Smith and the appearance of the Yorkshire sections of the Geological Survey memoirs in the latter half of the nineteenth century.

334. RUDLER, F.W. "Fifty Years' Progress in British Geology; Being an Address on the Opening of the Session 1887-8." *Proceedings of the Geologists Association*, 10 (1885), 234-272.

   Emphasizes the transformation to geology wrought by glacial theory, evolutionism and the rise of petrology. Has interesting remarks on international cooperation in geology à *propos* of the International Geological Congress.

335. SARJEANT, William A.S. "A History and Bibliography of the Study of Fossil Vertebrate Footprints in the British Isles." *Palaeogeography, Palaeoclimatology, Palaeoecology*, 16 (1974), 265-378.

A study by regions, listing and discussing mentions of fossil footprints in scientific literature mainly from the early nineteenth century. Extensively illustrated and with generous quotations from the source material.

336. TORRENS, Hugh. "Geological Communication in the Bath Area in the Last Half of the 18th Century." Pp. 215-247 in JORDANOVA, L.J., and PORTER, Roy S., eds. *Images of the Earth: Essays in the History of the Environment Sciences*. Chalfont St Giles, Bucks: British Society for the History of Science, 1979, pp. xx+282.

Shows the close social and geological connections among numerous amateur naturalists working in the southwestern counties of England in the last half of the eighteenth century. Argues that William Smith's grasp of the principle of the identification of strata by organized fossils rendered him superior to most of his contemporaries as a coal-mining prospector.

B. United States

337. ALLEN, R.C., and MARTIN, Helen M. "A Brief History of the Geological and Biological Survey of Michigan: 1837 to 1872, by R.C. Allen; 1872 to 1920, by Helen M. Martin." *Michigan History Magazine*, 6 (1922), 675-750.

338. CHAMBERLIN, Thomas C. "Seventy-five Years of American Geology." *Science*, 59 (1924), 127-135.

339. DERBY, Alice G., and PROSSER, Mary W. "A Bibliography of Ohio Geology. 2 Parts. Pt. 1. A subject index to the publications of the Geological Survey in Ohio, from its inception to and including Bulletin 8 of the fourth series, by Alice G. Derby. Part 2. A bibliography of the publications relating to the geology of Ohio, other than those of the State Geological Survey, by Mary W. Prosser." *Bulletin of the Geological Survey, Ohio*, series 4, no. 6 (1906).

340. FAIRCHILD, H. Le Roy. "Glacial Geology in America." *American Geologist*, 22 (1898), 154-189.

Shows the transition from the "Drift" theory, popular in the 1830s, to Agassiz's glacial ideas, first taken up in America by Edward Hitchcock.

341. FERGUSON, Walter K. *Geology and Politics in Frontier Texas 1845-1909.* Austin and London: University of Texas Press, 1969.

342. GOETZMANN, William H. *Exploration and Empire: The Explorer and the Scientist in the Winning of the American West.* New York: Knopf, 1966, pp. xxii+656.

   A general history of U.S. exploration and surveying, devoting much attention to geological matters. Separate chapters assess the work of Clarence King and Wesley Powell, in particular the utilization of scientific knowledge to shape exploitation of natural resources.

343. HAZEN, Robert M., ed. *North American Geology: Early Writings.* Benchmark Papers in Geology, 51. Stroudsburg, Pa.: Dowden, Hutchinson & Ross, 1979, xvii+356.

   Extracts covering the period up to the early nineteenth century, organized under "Earthquakes," "Fossils," "Medical Geology," "Mineralogy," "Physics of the Earth," "Formation and Classification of Rocks," "Field Geology" and "American Geology Comes of Age."

344. HAZEN, Robert M., and HAZEN, Margaret H. *Bibliography of American Geology Published 1669-1850.* Microcard Publications, no. 4. Boulder, Colo.: Geological Society of America, 1976, pp. 984.

   Contains 14,000 references.

345. JILLSON, Willard R. *Geological Research in Kentucky. A Summary Account of the Several Geological Surveys of Kentucky, Including a Complete List of Their Publications and a General Bibliography of 806 Titles Pertaining to Kentucky Geology.* Frankfurt: Kentucky Geological Survey, 1923, pp. 228.

346. LESLEY, J. Peter. "Historical Sketch of Geological Explorations in Pennsylvania and Other States." *Second Geological Survey of Pennsylvania, Report A.* Harrisburg and Pasadena: Board of Commissioners for the Second Geological Survey, 1876, pp. xxvi+200.

347. MENDENHALL, W.C. "Development and Present Status of Geology in North America." *Bulletin of the Geological Society of America,* 48 (1937), 349-364.

   Divided into four sections, "Early European Influences," "Early Work in America," "Post-Civil War Period" and

"Present Status." Emphasizes the role of economic and educational influences in recent times.

348. MERRILL, George P. "The Development of the Glacial Hypothesis in America." *Popular Science Monthly*, 68 (1906), 300-322.

349. MERRILL, George P. "Contributions to the History of American Geology." *Report of the Board of Regents of the Smithsonian Institution*, 1904, pp. 189-733. Reprinted in *The First One Hundred Years of American Geology*. New Haven, Conn.: Yale University Press, 1924, pp. xxi+773.

    Divides the century into four periods: the Maclurean, 1785-1819, named after the "father of American geology"; the Eatonian, marked by more careful mapping, from 1820 to 1829; the period of the state surveys, from 1830 to 1879; and the age of national surveys, from 1889. Strong mainly for the period after the founding of the state geological surveys.

350. OSPOVAT, Alexander M. "The 'Wernerian Era' of American Geology." Pp. 237-244 in ROSLER, Hans J., et al. *Abraham Gottlob Werner. Gedenkschrift aus Anlass der Wiederkehr seines Todestages nach 150 Jahren am 30 Juni 1967*. Freiberg: VEB, Deutscher Verlag für Glundstoffindustrie, 1976, pp. 317.

    Assesses the influence of Werner on the geology of Eaton, Silliman and Dana. Werner's work was not slavishly followed, but provided a framework within which research and teaching could proceed.

351. OSPOVAT, Alexander M. "Werner's Influence on American Geology." *Proceedings of the Oklahoma Academy for Science*, 40 (1960), 98-103.

352. PESTANA, Harold R. *Bibliography of Congressional Geology*. New York: Hafner Publishing Co., 1972, pp. 285.

    A brief discussion of the geological activities of Congress is followed by a 100-page bibliography extensively cross-indexed.

353. PESTANA, Harold R., and BONTA, Bruce D. "Congressional Geology." *Bulletin of the Geological Society of America*, 81 (1970), 899-904.

Lists Congressional geological reports published in the nineteenth and early twentieth centuries. Discusses the role of Congress in promoting geology.

354. PYNE, S.J. "From the Grand Canyon to the Marianas Trench: The Earth Sciences after Darwin." Pp. 165-192 in REINGOLD, Nathan, ed. *The Sciences in the American Context: New Perspectives*. Washington, D.C.: Smithsonian Institution Press, 1979, pp. 399.

    An essay on American geology from the late nineteenth century to the present, with an emphasis on the influence of plate tectonics on oceanography.

355. SCHNEER, Cecil J., ed. *Two Hundred Years of Geology in America. Proceedings of the New Hampshire Bicentennial Conference on the History of Geology*. Hanover, N.H.: University Press of New England, 1979, pp. xvi+385.

    Essays (separately listed here) dealing with aspects of the history of American geology, with an editorial introduction assessing larger themes.

356. SCHUCHERT, Charles. "A Century of Geology. The Progress of Historical Geology in North America." Pp. 60-121 in DANA, Edward S., et al. *A Century of Science in America, with Special Reference to the American Journal of Science, 1818-1918*. New Haven, Conn.: Yale University Press; London: Oxford University Press, 1918, pp. xii+458.

    Emphasizes the three growth points of early American geology, the scientific societies of Boston and Philadelphia and the work of Silliman at Yale and then the importance of the American Geological Society, founded in 1819. The bitter controversies surrounding Emmons's announcement of the Taconic System are assessed.

357. STEARNS, R.P. *Science in the British Colonies of America*. Urbana: University of Illinois Press, 1970, pp. xx+762.

    Discusses the work of pioneer American naturalists such as John Bannister and Cotton Mather, details their collections and emphasizes their connections with the Royal Society.

358. WHITE, George W. "Early Geological Observations in the American Mid-West." Pp. 415-425 in SCHNEER, C.J., ed. *Toward a History of Geology.* Cambridge, Mass., and London: M.I.T. Press, 1969, pp. vi+469.

   Deals chiefly with eighteenth-century naturalists and explorers such as Lewis Evans, Peter Kalm, Robert Rogers, Jonathan Carver, Thomas Hutchins and David Schopf.

359. WHITE, G.W. "History of Investigation and Classification of Wisconsinian Drift in North-Central United States." *Geological Society of America, Memoir,* 136 (1973), 3-34.

   Investigates changing interpretations of outwash deposits in the Ohio Valley from the early nineteenth century, particularly noting the shift of views which accompanied the rise of glacial theory.

360. WHITE, George W. "The History of Geology and Mineralogy as Seen by American Writers, 1803-1835: A Bibliographic Essay." *Isis,* 64 (1973), 197-214.

   Describes early American accounts of the history of geology from Samuel Miller (1803) onward.

361. WHITE, G. "Early American Geology." *The Scientific Monthly,* 76 (1953), 134-141. Reprinted in WHITE, George W. *Essays on History of Geology.* New York: Arno Press, 1978.

   Deals with geological writing in America up to the end of the eighteenth century, concentrating on the work of Thomas Hariot, John Smith, William Wood, John Clayton, Robert Beverley, John Bartram and Lewis Evans.

362. WHITE, George W., and SLANKER, Barbara O. *Early Geology in the Mississippi Valley; an Exhibition of Selected Works Held in the University of Illinois Library at Urbana, November 1962.* Urbana: University of Illinois, 1962. Reprinted in WHITE, George W. *Essays on History of Geology.* New York: Arno Press, 1978.

363. WILLIS, Bailey. "American Geology 1850-1900." *Science,* 96 (1942), 167-179.

   Includes a brief section on the development of geophysics, mineralogy and crystallography and assesses American contributions to the theory of mountain building.

364. WILSON, Leonard G. "The Emergence of Geology as a Science in the United States." *Journal of World History*, 10 (1967), 416-437.

    Emphasizes the utilitarian motives for the development of geology in the early United States and focuses upon the emergence of geology as a professional activity.

365. WINCHELL, Newton H. "Geological Notes from Early Explorers in the Minnesota Valley." *Bulletin of the Minnesota Academy of Natural Science*, 1 (1974), 89-101, 153-156.

C. Other
In alphabetical order by country or continent

ANTARCTICA

366. CRADDOCK, Campbell, ed. "The Geological Sciences in U.S. Antarctic Research." *Geological Times*, 11 (1966), 13-35.

AUSTRALIA

367. BRANAGAN, David F. "Samuel Stutchbury and Reverend W.B. Clarke. Not quite Equal and Opposite." Pp. 89-98 in STANBURY, Peter, ed. *100 Years of Australian Scientific Explorations*. Sydney, New York, Toronto and London: Holt, Rinehart and Winston, 1975, pp. 124.

368. BRANAGAN, David F., and TOWNLEY, K.A. "The Geological Sciences in Australia--A Brief Historical Review." *Earth Science Review*, 12 (1976), 323-346.

369. TOWNLEY, K.A. "History of the Bureau of Mineral Resources, Geology and Geophysics." Pp. 101-111 in JOHNS, R.K., ed. *History and Role of Government Geological Surveys in Australia*. Adelaide: South Australian Government Printer, 1976, pp. 111.

BELGIUM

370. DEWALQUE, Gustave. "Coup d'oeil sur la marche des sciences minerales en Belgique." *Bulletin de l'Académie Royale de Belgique*, 2nd ser., 30 (1870), 457-496.

An account of nineteenth-century Belgian geology and mineralogy, emphasizing the work of Dumont and d'Halloy.

371. LERICHE, Maurice. "L'Histoire de la géologie dans la région Gallo-Belge." *Revue de l'Université de Bruxelles*, 1928-1929, pp. 26.

CANADA

372. ADAMS, Frank D. "The History of Geology in Canada." Pp. 7-20 in TORY, H.M., ed. *A History of Science in Canada*. Toronto: Ryerson Press, 1939, pp. vi+152.

373. ELLS, Robert W. *A History of New Brunswick Geology*. Montreal: Gazette Printing Co., 1887.

374. GEOLOGICAL ASSOCIATION OF CANADA. "History of Canadian Geologists." *Proceedings of the Geological Association of Canada*, 23 (1971-1972), 1-41.

375. LEVERE, Trevor H., and HARRELL, Richard A., eds. *A Curious Field-book. Science & Society in Canadian History*. Toronto: Oxford University Press, 1974, pp. xi+233.

One chapter examines the development of Canadian geology, especially government patronage of the science through the Survey: how far was it a quest for pure knowledge or chiefly a utilitarian enterprise?

376. NEALE, E.R.W., ed. *The Earth Sciences in Canada. A Centennial Appraisal and Forecast*. Toronto: University of Toronto Press and Royal Society of Canada, 1968, pp. xi+259.

Essays by various hands on the history of Canadian geology, stressing the importance in recent times of the petroleum industry and the many facets of applied geology (with a major essay on the importance of the mineral industry to the national economy).

377. PARKS, W.A. "The Development of Stratigraphic Geology and Palaeontology in Canada." Presidential address. *Transactions of the Royal Society of Canada*, 16 (1922), 1-46.

Focuses chiefly on the period after about 1820 and stresses Canada's debts to American geologists. Useful

sections on Logan and the Canadian survey and on Dr.
G.M. Dawson's surveys of the region of the Great Plains.

CHINA

378. NEEDHAM, Joseph, and WANG LING. *Science and Civilization in China.* Vol. 3: *Mathematics and the Sciences of the Heavens and the Earth.* Cambridge: University Press, 1959, pp. xlvii+876.

Deals with Chinese meteorology, geography, cartography, geology, seismology and mineralogy.

CUBA

379. CONDE, José A. *Historia de la Geologia, Mineralogia y Paleontologia en Cuba.* La Habana: Publicaciones de la Junta Nacional de Arqueologia y Etnologia, 1957.

DENMARK

380. GARBOE, Axel. *Geologiens Historie i Danmark.* I. *Fra Myte til Videnskab. Fra de Aeldste Tider til 1835 (mod Norge Til 1814).* II. *Forskere og Resultalier. Fra 1835 til Nutiden.* Copenhagen: C.A. Reitzels Forlag, 1959-1961, pp. 283; 521.

A history of geological investigation in Denmark up to the present; rich in biographical detail.

FINLAND

381. HAUSEN, Hans. *The History of Geology and Mineralogy in Finland 1828-1918.* Helsinki: Societas Scientiarum Fennica, 1968, pp. 147.

Emphasizes the role of the Imperial Alexander University in promoting the science, and pays particular attention to the work of Nils Nordenskiold and Wilhelm Ramsay. A section deals with the important issue of quaternary geology.

FRANCE

382. ELLENBERGER, F. "Aux sources de la géologie française." *Histoire et Nature*, 15 (1979), 3-29.

    Discusses the history and historiography of French geology, and gives extensive bibliographical references, particularly for the history of ancient French volcanoes.

383. FURON, Raymond. "Histoire de la géologie de la France d'outre-mer." *Mémoires du Musée National d'Histoire Naturelle, Paris*, Ser. C, *Sciences de la Terre*, 5 (1955).

    Devoted to the history of geology in various sectors of the French Empire and of French expansion in Algeria, Tunisia, Morocco, French Sahara, Western and Equatorial Africa, Somalia, Madagascar, Indo-China, French Guiana and French territories in the South Seas and the Caribbean. Exploration, mapping and economic exploitation are extensively covered.

384. RUDEL, A. *Les Volcans d'Auvergne*. Clermont Ferrand: Volcans Editions, 1962, pp. 149.

    A well-illustrated narrative history of the discovery and geological understanding of the extinct volcanoes from the mid-eighteenth century to the present.

GERMANY

385. FISCHER, Walther. *Mineralogie in Sachsen von Agricola bis Werner: Die ältere Geschichte des Staatlichen Museums für Mineralogie und Geologie zu Dresden 1560-1820*. Dresden: Heinrich, 1939, pp. viii+347.

386. GUNTAU, M. "Bemerkungen zum System der geologisch-mineralogischen Wissenschaften in Deutschland am Ende des 18. Jahrhunderts." *Actes du XIIIe Congrès International d'Histoire des Sciences* [1971], 8 (1974), 99-106.

    Emphasizes the orientation of German geology and mineralogy to the needs of the extractive industries.

387. GUNTAU, Martin. "Die Bedeutung der Gangvererzung und der Entwicklung der Gangtheorie der sachsischen Erzgebirge für die Geschichte der Lager stattenlehre."

INHIGEO Zusammenfassung. VIII. Symposium. Münster und Bonn, 12-24 September 1978 (1978), 69-71.

Discusses rival theories of the formation of mineral veins chiefly surrounding the work of Werner in the eighteenth century.

388. LOTZE, Franz. "100 Jahre Forschung in der saxonischen Tektonik." *Zeitschrift der deutschen geologischen Gesellschaft*, 100 (1948), 321-337.

389. SCHMIDT, P. *Bibliographie in der DDR zur Geschichte der Geologie, Mineralogie, Geophysik und Paläontologie vorgelegten Arbeiten*. Freiberg: Bergakademie, 1978.

Major listing of German-language works in the history of geology.

ITALY

390. CAROBBI, Guido. "Il Contributo Italiano al Progresso della Mineralogia, negli Ultimi Cento Anni." *Un Secolo di Progresso Scientifico Italiano, 1839-1938*. Rome: Società Italiana Progr. Sci., 2 (1939), 429-451.

391. CERMENATI, Mario, and TELLINI, Achille. *Rassegna delle Scienze Geologiche in Italia*. 3 vols. Rome, 1891-1893, pp. 504; 340; 64.

392. GORTANI, Michele. "Italian Pioneers in Geology and Mineralogy." *Journal of World History*, 7 (1963), 503-519.

Chiefly discusses Targioni Tozzetti, Spallanzani and Arduino.

393. RODELICO, F. *L'Esplorazione Naturalistica dell'Appennino*. Florence: Le Monnier, 1963.

A history of the geographical and geological exploration of the Apennines.

JAPAN

394. PESTANA, Harold R. "History of Geology in Japan and Northern Asia: Documents Published by the United States Congress." *Japanese Studies in the History of Science*, no. 13 (1974), 69-73.

Shows how the geology of Japan was explored through Congressional initiative largely by American geologists from about the middle of the nineteenth century, until a generation of native geologists developed.

LUXEMBOURG

395. LUCIUS, Michel. "Aperçu historique sur les recherches géologiques concernant le pays de Luxembourg." *Bulletin du Société des Naturalistes Luxembourgeois*, 51 (1959), 130-141.

POLAND

396. CZARNIECKI, St. "Beispiele wissenschaftlicher Beziehungen zwischen polnischen und deutschen Gelehrten auf dem Gebeit der Geologie im Zeitalter der Aufklärung." *Zeitschrift für geologische Wissenschaften*, 8 (1980), 135-150.

Discusses Polish geology in the Enlightenment, particularly in the context of relationships between Polish students and German teachers.

397. WISNIOWSKI, Tadeusz. "Zarys Historii Nauk Geologiczych w Polsce i na Swiecie" [Historical Outline of the Geological Sciences in Poland and Elsewhere]. With Notes and Comments by Krystztof Jakubowski. *Prace Muzeum Ziemi*, no. 18, pt. 2 (1971), 3-53.

398. WISNIOWSKI, Tadeusz. "Esquisse d'une histoire de la géologie en Pologne." Pp. 87-106 in [Anon.] *Histoire sommaire des sciences en Pologne, publiée à l'Occasion du VIIe Congrès International des Sciences Historiques*. Cracow: Drukarnia Narodowa, 1933, pp. 154.

399. WOJCIK, Zbigniew. "Prace nad Historie Nauk Geologicznych w Zwiazku Radziechim i w Polsce" [Investigations on the History of Geological Sciences in USSR and in Poland]. *Prace Muzeum Ziemi*, no. 18, pt. 1 (1971), 87-104.

PORTUGAL

400. CARRINGTON DA COSTA, J. "Do Conhecimento Géologico de Portugal Continental." *Anais da Faculdade de Ciencias do Porto*, 26 (1941), 206-229.

SOUTH AFRICA

401. HAUGHTON, S.B. "South African Geology." Pp. 339-356 in BROWN, Alexander C., ed. *A History of Scientific Endeavour in South Africa. A Collection of Essays Published on the Occasion of the Centenary of the Royal Society of South Africa.* Rondebosch: Royal Society of South Africa, 1977, pp. xii+516.

SOUTH AMERICA

402. HAGEN, Victor W. von. *South America Called Them: Explorations of the Great Naturalists--Charles-Marie de la Condamine, Alexander von Humboldt, Charles Darwin, Richard Spruce.* New York: Knopf, 1945, pp. xii+311. 2nd ed. London: Hale, 1949, pp. xiv+410.

Biographical accounts of the South American explorations of De la Condamine, Alexander Von Humboldt, Charles Darwin and Richard Spruce.

403. HAGEN, Victor W. von. *South America: The Green World of the Naturalists. Five Centuries of Natural History in South America.* London: Eyre & Spottiswoode, 1951, pp. xvii+398.

Extracts from the writings of naturalists from the sixteenth century. Those of Darwin and Von Humboldt are of particular geological interest.

SPAIN

404. AZCONA, Juan M.L. de, and PARDO, José M.Y. *Contribución a la Historia de la Geología y Minería Españolas.* Madrid: Instituto Geológico y Minero de España, 1964.

405. SAMPELAVO, H., and RIOS, J.M. "Ahora Hace Cien Anos ...: Ojeada Retrospectiva." *Boletin del Instituto Geologico y Minero de Espana,* 60 (1948), i-xliii.

A brief history of geology with special attention devoted to Spain, including biographies of Spanish geologists.

SWEDEN

406. LINDROTH, Sven, ed. *Swedish Men of Science, 1650-1950.* Stockholm: Swedish Institute and Almquist and Wiksell, 1952, pp. 296.

Includes discussions of Linnaeus, Wallerius, Cronstedt, Bergman and Berzelius.

407. REGNELL, G. "On the Position of Palaeontology and Historical Geology in Sweden Before 1800." *Archiv för Mineralogi och Geologi*, 1 (1949), 1-64.

SWITZERLAND

408. BEER, Gavin R. de. *Travellers in Switzerland*. London, New York and Toronto: Oxford University Press, 1949, pp. xvii+585.

    A bibliographical resumé. Geologists cited include Gesner, Muralt, Scheuchzer, Guettard, De Luc, Saussure, Desmarest, Goethe, E.D. Clarke, Dolomieu, Humboldt, von Buch, Necker de Saussure, Lyell, de la Beche, J.D. Forbes, J. Ball, L. Agassiz, Hugi, Heer, Ruskin, E. Forces, W. Buckland, C.J.F. Bunbury, Benjamin Silliman, Sr., H. Spencer, A.R. Wallace, Bonney, Tyndall, Butler, T.H. Huxley, A.C. Ramsay, Prestwich, Owen, Whymper, Shaler, Lord Avebury, Fiske.

409. LUGEON, Maurice. "Cent ans de Géologie Vaudoise." *Suisse Contemporaine* (Lausanne), nos. 7-8 (1949), 12.

410. THAMS, J.C., ed. *The Development of Geodesy and Geophysics in Switzerland*. Zurich: Berichthaus, 1967.

U.S.S.R.

411. GUNTAU, Martin, ed. *Biographen bedeutender Geowissenschaften der Sowjetunion: 19 biographische Darstellungen zu bedeutenden Gelehrten der russischen und sowjetischen Geologiegeschichte*. Berlin: Akademie Verlag, 1979.

    Nineteen biographical portraits of leading Russian geologists from Lomonosov to S.A. Smirnov, N.S. Shatskij, A.P. Vinogradov and G.A. Gamburcev.

412A. TIKHOMIROV, Vladimir V. "Russian Geologists Abroad." *Archives Internationales d'Histoire des Sciences*, 12 (1959), 365-376.

Explores both the extent to which Russian scientists are obtaining geological education abroad (especially in the German mining academies) and also their fieldwork, particularly in China.

412B. TIKHOMIROV, V.V. "The Development of the Geological Sciences in the U.S.S.R. from Ancient Times to the Middle of the Nineteenth Century." Pp. 357-385 in SCHNEER, C.J., ed. *Toward a History of Geology*. Cambridge, Mass., and London: M.I.T. Press, 1969, pp. vi+469.

A chronologically comprehensive survey stressing the pioneer traveling and mapping activities of Lomonosov and Pallas in the eighteenth century.

6. BIOGRAPHICAL STUDIES

Contains both biographical works and interpretative and thematic studies focusing primarily on the geology of a particular individual. For more complete listings of obituary notices, tributes, etc., consult W.A.S. Sarjeant's *Geologists and the History of Geology* (item 20) and the *Dictionary of Scientific Biography*.

AGASSIZ

413. DAVIES, G.L. "The Tour of the British Isles Made by Louis Agassiz in 1840." *Annals of Science*, 24 (1968), 131-146.

    Agassiz's quest for former British glaciers.

414. GOULD, Stephen Jay. "Agassiz' Later Private Thoughts on Evolution: His Marginalia in Haeckel's *Naturliche Schöpfungsgeschichte* (1868)." Pp. 277-288 in SCHNEER, C.J., ed. *Two Hundred Years of Geology in America. Proceedings of the New Hampshire Bicentennial Conference on the History of Geology*. Hanover, N.H.: University Press of New England, 1979, pp. xvi+385.

    Shows Agassiz's deep antipathy to philosophies of evolution.

415. LURIE, Edward. *Louis Agassiz: Pied Piper of Science*. Chicago and London: University of Chicago Press, 1960, pp. xiv+449.

    In his early career in Europe, Agassiz worked within the comparative anatomy tradition of palaeontology pioneered by Cuvier, becoming an expert particularly on fossil fish, and pioneering in glacial theory. In his later life in America he mastered the natural history of the Continent. He achieved some public fame as an opponent of Darwinian evolution.

ANNING

416. LANG, W.D. "Mary Anning, of Lyme, Collector and Vendor of Fossils, 1799-1847." *Natural History Magazine*, 5 (1935), 64-81.

417. LANG, William D. "Mary Anning and the Pioneer Geologists of Lyme." *Proceedings of the Dorset Natural History and Archaeological Society*, 60 (1939), 142-164.

   Well-researched account of the discoverer and dealer in fossil vertebrates.

ARDUINO

418. STEGNANO, Giuseppe. *Il Veronese Giovanni Arduino e Il Suo Contributo al Progresso della Scienza Geologica*. Verona: Ministro dell'Istruzione Pubblica, 1929, pp. 42.

   Shows how Arduino's career combined interest in the geological structure of Italy with a profound concern for the technology of mining. He recognized the correlation between fossil types and the strata in which they were found.

ARGAND

419. LUGEON, M. "Emile Argand." *Bulletin de la Société Neuchateloise des Sciences Naturelles*, 65 (1940), 25-53.

   An account of the pioneer of Alpine tectonics, examining the techniques of geometrical projection which he developed and his theoretical investigations into orogeny.

ARRHENIUS

420. WALKER, J. "Arrhenius Memorial Lecture." *Journal of the Chemical Society*, (1928), 1380-1401.

   S.A. Arrhenius's *Text-book of Cosmic Physics* (1903) was the most distinguished attempt in its time to relate geology to developments in the chemical and physical sciences. This paper shows how much of

Arrhenius's geological chemistry--e.g., his attempted
chemical explanations of Ice Ages--was ignored.

BAILEY

421. MacGREGOR, A.G. "Memorial to Sir Edward B. Bailey, Kt.,
     M.C., F.R.S. (1881-1965)." *Proceedings of the Geological
     Society of America* (1966), 31-39.

    Bailey rose to become Director of the Geological
    Survey of Great Britain, and made important contributions
    to tectonics and metamorphism and to igneous geology.
    His major work was concerned with the tectonic inter-
    pretation of the Scottish Highlands.

BANKS

422. LYTE, C. *Sir Joseph Banks: Eighteenth Century Explorer,
     Botanist and Entrepreneur*. Newton Abbot: David and
     Charles, 1980, pp. 248.

    Emphasizes Banks's early interest in a geophysically
    based natural history science which would unite knowl-
    edge of all aspects of the globe, and his later concern
    for the utilitarian aspects of mineralogical knowledge.

BARBER

423. BARBER, C.T. *A Geologist in the Service of the Raj*.
     Henfield, Sussex: The Author, 1978, pp. ix+245.

    A well-illustrated autobiographical account of work
    on the Indian Geological Survey and of prospecting for
    oil in Burma.

BARRANDE

424. WOODWARD, Henry. "Sketch of the Life of Joachim Barrande,
     of Prague." *Geological Magazine*, 20, no. 12 (1883),
     529-533.

    Barrande pioneered in geological explorations of the
    Danube basin, applying the concepts of the Silurian,
    and making major developments in the study of fossil
    metamorphism. His Cuvierian background led to hostility
    to evolutionism.

BARRELL

425. GREGORY, H.E. "Memorial to Joseph Barrell." *Bulletin of the Geological Society of America*, 34 (1923), 18-28.

    Barrell was primarily interested in the philosophical aspects of geology, exploring the theoretical relationships among volcanic phenomena, magma and metamorphism, and pursuing an understanding of sedimentation.

BARROIS

426. PRUVOST, P. "Charles Barrois." *Bulletin de la Société Géologique de France*, 5th ser., 10 (1950), 231-262.

    Emphasizes the importance of Barrois's researches on the primary geology of Northern Spain and the Sierra Nevada, and his distinguished mapping of Brittany. His religious commitments led him to avoid involvement in the Darwinian controversies.

BEDDOES

427. STOCK, J.E. *Memoirs of the Life of Thomas Beddoes, M.D.* London and Bristol: J. Murray, 1811, pp. v+413.

    Touches upon Beddoes's chemically and experimentally based support for the Huttonian theory of the igneous origin of crystalline rocks, and shows his close connections with mineralogically active circles at the end of the eighteenth century.

BERGMAN

428. CARLID, Göte, and NORDSTRÖM, Johan, eds. *Torbern Bergman's Foreign Correspondence*. Vol. 1: *Letters from Foreigners to Torbern Bergman*. With an Introductory Biography by Hugo Olsson. Stockholm: Almqvist and Wiksell, 1965, pp. lvi+466.

429. HEDBERG, Hollis D. "The Influence of Torbern Bergman (1735-1784) on Stratigraphy: A Résumé." Pp. 186-191 in SCHNEER, C.J., ed. *Toward a History of Geology*. Cambridge, Mass., and London: M.I.T. Press, 1969, pp. vi+469.

Argues that Bergman was important in the emergence
of historical geology in the eighteenth century through
his desire to link analysis and classification of mineral
substances to their position in the order of the strata,
thus paving the way for a science of rocks based on time
and process.

BERINGER

430. BERINGER, Johann B.A. *The Lying Stones of Dr. Johan Bartholomew Adam Beringer Being His Lithographiae Wirceburgensis*. Trans. by Melvin E. Jahn and Daniel J. Woolf. Berkeley and Los Angeles: University of California Press, 1963, pp. xiv+221.

    Beringer is best known as the eighteenth-century
German professor hoaxed by students who planted fake
"fossils" in his path. The translators present a sympathetic account of Beringer as the victim of academic
politics, and show the plausibility of his palaeontological views in the context of their time.

BERTRAND

431. Termier, Pierre. "Marcel Bertrand (1847-1907)." *Bulletin de la Société Géologique de France*, ser. 4, no. 8 (1908), 163-204.

    Always concerned with the large-scale problems of
geology, Bertrand made important contributions to the
understanding of the *nappe* structure of the Alps and
to orogenesis in general. He also devoted much attention
to the sedimentary cycle.

BERZELIUS

432. FRÄNGSMYR, Tore. "The Geological Ideas of J.J. Ber-zelius." *The British Journal for the History of Science*, 9 (1976), 228-236.

    Shows that the Swedish chemist was an empirical
geologist of some stature, who applied theory and
glacialism to his Scandinavian experience.

BONNEY

433. [WATTS, William W.]. "Thomas George Bonney--1833-1923." *Proceedings of the Royal Society of London*, ser. B, 99 (1927), xvii-xxvii.

Emphasizes Bonney's contributions to the development of petrology in Britain and the importance of his volcanic and Alpine studies. Bonney was one of the leading early clerical champions of Darwinian evolutionism and wrote widely on relations between religion and modern science.

BOWEN

434. LANGWILL, C.R., and ROGERS, J. *Bowen Volume, Part I, American Journal of Science*. New Haven, Conn., 1952, pp. viii+627.

N.L. Bowen was a geophysicist who worked most of his life at the Geophysics Laboratory at Washington, D.C., establishing the physico-chemical principles relevant to the fractional crystallization of magmas, and advancing igneous petrology to a theoretical science.

BRONGNIART

435. LAUNAY, Louis A.A. de. *Les Brongniarts, une grande famille de savants*. Paris: Rapilly, 1940, pp. 208.

Alexandre Brongniart was distinguished chiefly for his collaboration with Cuvier in the reconstruction of extinct fossil remains. His son, Adolphe, became a leading student of palaeobotany.

BUCH, VON

436. DECHEN, H. von. *Leopold von Buch, sein Einfluss auf die Entwicklung der Geognosie*. Bonn, 1853.

Traces the life of one of Europe's most eminent amateur traveler-geologists, trained by Werner, although later modifying his work. Assesses von Buch's theory of elevation craters to explain volcano-like phenomena.

437. GUNTAU, M. "Leopold von Buch: Gedanken zu seinen Leben und Wirken als Geologie." *Zeitschrift für geologische Wissenschaft*, 2 (1974), 1371-1383.

Emphasizes von Buch's shift from a Neptunist to a Vulcanist stance and evaluates his theory of elevation craters.

438. GUNTAU, Martin. "Leopold von Buch 1774-1853. Kolloquium aus Anlass der Wiederkehr seines Geburtstages nach 200 Jahren." *Zeitschrift für geologische Wissenschaft*, 2 (1974), 1363-1365.

439. MATHÈ, Gerhard. "Leopold von Buch und seine Bedeutung für die Entwicklung der Geologie. Gedanken anlässlich seines 200. Geburtstages am 26 April 1974." *Zeitschrift für geologische Wissenschaft*, 2 (1974), 1395-1404.

BUCKLAND

440. GORDON, Mrs. *The Life and Correspondence of William Buckland D.D., F.R.S., Sometime Dean of Westminster. Twice President of the Geological and First President of the British Association*. London: Murray, 1894, pp. xvi+288.

Lively letters of the man who pioneered geology at Oxford, was one of the last respectable geologists who clung to the notion of a biblical deluge of geological significance and was one of the earliest champions of glacial theory.

BUFFON

441. ROGER, J. "Buffon. *Les Epoques de la Nature*: Edition critique." *Mémoires du Museum National d'Histoire Naturelle*. Ser. C, Vol. X (1963).

A critical edition which shows how Buffon's geological ideas modified from an essentially cyclical vision of Earth history to one which stressed more evolutionary accounts of the history of the Earth and of life.

CATCOTT

442. NEVE, Michael, and PORTER, Roy. "Alexander Catcott: Glory and Geology." *The British Journal for the History of Science*, 10 (1977), 37-60.

Argues that Catcott was a pivotal figure, both a follower of the anti-Newtonian, biblical natural philosopher John Hutchinson, and an accomplished fieldworker (which led to his being respected by later geologists). Investigates instances where his religious philosophy clashed with the evidence of his eyes.

CHAMBERLIN

443. CHAMBERLIN, Rollin T. "Biographical Memoir of Thomas Chrowder Chamberlin, 1843-1928." *Biographical Memoirs of the National Academy of Science*, 15 (1934), 305-407.

Though probably most famous for his refutation of Laplace's nebular hypothesis, Chamberlin spent most of his career as a working survey geologist, chiefly on the Wisconsin Survey, contributing much to the understanding of glaciation.

CHAMBERS

444. MILLHAUSER, Milton. *Just Before Darwin: Robert Chambers and "Vestiges."* Middletown, Conn.: Wesleyan University Press, 1959, pp. ix+246.

Chambers published his *Vestiges of the Natural History of Creation* anonymously in 1844. Though much abused by the scientific elite, it became easily the most popular pro-evolutionary tract before Darwin's *Origin*, arguing that evolutionism was simply the inevitable consequence of the universal operation of natural law.

CHARPENTIER

445. BALMER, Heinz. "Jean de Charpentier 1786-1855." *Gesnerus*, 26 (1969), 213-232.

Charpentier was the first to develop the notion of vast extensions of ice sheets in former times, the product of an Ice Age, evidenced by the effects of glaciers upon rock and valley forms. His ideas were enthusiastically taken up and popularized by Agassiz.

446. ENGEWALD, G.-R. "Einige Gedanken zum Erscheinen der ersten farbigen petrographischen Karten Sachsens von Johann Friedrich Wilhelm von Charpentier vor 200

Jahren." *Zeitschrift für geologische Wissenschaften*, 8 (1980), 159-169.

Discusses the eighteenth-century geological map of Saxony by J.F.W. von Charpentier.

CLARKE

447. OTTER, William. *The Life and Remains of the Reverend Edward Daniel Clarke LL.D., Professor of Mineralogy in the University of Cambridge.* London: Dove, 1824, pp. xii+670.

    Shows how Clarke's interest in geology and mineralogy arose largely from his passion for travel.

CLOOS

448. BALK, R. "Memorial to Hans Cloos (1886-1951)." *Proceedings of the Geological Society of America* (1963), 87-94.

449. [WILSON, G.]. "Professor Hans Cloos." *Proceedings of the Geological Society of London*, no. 1515 (1954), cxxvii-cxxviii.

    Examines Cloos's lifelong pioneering work on the tectonics of granite, which opened up the study of the flow-textures of solidifying magma. Cloos developed techniques of replicating tectonic processes in the laboratory.

CONYBEARE, W.D.

450. NORTH, F.J. "Dean Conybeare, Geologist." *Transactions of the Cardiff Naturalists' Society*, 66 (1933), 15-68.

    Stresses the importance of W.D. Conybeare (with William Phillips) as the author of the first major stratigraphical textbook of England and Wales, and discusses his palaeontological work.

COPE

451. BOWLER, Peter J. "Edward Drinker Cope and the Changing Structure of Evolutionary Theory." *Isis*, 68 (1977), 249-265.

Cope's palaeontological work was primarily focused on evidence of changing morphological structures, in which he believed he discerned the "law of the acceleration of growth." Explores Cope's neo-Lamarckianism.

452. OSBORN, H.F. *Cope, Master Naturalist.* Princeton, N.J.: Princeton University Press, 1931, pp. xvi+740.

Emphasizes the importance of Cope's fundamental researches into the fossil fauna of the American midwest.

CORDIER

453. [JAUBERT, Compe]. *Notice sur la vie et les travaux de P.L.A. Cordier, suivi d'une liste chronologique et raisonné de ses ouvrages.* 2nd ed., revised and augmented, with his posthumous memoir "Sur l'origine des roches calcaires et des dolomies." Paris: Benjamin Duprat et Mallet-Bachelier, 1862, pp. 83.

Cordier carried out major surveys of French mineral resources. His most important contribution to theoretical geology lay in his studies of Earth cooling, and his hypothesis that consolidation had taken place from the exterior to the interior.

COTTA

454. WAGENBRETH, Otfried. "Bernhard von Cotta. Leben und Werk eines deutschen Geologen im 19. Jahrhundert." *Freiberger Forschrift,* D. 36. Leipzig: VEB Deutscher Verlag für Grundstoff Industrie, 1965, pp. 134.

Much of Cotta's life was devoted to teaching at Freiberg. He did important work in developing the science of ore deposits and was an ardent defender of evolutionism.

CROLL

455. [Anon.]. "Dr. Croll's Life and Work." *Geological Magazine,* 34 (1897), 71-77.

James Croll was especially concerned with the geographical understanding of climate and time, exploring the possibility that changes in the eccentricity of the Earth's orbit had been responsible for Ice Ages.

CUVIER

456. COLEMAN, William. *Georges Cuvier, Zoologist: A Study in the History of Evolution Theory*. Cambridge, Mass.: Harvard University Press, 1964, pp. x+212.

    Rescues Cuvier from his common reputation as a religiously inspired Catastrophist in geology and dogmatic anti-evolutionist in biology by demonstrating the fundamental importance of his work in comparative anatomy for the reconstruction of newly discovered fossil vertebrates, and thence for the formulation of a geologically based history of life. Important emphasis on Cuvier's Aristotelianism, his stress on form and function.

457. OUTRAM, D., ed. *The Letters of Georges Cuvier*. Chalfont St. Giles, Bucks: The British Society for the History of Science, 1980, pp. 101.

    A calendar, with abstracts of all the known correspondence, much of which is of geological interest.

458. VIENOT, John P. *Le Napoléon de l'intelligence: Georges Cuvier, 1769-1832*. Paris: Fischbacher, 1932, pp. 249.

    Though perhaps most widely regarded in the history of geology as a Catastrophist and anti-evolutionist, Cuvier's main work lay in the patient reconstruction of fossil vertebrates by the methods of comparative anatomy. His work established the reality of extinction, showed that the Earth had gone through a series of major transformations and helped to establish a long timescale.

DANA

459. GILMAN, Daniel C. *Life of James Dwight Dana, Scientific Explorer, Mineralogist, Geologist, Zoologist, Professor in Yale University*. New York: Harper, 1899, pp. 409.

    An all-around naturalist and geologist, Dana's leading achievements lay in his studies of corals, where he bore out Darwin's theory of coral islands and reefs. He also developed the geosynclinal-contraction hypothesis of mountain building.

DARWIN, Charles

460. BARLOW, N. *The Autobiography of Charles Darwin, 1809-1882.* London: Collins, 1958, pp. 253.

    The first publication of an unexpurgated version of Darwin's autobiography, important to the historian of geology for reminding him that Darwin's first area of scientific competence was geology, and that Darwin viewed the terraqueous globe on the voyage of the *Beagle* through the Uniformitarian spectacles of Lyell's *Principles of Geology.*

461. CONRY, Y. *Correspondance entre Charles Darwin et Gaston de Saporta.* Paris: Galien, 1972, pp. 151.

    Prefaced by a long (seventy pp.) essay on palaeobotany in the nineteenth century, and its relations with taxonomy, plant distribution and geological theory.

462. GEIKIE, A. *Charles Darwin as Geologist.* Cambridge: Cambridge University Press, 1909, pp. 91.

    Emphasizes Darwin's debt as an evolutionist to the naturalism and gradualism of Lyell's Uniformitarian geology, as well as discussing his theory of coral reefs and his work on the parallel roads of Glen Roy.

463. ROMER, A.S. "Darwin and the Fossil Record." Pp. 130-152 in BARNETT, S.A., ed. *A Century of Darwin.* London: Heinemann, 1958, pp. xvi+376.

    A survey piece, retrospective in tone but including a useful description of Darwin's fossil collecting in South America and the role of palaeontology generally in evolutionary theory.

464. RUDWICK, Martin J.S. "Darwin and Glen Roy: A 'Great Failure' in Scientific Method?" *Studies in the History and Philosophy of Science*, 5 (1974), 97-185.

    Examines Darwin's attempt to explain the parallel "roads" of Glen Roy by analogy with his experience of raised sea-beaches in South America, and Darwin's later recognition of the inadequacy of this theory in the light of glacial theory.

465. STODDART, D.R. "Darwin, Lyell and the Geological Significance of Coral Reefs." *The British Journal for the History of Science*, 9 (1976), 199-218.

Darwin's new and essentially correct view of the formation of coral reefs was deeply indebted to the gradualistic vision of geology which he had taken from Lyell.

466. YONGE, C.M. "Darwin and Coral Reefs." Pp. 245-266 in BARNETT, S.A., ed. *A Century of Darwin*. London: Heinemann, 1958, pp. xvi+376.

    A simplified account of Darwin's work on coral formations, followed by a resumé of modern theories.

DARWIN, Erasmus

467. KING-HELE, Desmond G. *Doctor of Revolution: The Life and Genius of Erasmus Darwin*. London: Faber and Faber, 1978, pp. 361.

    Shows Erasmus Darwin's very varied interests in the Earth sciences, taking in such phenomena as soil composition and artesian wells. Erasmus Darwin had a theory of an Earth progressing from a chaotic condition to habitability, which served as a backdrop to his ideas of organic evolution.

DAVIS

468A. BRYAN, K. "William Morris Davis--Leader in Geomorphology and Geography." *Annals of the Association of American Geographers*, 25 (1935), 23-31.

    Davis is easily the single most influential figure in geomorphology over the last century. Building on his vast experience of the vastnesses of the American landscape, Davis formulated the idea of the cycle of erosion in the development of river valleys, as part of his conception that present-day landscape had evolved from a long-continued and law-governed congruence of forces. See also item 115.

DAVY

468B. SIEGFRIED, R., and DOTT, R.H., Jr. *Humphry Davy on Geology*. Madison: The University of Wisconsin Press, 1980, pp. xliv+169.

Prints for the first time Davy's 1805 geological lectures to the Royal Institution, with a historical introduction.

469. SIEGFRIED, R., and DOTT, R.H., Jr. "Humphry Davy as Geologist 1805-1829." *The British Journal for the History of Science*, 9 (1976), 219-227.

Uses Davy's Royal Institution Lectures on geology to show his Vulcanist leanings but powerful criticisms of full Huttonian Uniformitarianism and Plutonism. Davy emphasized the harmony of religion and science and the economic potential of geology.

DAWSON

470. ADAMS, F.D. "Memoir of Sir William Dawson." *Bulletin of the Geological Society of America*, 11 (1899), 550-557.

Dawson, the leading Canadian geologist of the nineteenth century after Logan, made his most fundamental contributions in palaeobotany, not least discovering *Psilophyton*, the earliest land plant then known.

DE LA BECHE

471. McCARTNEY, Paul J. *Henry De La Beche: Observations on an Observer*. Edited and with foreword by Douglas A. BASSETT. Cardiff: Friends of the National Museum of Wales, 1977, pp. xiv+78.

Shows how De la Beche saw accurate factual observation as the most pressing priority in geology in the 1830s, relating this to his pioneering mapping work. Based upon extensive work on hitherto unused De la Beche papers.

472. RUDWICK, M.J.S. "Caricature as a Source for the History of Science: De la Beche's Anti-Lyell Sketches of 1831." *Isis*, 66 (1975), 534-560.

Shows that De la Beche's cartoons lampooning Lyell's Uniformitarianism contained in visual form searching criticism of Lyell's theoretical stance, his views on time and his steady-state presuppositions.

DE LUC

473. TUNBRIDGE, Paul A. "Jean André de Luc, F.R.S. (1727-1817)." *Notes and Records of the Royal Society of London*, 26 (1971), 15-33.

    Emphasizes that De Luc was no mere scriptural geologist but had made extensive observations particularly in the Alpine region of Europe. His chemical and meteorological interests are also explored.

DE MAILLET

474. CAROZZI, A.V. "De Maillet's *Telliamed* (1748): An Ultra-Neptunian Theory of the Earth." Pp. 80-99 in SCHNEER, C.J., ed. *Toward a History of Geology*. Cambridge, Mass., and London: M.I.T. Press, 1969, pp. vi+469.

    De Maillet denied that land forms were primary; they had gradually emerged over time as a result of the action of tides and currents creating solid land from ocean sediments. Similar forces were continually destroying the continents.

DESMAREST

475. TAYLOR, Kenneth L. "Nicolas Desmarest and Geology in the Eighteenth Century." Pp. 339-356 in SCHNEER, C.J., ed. *Toward a History of Geology*. Cambridge, Mass., and London: M.I.T. Press, 1969, pp. vi+469.

    Shows how Desmarest was an actualist without being a Uniformitarian, and accepted the volcanic origin of many basalts without being a thorough-going Plutonist.

DOLOMIEU

476. LACROIX, Alfred. *Déodat Dolomieu, Membre de l'Institut National (1750-1801). Sa Vie aventureuse--sa captivité--ses oeuvres--sa correspondance*. 2 vols. Paris: Perrin, 1921, pp. lxxx+255.

    Chronicles Dolomieu's extensive geological travels in Italy, Sicily, the Pyrenees and France, and later with Napoleon in Egypt. Dolomieu's reputation rests chiefly on his astute empirical observation.

477. TAYLOR, K. "The Geology of Dolomieu." *Actes du XII Congrès International d'Histoire des Sciences,* 7 (1971), 49-53.

Important for showing how Dolomieu, like many late eighteenth-century geologists, could be both a "Neptunist," emphasizing the role of *débacles* in shaping the landscape, and a Vulcanist, pointing out the formerly greater extent of volcanic activity.

DUFRENOY

478. DAUBRÉE, A. "Dufrénoy." *École polytechnique. Livre du centènaire, 1794-1894,* i (Paris, 1895), 375-381.

Dufrénoy was largely responsible for drawing up the first modern geological map of France (1830-1838). He was noted as a teacher of mineralogy and applied geology.

DU TOIT

479. GEVERS, T.W. *The Life and Work of Dr Alex. L. du Toit.* Geological Society of South Africa, Annexure to Vol. 52. Alex. L. du Toit Memorial Lectures No. 1. Johannesburg: Geological Society of South Africa, 1950, pp. 109.

480. HAUGHTON, S.H. "Alexander Logie du Toit 1878-1948." *Obituary Notices of the Fellows of the Royal Society of London,* 6, no. 18 (1949), 385-395.

Examines Du Toit's support, using South African evidence, for Wegener's theory of Continental Drift, comparing the continent with South America and proposing an original supercontinent, Gondwanaland, distinct from the northern continent of Laurasia.

EATON

481. McALLISTER, Ethel M. *Amos Eaton: Scientist and Educator, 1776-1842.* Philadelphia: University of Pennsylvania Press; London: Oxford University Press, 1941, pp. xiii+587.

Eaton pioneered the application of Wernerian geology and mineralogy to American conditions, attempting to correlate American with European formations. He made important contributions to botany and scientific education.

EHRENBERG

482. LOCKER, S. "Christian Gottfried Ehrenberg (1795-1876) und die mikrogeologische Sammlung." *Zeitschrift für geologische Wissenschaften*, 8 (1980), 231-238.

Ehrenberg made important contributions to microbiology and micropalaeontology.

ELIE DE BEAUMONT

483. BERTRAND, J. *Eloge historique de Elie de Beaumont.* Paris, 1875.

Elie de Beaumont was in charge of compiling the Eastern division of the official geological map of France, completed in 1831. His main contribution to geological thought was the notion that the mountain regions of the globe were the product of sudden catastrophic elevation.

484. SAINTE CLAIRE DEVILLE, Charles. *Coup d'oeil historique sur la géologie et sur les travaux d'Elie de Beaumont.* Leçons professées au Collège de France, Mai-Juillet, 1875. Vol. 1. Paris, 1878, pp. 381-582.

ESKOLA

485. BARTH, T.F.W. "Memorial to Pentti Eskola (1883-1964)." *Bulletin of the Geological Society of America*, 76, no. 9 (1965), 117-120.

An account of the leading exponent of the geology of the Precambrian in Finland, applying physico-chemical principles to the problems of metamorphism and laying foundations for future studies of metamorphic petrology.

FALCONER

486. MURCHISON, Charles, ed. *Palaeontological Memoirs and Notes of the Late Hugh Falconer, A.M., M.D. ... with a Biographical Sketch of the Author.* 2 vols. Vol. 1: *Fauna Antiqua Sivalensis*. Vol. 2: *Mastodon, Elephant, Rhinoceroses, Ossiferous Caves, Primaeval Man and his Contemporaries.* "Biographical Sketch" (Vol. 1, pp. xxiii-liii). London: Hardwicke, 1868, pp. lvi+590; xiv+675.

Demonstrates Falconer's immense contributions to the palaeontology and zoology of India, Kashmir and Tibet and his work on the history of primeval man.

FAUJAS DE ST. FOND

487. FAUJAS DE SAINT FOND, Barthélémy. *A Journey through England and Scotland to the Hebrides in 1784.* Edited with Notes and a Memoir of the Author by Archibald GEIKIE. 2 vols. Glasgow: Hopkins, 1907, pp. xxxii+356; ix+375.

    This translation of Faujas de St. Fond's British tour contains an important assessment of his geological significance, particularly in the understanding of ancient volcanoes.

FEATHERSTONHAUGH

488. EYLES, J.M. "G.W. Featherstonhaugh (1780-1866), FRS, FGS, Geologist and Traveller." *Journal of the Society for the Bibliography of Natural History*, 8, pt. 4 (1978), 381-395.

    Born in England, Featherstonhaugh made his name in America as a geologist, influenced by the teachings of William Buckland. An appendix prints some of his correspondence.

FORBES, Edward

489A. BROWNE, Janet. "The Making of the *Memoir* of Edward Forbes, F.R.S." *Archives of Natural History*, 10, pt. 2 (1981), 205-219.

    A survey of Forbes's relationship with the Royal School of Mines and the politics of publishing his biography, including some comments on Archibald Geikie.

489B. WILSON, George, and GEIKIE, Archibald. *Memoir of Edward Forbes, F.R.S.* Cambridge and London: Macmillan; Edinburgh: Edmonston and Douglas, 1861, pp. xi+589.

    Forbes was an enthusiastic supporter of Lyellian geology, much concerned with marine science and marine geology. He did important palaeontological work for the Geological Survey.

FORSTER, J.R.

490. HOARE, M. *The Tactless Philosopher: Johann Reinhold Forster, 1729-98*. Melbourne: The Hawthorn Press, Ltd, 1976, pp. x+419.

Important biography of the mineralogist and naturalist who accompanied Cook to the South Seas.

491. HOARE, Michael E. "Johann Reinhold Forster (1729-1798): Problems and Sources of Biography." *Journal of the Society for the Bibliography of Natural History*, 6, pt. 1 (1971), 1-8.

FRENZEL

492. URBAN, G. "David Frenzels kurzer Bericht über die versteinerten Hölzer in Chemnitz (1750), die erste Erwähnung des versteinerten Waldes von Karl-Marx-Stadt." *Zeitschrift für geologische Wissenschaften*, 8 (1980), 151-158.

Discusses the work of the Chemnitz mineralogist and palaeontologist D. Frenzel.

FÜCHSEL

493. MOLLER, R. "Mitteilungen zur Biographie George Christian Füchsels." *Freiberger Forschungsheft*, Series D, 44. Leipzig, 1963.

Useful account of the little-known mid-eighteenth-century German stratigrapher, who pressed the distinction between primary and secondary formations, and insisted upon a rigorous actualism. His map of Thuringia is one of the earliest published geological maps.

GEIKIE, Archibald

494. GEIKIE, Archibald. *A Long Life's Work: An Autobiography*. London: Macmillan, 1924, pp. xii+426.

Discusses most of the great geological figures of Victorian England, and demonstrates the mystique geology held for the age as a source of quasi-religious experience, natural beauty and athletic exercise in the open air. The most important scientific sections deal with Geikie's work on ancient volcanoes.

495. OLDROYD, D. "Sir Archibald Geikie (1835-1924), Geologist, Romantic Aesthete, and Historian of Geology: The Problem of the Whig Historiography of Science." *Annals of Science*, 37 (1980), 441-462.

Investigates the long-term impact of Geikie's Whig views of the history of geology upon views of the development of the science. Shows the interconnections of Geikie's many interests in shaping his geology and historical outlook.

GEIKIE, James

496. NEWBIGIN, Marion I., and FLETT, John S. *James Geikie: The Man and the Geologist*. Edinburgh: Oliver & Boyd; London: Gurney and Jackson, 1917, pp. xi+227.

Geikie's major work was his synthesis of glacial studies, published in his *The Great Ice Age* of 1874, which argues that ice ages are interrupted by milder, interglacial periods.

GERHARD

497. BIELEFELDT, E. "Carl Abraham Gerhard--ein Berliner Geologe der Aufklärung." *Zeitschrift für geologische Wissenschaften*, 8 (1980), 207-215.

Gerhard (1738-1821) was the founder of the Mining Academy of Berlin.

GERSDORF

498. LEMPER, E.-H. "Adolf Traufott von Gersdorf (1744-1807) und die Oberlausitzische Gesellschaft der Wissenschaften zu Görlitz." *Zeitschrift für geologische Wissenschaften*, 8 (1980), 217-230.

Von Gersdorf was a many-sided naturalist, connected with the Freiberg Mining Academy and deeply involved in utilitarian mining projects.

GILBERT

499. DAVIS, William M. "Grove Karl Gilbert." *American Journal of Science*, 46 (1918), 669-681.

500. MENDENHALL, W.C. "Memorial to Grove Karl Gilbert." *Bulletin of the Geological Society of America*, 31 (1920), 26-45.

   Traces Gilbert's long and fruitful association with Wesley Powell on the U.S. Geological Survey, during which he accomplished his most important work on subaerial erosion and developed his theories on river valleys.

501. PYNE, Stephen J. "Certain Allied Problems in Mechanics: Grove Karl Gilbert at the Henry Mountains." Pp. 225-238 in SCHNEER, C.J., ed. *Two Hundred Years of Geology in America. Proceedings of the New Hampshire Bicentennial Conference on the History of Geology*. Hanover, N.H.: University Press of New England, 1979, pp. xvi+385.

   Stresses Gilbert's purely Newtonian approach to problems of geological mechanics.

502. PYNE, Stephen J. *Grove Karl Gilbert: A Great Engine of Research*. Austin and London: University of Texas Press, 1980, pp. xiv+306.

   Explores Gilbert's career as a pioneer American geologist, protagonist of the concept of the graded stream and theorist of lunar origins.

GOETHE

503. WELLS, George A. "Goethe's Geological Studies." *Publications of the English Goethe Society*, 35 (1964/5), 92-137.

   As with his biological thinking, Goethe's geological outlook was concerned to discover certain general "types" of which the different kind of actual rocks were variants. His theory of the origin of continents followed Werner in being largely chemical, and he showed much interest in the geomorphological role of glaciers.

GOLDSMITH

504. PITMAN, J.H. *Goldsmith's Animated Nature.* New Haven: Yale University Press, 1924, pp. 159.

   Analyzes Oliver Goldsmith's 1774 popularization of knowledge about the Earth and the animal and vegetable kingdoms.

GRABAU

505. SUN, Y.C. "Professor Amadeus William Grabau. Biographical Note." *Bulletin of the Geological Society of China,* 27 (1947), 1-26.

   Much of Grabau's geology was accomplished in China where he developed sedimentological studies, and advanced theories about the classification of sedimentary rocks. He was deeply interested in the rhythmicality of Earth history, and favored the Continental Drift theories of Wegener.

GRAY

506. DUPREE, A. Hunter. *Asa Gray, 1810-1888.* Cambridge, Mass.: Harvard University Press, 1959, pp. xvi+505.

   Gray was America's leading botanist of the mid-nineteenth century. He became the American champion of evolutionism, though not fully accepting the anti-teleology of Darwin's natural selection. He became involved in geological debates about Catastrophism and the relationship between Genesis and geology.

GREENOUGH

507. RUDWICK, Martin J.S. "Hutton and Werner Compared: George Greenough's Geological Tour of Scotland in 1805." *The British Journal for the History of Science,* 1 (1962), 117-135.

   Shows how the skeptical George Greenough found that field evidence gave little consistent support to the ideas of either the Plutonists or the Neptunists.

Biographical Studies 107

GRIFFITH

508. DAVIES, G.L. Herries, and MOLLAN, R.C., eds. *Richard Griffith 1784-1878*. Dublin: Royal Dublin Society, 1980, pp. v+221.

Studies of the geological surveyor and mapper of Ireland, exploring his mapping work, connections with government and scientific societies, road building and engineering, and mines operations.

HALL, James

509. CLARKE, John M. *James Hall of Albany, Geologist and Paleontologist, 1811-1898*. Albany, N.Y.: The Author, 1921, pp. 565.

Traces Hall's work with the New York Geological Survey, during which he built up his unrivalled collection of fossils leading to the founding of the State palaeontological museum. His later work was concerned with orogeny.

HALL, Sir James

510. EYLES, V.A. "Sir James Hall, Bt. (1761-1832)." *Endeavour*, 20 (1961), 210-216.

Emphasizes that Hall put Hutton's theory of the Earth on a more empirical footing by his experiments on the fusion of limestones and basalt.

HALLEY

511. RONAN, Colin A. *Edmond Halley: Genius in Eclipse*. London: Macdonald, 1970, pp. xii+251.

Contains a brief discussion of Halley's geophysics and notions of geomagnetism and tidal action.

512. RONAN, Colin A. "Edmond Halley and Early Geophysics." *Geophysical Journal*, 15 (1968), 241-248.

Examines Halley's work on geomagnetism, on the aurora and the behavior of the Trade Winds, and discusses his attempts to ascertain the age of the Earth.

513. SCHAFFER, S. "Halley's Atheism and the End of the World." *Notes and Records of the Royal Society of London*, 32 (1977), 17-40.

   Shows how Halley's speculations that the globe might be far older than the 6000 or so years suggested by the Bible helped to earn him his reputation as an "atheist."

HAMILTON

514. FOTHERGILL, Brian. *Sir William Hamilton--Envoy Extraordinary*. London: Faber and Faber, 1969, pp. 459.

   A rounded biography which recognizes the importance of Hamilton's sober, factual, detailed studies of Vesuvius and Etna from the 1760s, published in *Philosophical Transactions*, in the development of "Vulcanism." Hamilton's contacts with Italian geologists are touched upon.

515. SLEEP, Mark C.W. "Sir William Hamilton (1730-1803): His Work and Influence in Geology." *Annals of Science*, 25 (1969), 319-338.

   An account of Hamilton's careful observations of Vesuvius from the 1760s emphasizing Hamilton's injunction that strict empiricism was the first desideratum in the Earth sciences.

HARKER

516. SEWARD, Albert C., and TILLEY, Cecil E. "Alfred Harker, 1859-1939." *Obituary Notices of the Fellows of the Royal Society of London*, 3 (1940), 197-216.

   Brings out Harker's steady application to the development of petrology in England, and the importance of his works on metamorphic structures. His role in the "Cambridge School of Geology" is stressed.

HAUG

517. JACOB, Charles. "La Vie et l'oeuvre d'Emile Haug." *Revue Générale des Sciences*, 39 (1928), 261-271.

518. MARGERIE, E. de. "Discours aux funerailles d'Emile Haug." *Notices et Discours. Académie des Sciences*, 2nd ser., 1 (1937), 152-167.

Emphasizes the breadth of Haug's geological researches and vision, and in particular his work on geosynclines.

HAÜY

519. WHITLOCK, Herbert P. "René-Just Haüy and His Influence." Pp. 92-98 in KUNZ, George F., WHITLOCK, Herbert P., and WHERRY, Edgar T., eds. "The Abbé Réné-Just Haüy Celebration." *American Mineralogist*, 3 (1918), 49-136.

    Underlines the importance of Haüy's transformation of crystallography and the fruitfulness of his geometrical approach for nineteenth-century mineralogy.

HERSCHEL, William

520. LUBBOCK, Constance A., ed. *The Herschel Chronicle: The Life-Story of William Herschel and His Sister Caroline Herschel*. Cambridge: The University Press, 1933, pp. 388.

    William Herschel had extensive geological interests, discussing the relationships between terrestrial volcanoes and craters that could be found on the Moon, and speculating about the internal composition of the Sun. He made geological observations on his travels, and was a correspondent of James Hutton.

HILL

521. ALEXANDER, Nancy S. *Father of Texas Geology, Robert T. Hill*. Bicentennial Series in American Studies IV. Dallas, Texas: Southern Methodist University Press, 1976, pp. xii+317.

    A life of the pioneer geologist of the Texan Geological Survey, later an independent oil and mining geological consultant and journalist.

HIND

522. MORTON, W.L. "Henry Youle Hind, Geologist (1823-1908)." *Proceedings of the Geological Association of Canada*, 23 (1971), 25-29.

HOBBS

523. PORTER, R. *William Hobbs: The Earth Generated and Anatomized*. Ithaca: Cornell University Press; London: British Museum (Natural History), 1981, pp. 157.

An edition of a hitherto unpublished manuscript by an obscure early eighteenth-century Dorset amateur who viewed the Earth as organic and alive and as of considerable antiquity. Includes some important early diagrams.

HOFF, Von

524. REICH, Otto. *Karl Ernst Adolf von Hoff, Der Bahnbrecher moderner Geologie, eine wissenschaftliche Biographie*. Leipzig: Verlag von Veit, 1905, pp. vii+144.

Shows how Von Hoff's joint interests in geography and geology led him to a physical geology which emphasized the role of gradual and continuous processes in the formation of land forms.

HOLMES

525. DUNHAM, K.C. "Arthur Holmes." *Biographical Memoirs of Fellows of the Royal Society*, 12 (1966), 291-310.

Holmes did pioneer work applying radioactivity physics to concepts of geological time and the thermal history of the Earth. He made important contributions to granite petrology.

HOOKE

526. DAVIES, Gordon L. "Robert Hooke and His Conception of Earth-History." *Proceedings of the Geological Association*, 75 (1964), 493-498.

Shows that Hooke had a dynamic notion of Earth history, in which the agency of continental upthrust, and thereby constructive change, was earthquakes. Hooke saw fossilized animal remains, buried deep in the Earth, as evidence of such upheavals.

527. 'ESPINASSE, M. *Robert Hooke*. London: Heinemann, 1956, pp. viii+192.

Biographical Studies

The standard biography with a useful discussion of his *Micrographia*.

528. GUNTHER, R.T. *The Life and Work of Robert Hooke*. Vol. IV: *Early Science in Oxford*. London: Dawson's, 1930; reprinted 1968, pp. 396.

    Hooke's correspondence, here printed, contains items of interest for the history of palaeontology.

529. OLDROYD, David R. "Robert Hooke's Methodology of Science as Exemplified in his *Discourse of Earthquakes*." *The British Journal of the History of Science*, 6 (1972), 109-130.

    Examines the relationship between Hooke's geological writings and his stated methodology of induction.

HUMBOLDT

530. BAUMGÄRTEL, Hans. "Alexander von Humboldt: Remarks on the Meaning of Hypothesis in Historical Geological Researches." Pp. 19-34 in SCHNEER, C.J., ed. *Toward a History of Geology*. Cambridge, Mass., and London: M.I.T. Press, 1969, pp. vi+469.

    Examines Humboldt's ambition to construct a fully theorized general science of the interlocking of the totality of physical forces that shape the configurations of the terraqueous globe, an ambition particularly realized in *Kosmos*.

531. BOTTING, Douglas. *Humboldt and the Cosmos*. London: Michael Joseph, 1973, pp. 295.

    A pictorial biography which stresses the aesthetic component in Humboldt's desire for an interconnected science of the globe.

532. MEYER-ABICH, A. *Alexander Von Humboldt*. Bonn: Internationales, 1969, pp. 169.

    The most penetrating biography to date, with a good study of Humboldt's scientific works.

HUNT

533. ADAMS, Frank D. "Biographical Memoir of Thomas Sterry Hunt 1826-1892." *Biographical Memoirs of the National Academy of Science*, 15 (1932), 207-238.

As a geologist Hunt played a major part in Logan's elucidation of the Laurentian and Huronian systems. His controversial attempts to provide chemically based theories of Earth history were not well received.

534. DOUGLAS, James. *A Memoir of Thomas Sterry Hunt, M.D., Ll.D.* Philadelphia: MacCalla & Co., 1898, pp. 61.

HUNTER, John

535. JONES, F. Wood. "John Hunter as a Geologist." *Annals of the Royal College of Surgeons of England*, 12 (1953), 219-245.

Shows how Hunter's medical interest in comparative anatomy led him to study fossil vertebrate remains. His awareness of the depth of strata and of the distinct fossil types found therein suggested to him a high antiquity for the Earth.

HUTTON

536. BAILEY, E.B. *James Hutton--The Founder of Modern Geology*. Foreword by J.E. Richey. London, Amsterdam and New York: Elsevier, 1967, pp. xii+161.

Sound biography of James Hutton as a geologist, though it says little of his extensive interests in natural philosophy, chemistry or metaphysics. Extensive discussion of the role of particular instances of fieldwork (e.g., on Arran) in the genesis of Hutton's geology, but little about the wider metaphysics which underpin Hutton's geological theories.

537. [BAILEY, E.B., et al.]. *James Hutton 1726-1797: Commemoration of the 150th Anniversary of His Death.* Pt. iv of vol. lviii of the *Proceedings*, Section "B," of the *Royal Society of Edinburgh*, 1950.

Contains articles on the life and work of Hutton by M. MacGregor, Sir E.B. Bailey, G.W. Tyrrell, V.A. Eyles and S.I. Tomkeieff.

Biographical Studies

538. CRAIG, G.Y., ed. *James Hutton's Theory of the Earth: The Lost Drawings.* Text by G.Y. Craig, D.B. McIntyre, C.D. Waterston. Edinburgh: Scottish Academic Press in association with the Royal Society of Edinburgh and the Geological Society of London, 1978, pp. 67+portfolio of plates.

    Reproductions of the recently discovered drawings made by Clerk of Eldin to accompany James Hutton's *Theory of the Earth*, with important biographical and geological commentary.

539. DEAN, D.R. "James Hutton and His Public, 1785-1802." *Annals of Science*, 30 (1973), 89-105.

    Proves through numerous examples that, Playfair to the contrary, Hutton's theory was *not* ignored upon its first appearance; it was noticed, summarized and rejected.

540. DOTT, Robert H., Jr. "James Hutton and the Concept of a Dynamic Earth." Pp. 122-141 in SCHNEER, C.J., ed. *Toward a History of Geology.* Cambridge, Mass., and London: M.I.T. Press, 1969, pp. vi+469.

    Argues that Hutton's chief contribution to geology was not his Uniformitarian method but his conception of an Earth that was active, and in which forces of destruction and rebuilding were continually finely balanced. Brings out the key role of central heat in this theory.

541. EYLES, Victor A. *Introduction to James Hutton's System of the Earth, 1785: Theory of the Earth, 1788: Observations on Granite, 1794: Together with Playfair's Biography of Hutton. (Facsimiles of the Original Editions).* Foreword by George W. White. Darien, Conn.: Hafner, 1970, pp. xxiii+203.

    Reprints Hutton's first short announcement (1785) of his theory of the Earth--a notably theoretical statement--together with the first extensive account of the theory, first published in *Transactions of the Royal Society of Edinburgh* for 1788, together with the less important reflections on granite and Playfair's biographical memoir (still the major source of information). Dr. Eyles's introduction contains an important statement of Hutton's merits as a fieldworker.

542. GERSTNER, Patsy A. "James Hutton's Theory of the Earth and His Theory of Matter." *Isis*, 59 (1968), 26-31.

Examines notions of heat, expansion and consolidation in Hutton's *Theory of the Earth* in the light of his physical theory of the existence of two separate sorts of matter.

543. GERSTNER, Patsy A. "The Reaction to James Hutton's Use of Heat as a Geological Agent." *The British Journal of the History of Science*, 5 (1971), 353-362.

Shows that Hutton's conception of a regenerating internal heat won little acceptance, though his arguments for the igneous origin of particular rocks were more sympathetically received.

544. GRANT, R. "Hutton's Theory of the Earth." Pp. 23-38 in JORDANOVA, L.J., and PORTER, Roy S., eds. *Images of the Earth: Essays in the History of the Environmental Sciences*. Chalfont St Giles, Bucks: British Society for the History of Science, 1979, pp. xx+282.

Argues that the ultimate intellectual determinant of Hutton's *Theory of the Earth* was his theology, a form of Deism in which God had designed the Earth to continue in a state of perfection. Hence, the claim commonly made that Hutton separated geology from theology is erroneous.

545. LAUDAN, Rachel. "The Problem of Consolidation in the Huttonian Tradition." *Lychnos* (1977-1978; pub. 1979), 195-206.

Stresses the outstanding difficulties of Hutton's theory of consolidation by the action of a universal central heat, and suggests this was a major reason for the slow acceptance of Huttonian geology.

546. O'ROURKE, J.E. "A Comparison of James Hutton's *Principles of Knowledge* and *Theory of the Earth*." *Isis*, 69 (1978), 4-20.

Examines Hutton's geology in the light of his epistemology and philosophy of knowledge.

547. TOMKEIEFF, S.I. "James Hutton and the Philosophy of Geology." *Proceedings of the Royal Society of Edinburgh*, 63 (1950), 387-400.

Investigates the relationship between Hutton's concept of the geological cycle and his physical notion of time as an integrating force.

548. TOMKEIEFF, S.I. "James Hutton's 'Theory of the Earth,' 1795." *Proceedings of the Geological Association*, 57 (1946), 322-328.

    Stresses the key role played by the notion of cycle and circulation in Hutton's geology.

HUXLEY, T.H.

549. PARADIS, J.C. *T.H. Huxley: Man's Place in Nature*. Lincoln: University of Nebraska Press, 1978, pp. xi+226.

    Paradis briefly discusses Huxley's palaeontology but concentrates his attention on his scientific naturalism and his role in the evolutionary debates.

JAMESON

550. JAMESON, R. *Elements of Geognosy, 1808*. A facsimile reprint with an Introduction by J.M. SWEET. New York: Hafner, 1976, pp. xxiv+xvi+368.

    Contains a valuable introduction assessing Jameson's influence in popularizing Werner's geology.

551. SWEET, Jessie M., and WATERSTON, Charles D. "Robert Jameson's Approach to the Wernerian Theory of the Earth, 1796." *Annals of Science*, 23 (1967), 81-95.

    Examines Jameson's early and lasting attachment to the Wernerian theory, and his scientific contacts with John Walker and Richard Kirwan.

JEFFERSON

552. MARTIN, Edwin T. *Thomas Jefferson: Scientist*. London, New York and Toronto: Abelard-Schuman, 1952, pp. x+289.

    Jefferson had a deep interest in the natural history of Virginia, and defended America from charges, such as those contained in Buffon's natural history, that

America had a decadent physical environment, using the evidence of vast fossil remains to prove that the continent could sustain complex and high forms of life.

JUKES

553. BROWNE, C.A., ed. *Letters and Extracts from the Addresses and Occasional Writings of J. Beete Jukes, M.A., F.R.S., F.G.S. Edited, with Connecting Memorial Notes, by His Sister.* London: Chapman and Hall, 1871, pp. xx+596.

    The letters record in some detail Jukes's important work on the Geological Survey of England in the 1840s, especially in the West Midlands, and his crucial work organizing the Irish Survey in the 1850s.

KANT

554. O'ROURKE, J.E. "Kant's Significance for Geology." *INHIGEO Zusammenfassung, VIII. Symposium, Münster und Bonn, 12-24 September 1978* (1978), 213-215.

    Kant stressed the regulative power of natural law and saw the cosmos in terms of gradual evolution.

KING

555. WILKINS, Thurman. *Clarence King: A Biography.* New York: Macmillan, 1958, pp. ix+441.

    A popular narrative account of the American geologist who pioneered the survey of the Sierra Nevada.

LAMARCK

556. CAROZZI, Albert V. "Lamarck's Theory of the Earth: Hydrogéologie." *Isis*, 55 (1964), 293-307.

    Lamarck's studies of the global erosive effects of running water led him to postulate a system of geological forces of cyclic destruction and renewal taking place over an unlimited time-scale.

557. CAROZZI, Albert V. "Editor's Introduction." Pp. 1-14 in LAMARCK, J.B. *Hydrogeology.* Translated and with in-

troduction by Albert V. Carozzi. Urbana: University of Illinois Press, 1962, pp. viii+152.

LAPWORTH

558. BOULTON, W.S. "The Work of Charles Lapworth." *Advancement of Science*, 7 (1951), 433-442.

    Surveys Lapworth's classic work on the Ordovician strata of the Southern Uplands of Scotland. By using graptolites as an index Lapworth showed that the outcrops were repetitions of comparatively few bands constituting a series of overfolds.

559. WATTS, William W. "The Geological Work of Charles Lapworth, M.Sc., Ll.D., F.R.S., F.G.S., Professor of Geology and Physiography at the University of Birmingham." Special Supplement to Vol. XIV, *Proceedings of the Birmingham Natural History and Philosophical Society*. Birmingham: The Birmingham Printers for the Birmingham Natural History and Philosophical Society, 1921, pp. 51.

LATROBE

560. LINTNER, Stephen F., and STAPLETON, Darwin H. "Geological Theory and Practice in the Career of Benjamin Henry Latrobe." Pp. 109-119 in SCHNEER, C.J., ed. *Two Hundred Years of Geology in America. Proceedings of the New Hampshire Bicentennial Conference on the History of Geology*. Hanover, N.H.: University Press of New England, 1979, pp. xvi+385.

    Examines the wide-ranging geological interests of the architect-engineer.

LAVOISIER

561. CAROZZI, A.V. "Lavoisier's Fundamental Contribution to Stratigraphy." *Ohio Journal of Science*, 65 (1965), 65-84.

    Argues that Lavoisier was the first geologist to describe transgressive and regressive overlaps.

562. RAPPAPORT, Rhoda. "The Early Disputes Between Lavoisier and Monnet, 1777-1781." *The British Journal for the History of Science*, 4 (1969), 233-244.

Shows that the rivalry was largely professional, centering on Lavoisier's denial of Monnet's right to appropriate joint geological data.

LEHMANN

563. FREYBERG, Bruno von. *Johann Gottlob Lehmann (1719-1767). Ein Arzt, Chemiker, Metallurg, Bergmann, Mineraloge und grundlergender Geologe*. Erlangen: Verlag Universitätsbund Erlangen, 1955, pp. 159.

Lehmann pioneered the classification of different kinds of rock formation and strata, and was especially concerned with sedimentary rocks. He had a lifelong interest in the chemical aspects of mineralogy and geology.

LHWYD

564. GUNTHER, R.T. *Life and Letters of Edward Lhwyd, Second Keeper of the Museum Ashmoleanum. Early Science in Oxford*, XIV. Oxford: Oxford University Press, 1945, pp. xv+576.

Many letters relate to Lhwyd's extensive travels through the British Isles collecting fossils and minerals. Lhwyd's own deep uncertainties regarding the origins and nature of fossils appear in many letters, particularly those to John Ray.

565. JAHN, Melvin E. "A Note on the Editions of Edward Lhwyd's *Lithophylacii Britannici Ichnographia*." *Journal of the Society for the Bibliography of Natural History*, 6 (1972), 86-97.

566. JAHN, Melvin E. "A Note on the Correspondence of Edward Lhuyd." *Journal of the Society for the Bibliography of Natural History*, 6 (1971), 61-62.

Biographical Studies

LINNAEUS

567. BLUNT, Wilfrid. *The Compleat Naturalist. A Life of Linnaeus*. With an Appendix by William T. Stearn. London: Collins, 1971, pp. 256.

    Relevant especially for its accounts of Linnaeus's early travels in the north of Scandinavia, and for its discussion of the dissemination of Linnaean ideas and classification by Linnaeus's pupils such as Solander.

LISTER

568. JACKSON, J. Wilfrid. "Martin Lister and Yorkshire Geology and Conchology." *The Naturalist* (January-March 1945), 1-11.

    Discusses Lister's fossil discoveries, identifications and collections in the light of his Yorkshire connections; examines his conchological interests; and discusses Lister's awareness of Yorkshire coal deposits.

LOGAN

569. BELL, R. *Sir William Logan and the Geological Survey of Canada*. Ottawa, 1877.

    Traces Logan's lifelong work with the Geological Survey of Canada, and gives credit for his interpretative work on the structural geology of Quebec.

570. HARRINGTON, Bernard J. *Life of Sir William Logan, Kt., Ll.D., F.R.S., F.G.S., &c. First Director of the Geological Survey of Canada. Chiefly Compiled from His Letters, Journals and Reports*. London: Sampson Low, Marston, Searle and Rivington, 1883, pp. xv+432.

LOMONOSOV

571. PARRY, Albert. "Mikhail Lomonosov. One-Man University." Chapter 1, pp. 25-37, of *The Russian Scientist*. Russia Old and New Series. New York: Macmillan Co.; London: Collier-Macmillan, 1972, pp. 8+196.

572. TIKHOMIROV, V.V. "Lomonosov und die Geologie in Russland des 18. Jahrhunderts." *Zeitschrift für geologische Wissenschaft*, 8 (1980), 107-113.

Emphasizes Lomonosov's pioneer stratigraphical work and his contributions to economic geology.

LYELL

573. BAILEY, E.B. *Sir Charles Lyell*. London: Thomas Nelson, 1962, pp. 214.

    A lucid and straightforward biography, based principally on the printed *Life and Letters* (item 576).

574. BARTHOLOMEW, M. "The Singularity of Lyell." *History of Science*, 17 (1979), 276-293.

    Lyell's insistence on absolute steady-state Uniformitarianism in the history of the Earth *and* the history of life won few followers, most geologists being either Progressionists or, later, Evolutionists when interpreting the fossil record. Lyell's immense popularity stemmed largely from his writing easily the most accomplished general textbook of geology.

575. DEAN, D.R. "Graham Island, Charles Lyell, and the Craters of Elevation Controversy." *Isis*, 71 (1980), 571-588.

    The temporary emergence of a submarine volcano in 1831 involved Lyell in controversies lasting thirty years.

576. LYELL, Katherine M., ed. *Life, Letters, and Journals of Sir Charles Lyell, Bart*. 2 vols. London: Murray, 1881, pp. xi+475; ix+489.

    Lyell's letters reveal much that is never stated in his printed geological writings about the roots and motives of his adoption of Uniformitarianism.

577. McCARTNEY, Paul J. "Charles Lyell and G.B. Brocchi: A Study in Comparative Historiography." *The British Journal for the History of Science*, 9 (1976), 175-189.

    Explores Lyell's indebtedness to Brocchi for his knowledge of the history of Italian geology.

578. OSPOVAT, D. "Lyell's Theory of Climate." *Journal of the History of Biology*, 10 (1978), 317-339.

    Shows how Lyell's theory of climate lay at the heart of his interpretation of Earth history. The elevation and depression of sections of the Earth's crust were thought to promote major climatic changes, one more argument against a directional history of the Earth.

579. PAGE, Leroy E. "The Rivalry Between Charles Lyell and Roderick Murchison." *The British Journal for the History of Science*, 9 (1976), 156-165.

Indicates how the rivalry went beyond contrasting ideas in geology, encompassing distinctive social ambitions, politics and religious outlooks.

580. PORTER, Roy. "Charles Lyell, l'Uniformitarismo e l'Atteggiamento del Secolo XIX verso la Geologia dell'Illuminismo." Pp. 395-433 in SANTUCCI, A., ed. *Eredità dell'Illuminismo*. Bologna: Società Editrice il Mulino, 1979, pp. 462.

Argues that the origins of Uniformitarianism lie not primarily as a geological methodology but in the naturalism of the Enlightenment which stressed the sovereignty of natural law and the emergence of order through gradual and continuous changes. Hutton and Lamarck in particular should be seen as thinkers of the Enlightenment.

581. PORTER, Roy. "Charles Lyell and the Principles of the History of Geology." *The British Journal for the History of Science*, 9 (1976), 91-103.

Shows how the historical account of geology prefatory to Lyell's *Principles* was polemically designed to pave the way for his testament of Uniformitarianism.

582. RUDWICK, M.J.S. "The Strategy of Lyell's *Principles of Geology*." *Isis*, 61 (1970), 5-33.

Internal analysis demonstrating the unity of purpose underlying the three volumes of the *Principles*, in particular pointing out Lyell's *geological* reasons for attacking Lamarckian evolutionism.

583. RUDWICK, Martin J.S. "Charles Lyell, F.R.S. (1797-1875) and His London Lectures on Geology, 1832-33." *Notes and Records of the Royal Society of London*, 29 (1975), 231-263.

Investigates Lyell's geological lectures at the Royal Institution and his brief tenure in the Geology chair at King's College, London, which he resigned because remuneration was not commensurate with expenditure of time. The content of the lectures is examined.

584. RUDWICK, M.J.S. "Historical Analogies in the Geological Work of Charles Lyell." *Janus*, 64 (1977), 89-108.

    Lyell's use of historical, linguistic and demographic models in framing his "principles" of geological method go toward a reassessment of his originality.

585. RUDWICK, M.J.S. "Charles Lyell Speaks in the Lecture Theatre." *The British Journal for the History of Science*, 9 (1976), 147-155.

    Generous extracts from hitherto unpublished lectures delivered by Lyell in London in 1832-1833, with linking commentary.

586. RUDWICK, M.J.S. "Transposed Concepts from the Human Sciences in the Early Work of Charles Lyell." Pp. 67-83 in JORDANOVA, L.J., and PORTER, Roy, eds. *Images of the Earth*. Chalfont St Giles, Bucks: The British Society for the History of Science, 1979, pp. xx+282.

    Argues that science frequently appropriates and deploys metaphors and images taken from other fields of discourse, and uses as example the incorporation by Charles Lyell into his Uniformitarian geology of such everyday concepts as money and cash-flow, population statistics and the metaphor of Nature as a book.

587. WILSON, Leonard G. *Charles Lyell. The Years to 1841: The Revolution in Geology*. New Haven, Conn., and London: Yale University Press, 1972, pp. xiii+553.

    The first volume of a proposed three-volume exhaustive biography arguing that Lyell wrought a revolution with the statement of Uniformitarianism in his *Principles of Geology* (1830-1833). Contains generous quotations from unpublished Lyell manuscripts.

588. WILSON, L.G. *Sir Charles Lyell's Scientific Journals on the Species Question*. New Haven, Conn.: Yale University Press, 1970, pp. lxi+572.

    Prints journals dating chiefly from the late 1850s in which Lyell assesses the consequences of theories of the transmutation of species for his geological and biological Uniformitarianism and also for his personal faith in the uniqueness and dignity of man.

589. WILSON, L.G. "The Development of the Concept of Uniformitarianism in Lyell's Mind." *Proceedings of the 10th International Congress of the History of Science*, 2 (1964), 992-996.

590. WILSON, L.G. "Lyell and the Species Question." *American Scientist*, 59 (1971), 43-55.

   Shows how Lyell's Uniformitarianism led him to deny that the fossil record gave evidence for the progressive development of life. Lyell at length came to accept his friend Darwin's evolutionism and in *The Antiquity of Man* (1863) argued for the high antiquity of the species.

591. WILSON, L.G. "The Intellectual Background to Charles Lyell's *Principles of Geology*." Pp. 426-443 in SCHNEER, C.J., ed. *Toward a History of Geology*. Cambridge, Mass., and London: M.I.T. Press, 1969, pp. vi+469.

   Argues the revolutionary nature of Lyell's emphasis upon gradual causation, and shows how it was Lyell's continental fieldwork in 1828-1829 that led him to a Uniformitarian viewpoint.

MacCULLOCH

592. CUMMING, David A. "A Description of the Western Islands of Scotland; John Macculloch's Successful Failure." *Journal of the Society for the Bibliography of Natural History*, 8 (1977), 270-285.

   Discusses the geological explorations by MacCulloch leading to the publication of his *A Description of the Western Isles of Scotland* (1819).

593. EYLES, V.A. "John MacCulloch and His Geological Map: An Account of the First Geological Survey of Scotland." *Annals of Science*, 2 (1937), 114-129.

   Assesses MacCulloch's mapping work in Scotland and the government patronage he received.

MACLURE

594. MORTON, S.G. *Memoir of William Maclure, Esq.* Philadelphia and Pasadena: Academy of Natural Sciences of Philadelphia, 1841, pp. 34.

Maclure gave the first connected accounts of the geology of the United States. As a Wernerian, he divided America into areas of primary rocks, transition rocks, floetz and secondary rocks and alluvial rocks. He did pioneer work on American geological mapping.

MANTELL

595. CURWEN, E.C., ed. *The Journal of Gideon Martell.* Oxford: Oxford University Press, 1940, pp. 315.

The journal reveals some of the breadth of enthusiasm and energies of the Sussex doctor who did much to popularize knowledge of extinct saurians in the early Victorian period.

MARSH

596. SCHUCHERT, C., and C.M. LEVENE. *O.C. Marsh, Pioneer in Palaeontology.* New Haven, Conn.: Yale University Press, 1940, pp. xxi+541.

Vertebrate palaeontologist to the U.S. Geological Survey, Marsh built up huge fossil collections at the Peabody Museum at Yale. His main achievements lay in the reconstruction of fossil horses from the Eocene.

MENDES da COSTA

597. WHITEHEAD, Peter J.P. "Emanuel Mendes da Costa (1717-91) and the Conchology, or Natural History of Shells." *Bulletin of the British Museum (Natural History) History Series*, 6, no. 1 (1978), 1-24.

Mendes da Costa was a leading fossil and mineral collector and dealer in London in the mid-eighteenth century with extensive geological contacts.

Biographical Studies

MICHELL

598. GEIKIE, A. *A Memoir of John Michell*. Cambridge: University Press, 1918, pp. 108.

    The only biographical account of one of the more important eighteenth-century Woodwardian professors of geology at Cambridge, including Michell's pioneering discussion of the order of the strata across parts of central England, as recognized later by John Farey.

MILLER

599. MACKENZIE, William M. *Hugh Miller: A Critical Study*. London: Hodder and Stoughton, 1905, pp. vii+246.

    Stresses Miller's real achievements in the reconstruction of fossil fish, particularly in the Old Red Sandstone, as well as his attempts to synthesize modern geological knowledge with the broad patterns of cosmogony dictated in *Genesis*.

MILNE

600. STRAHAN, Aubrey. "The Anniversary Address of the President. 'John Milne.'" *Proceedings of the Geological Society of London* (1913-1914), liv-xciv. In *Journal of the Geological Society of London*, 70 (1914).

    As professor of geology at Tokyo, Milne became a pioneer of seismology, developing apparatus for quantitative measures of seismic activity and calling for worldwide recording of earthquake events.

MONNET

601. CLOUGH, Robert T. *A Treatise on the Exploitation of Mines. Antoine Grimoald Monnet. A Forgotten French Chemist and Metallurgist 1734-1817*. Leeds: The Author, 1974, pp. xvi+43.

    A facsimile with historical introduction. See also item 562.

MURCHISON

602. GEIKIE, A. *Life of Sir Roderick I. Murchison, Bart.: K.C.B., F.R.S.: Some-Time Director-General of the Geological Survey of the United Kingdom. Based on His Journals and Letters with Notices of His Scientific Contemporaries and a Sketch of the Rise and Growth of Palaeozoic Geology in Britain.* 2 vols. London: Murray, 1875, pp. xiii+387; vii+375.

    Powerfully establishes the enormous pioneering geological traveling undertaken by Murchison, especially in Russia, to establish the nature of geological systems once ill-distinguished as "primitive" or as "grauwacke." Revealing insights into Murchison's social snobbery and intellectual authoritarianism.

603. SECORD, James A. "King of Siluria: Roderick Murchison and the Imperial Themes in Nineteenth Century British Geology." *Victorian Studies*, 25, no. 4 (1982), 413-442.

    Roderick Murchison, stratigraphical geologist and founder of the Silurian system, began his career as a soldier and ended as a famous friend of explorers. Through an analysis of the military and imperial metaphors in Murchison's geological work, this essay explores the underlying connections between these seemingly disparate endeavors.

604. THACKRAY, J. "Essential Source-Material of Roderick Murchison." *Journal of the Society for the Bibliography of Natural History*, 6 (1972), 162-170.

    A listing of the major holdings of Murchison manuscripts.

605. THACKRAY, J.C. "R.I. Murchison's *Geology of Russia* (1846)." *Journal of the Society for the Bibliography of Natural History*, 8, pt. 4 (1978), 421-433.

    A bio-bibliographical study.

OMALIUS d'HALLOY

606. DUPONT, Edouard. *D'Omalius d'Halloy, 1783-1875.* Brussels: Musée d'Histoire Naturelle de Belgique, 1897, pp. 96.

Omalius d'Halloy was prominent in exposing the limitations of both Wernerian and Uniformitarian geology when confronted with stratigraphical field evidence in France. He supported von Buch's theory of craters of elevation and was an early proponent of the glacial hypothesis.

ORBIGNY, d'

607. FISCHER, P. "Notice sur la vie et sur les travaux d'Alcide d'Orbigny." *Bulletin de la Société Géologique de France*, ser. 3, 6 (1878), 434-453.

    Shows how d'Orbigny's career fell into two parts, the first mainly given over to natural historical travels in South America, the latter mainly concerning the palaeontological history of France.

608. HERON-ALLEN, Edward. "Alcide d'Orbigny, His Life and Work." *Journal of the Royal Microscopical Society* (1917), 1-105.

OSBORN

609. GREGORY, W.K. "Biographical Memoir of Henry Fairfield Osborn 1857-1935." *Biographical Memoirs of the National Academy of Sciences*, 19 (1938), 53-119.

    Chiefly a vertebrate palaeontologist, Osborn was an early enthusiast for evolutionary theory, through his work focusing upon the problem of the adaptive diversification of life.

610. OSBORN, Henry F. *Fifty-Two Years of Research; Observation and Publication 1877-1929. A Life Adventure in Breadth and Depth. With Complete Bibliography, Chronologic and Classified by Subject 1877-1929.* New York: Charles Scribner's Sons, 1930, pp. 160.

OWEN, David

611. HENDRICKSON, Walter B. *David Dale Owen: Pioneer Geologist of the Middle West*. Indianapolis: Indiana Historical Bureau, 1943, pp. vii+180.

    Son of Robert Owen the factory-owner and socialist, D.D. Owen, who was particularly skilled in palaeozoic formations, did important work on the Indiana Geological Survey.

OWEN, Richard

612. OWEN, Rev. Richard. *The Life of Richard Owen*. With the scientific portions revised by C.D. Sherborn. With an essay on Owen's position in anatomical science by Thomas H. Huxley. 2 vols. London: Murray, 1894, pp. 409.

Owen's chief work lay in zoological and palaeontological comparative anatomy, contributing notably to the reconstruction of Archaeopteryx. He crossed swords with Huxley over Darwinian evolution and man's place in Nature.

PALLAS

613. WENDLAND, F., and JUBITZ, K.B. "Der Beitrag von Peter Simon Pallas (1741-1811) zum Weltbild der Geowissenschaften. Eine Bestandsanfrahme." *Zeitschrift für geologische Wissenschaft*, 8 (1980), 119-133.

Examines the contribution of Pallas's travels across Russia to his overall geological views.

PARKINSON

614. KNIGHT, D. "Chemistry in Palaeontology: The Work of James Parkinson (1755-1824)." *Ambix*, 21 (1974), 78-85.

Examines attempts by Parkinson and his contemporaries to find chemically satisfactory theories of fossilization.

615. THACKRAY, J. "James Parkinson's *Organic Remains of a Former World* (1804-1811)." *Journal of the Society for the Bibliography of Natural History*, 7, pt. 4 (1976), 451-466.

A bio-bibliographical study emphasizing Parkinson's shifting outlook between the first and later volumes.

PEIRCE

616. DUSEK, Val. "Geodesy and the Earth Sciences in the Philosophy of C.S. Peirce." Pp. 265-275 in SCHNEER, C.J., ed. *Two Hundred Years of Geology in America. Proceedings of the New Hampshire Bicentennial Conference on the History of Geology.* Hanover, N.H.: University Press of New England, 1979, pp. xvi+385.

Explores the relations between Peirce's geological researches and his philosophy of pragmatism.

PENCK

617. SÖLCH, J. "Albrecht Penck." *Mitteilungen der geographischer Gesellschaft in Wien*, 89, Heft 7-12 (1946), 88-122.

Pioneer of the Quaternary, Penck ranged freely from prehistory, anthropogeography and climatology to geomorphology. Penck's major achievement lay in establishing the fourfold division of the Pleistocene glaciation of the Alps.

PHILLIPS, John

618. COLLINGE, Walter E. "John Phillips, the First Keeper of the Yorkshire Museum, York." *Yorkshire Philosophical Society, Annual Report* (1925), 39-46.

Traces Phillips's rise from his geological apprenticeship at the hands of William Smith to his tenure in the Oxford chair of geology. Stresses his work on Yorkshire geology, especially the coal measures.

PLAYFAIR

619. JEFFREY, F. *Memoir of John Playfair.* Edinburgh: privately printed, 1822, pp. 31.

Friend, supporter and popularizer of James Hutton, it was Playfair's *Illustrations of the Huttonian Theory of the Earth* that familiarized most nineteenth-century geologists with Hutton's ideas.

620. WHITE, George W. "Biography of Playfair." Pp. xv-xviii in PLAYFAIR, John. *Illustrations of the Huttonian Theory of the Earth*. New York: Dover Publications, 1964, pp. xx+528.

Shows how Playfair's *Illustrations* placed Hutton's *Theory* in a more empirical, hence more acceptable, light.

PLOT

621. CHALLINOR, J. "Dr Plot and Staffordshire Geology." *Transactions of the North Staffordshire Field Club*, 79 (1945), 29-67.

Robert Plot made important contributions to the study of the geology of Oxfordshire and Staffordshire in the seventeenth century, and took part in the debate on the origin and nature of fossils.

POWELL

622. GILBERT, G.K., et al., eds. *John Wesley Powell, a Memorial*. Chicago, 1903, pp. 75.

Emphasizes Powell's immense influence as head of the U.S. Survey of Utah, Colorado and Arizona, exploring canyon geology and demonstrating how geological and climatic causes jointly produced the aridity of the region.

623. TERRELL, John U. *The Man Who Rediscovered America: A Biography of John Wesley Powell*. New York: Weybridge and Talley, 1969, pp. 281.

PRESTWICH

624. PRESTWICH, G. *Life and Letters of Sir Joseph Prestwich*. Edinburgh: Blackwood, 1899, pp. xvi+444.

Valuable for its letters referring to Prestwich's part in debates on the antiquity of man in the 1860s and his contributions to glacial and post-glacial geology. Revealing about the institutions of late Victorian English geology.

PREVOST

625. LAURENT, G. "Actualisme et antitransformisme chez Constant Prévost." *Histoire et Nature*, 8 (1976), 33-52.

   Discussion of the French geologist who shared Lyell's actualism and hostility to evolutionism (but who did not wholly accept Lyell's Uniformitarianism).

RAMSAY

626. GEIKIE, A. *Memoir of Sir Andrew Crombie Ramsay*. London: Macmillan, 1896, pp. xi+397.

   Geikie, a Scottish geologist who came to London and made good, was a particularly suitable biographer for Ramsay. Geikie discusses Ramsay's pioneering glacial work, and emphasizes his qualities as teacher and administrator at the head of the Geological Survey.

RASPE

627. CAROZZI, Albert V. "The Geological Contribution of Rudolf Erich Raspe (1737-1794)." *Archives of Science, Genève*, 22, pt. 3 (1969), 625-643.

   Utilizing the earlier work of Hooke, Raspe helped to give earthquakes universal significance as agents of crustal uplift. Raspe tended to be a Uniformitarian in his geology.

628. CARSWELL, J.P. *The Prospector: Being the Life and Times of R.E. Raspe, 1737-94*. London: Cresset, 1950, pp. x+288.

   Shows how becoming a functionary could assist an aspiring young scholar, while eventually frustrating the desire for scientific fame.

629. RASPE, R.E. *An Introduction to the Natural History of the Terrestrial Sphere*. Translated and Edited by A.N. IVERSEN and A.V. CAROZZI. New York: Hafner, 1970, pp. cxvii+191.

   Contains an important introduction discussing Raspe's contributions to volcanic geology.

RAY

630. GUNTHER, R.W.T. *Further Correspondence of John Ray.*
London: Ray Society, 1928, pp. xxiv+322.

Includes numerous letters to Lhwyd written late in
Ray's life, expressing his uncertainties as to the
origin of fossils.

631. LANKESTER, E.R. *The Correspondence of John Ray: Consisting of Selections from the Philosophical Letters Published by Dr. Derham and Original Letters of John Ray, in the Collection of the British Museum.* London:
Printed for the Ray Society, 1848, pp. xvi+502.

Ray's correspondence indicates the importance of the
network of natural historians including Martin Lister
and Robert Plot for building a knowledge of the geographical distribution of fossils and minerals in late
seventeenth-century England.

632. RAVEN, Charles E. *John Ray, Naturalist, His Life and Works.* Cambridge: University Press, 1942, pp. xix+502.

Contains an important discussion of Ray's geological
ideas in the context of his views of the nature of
fossils, his benevolist natural theology and his extensive observations on continental travels.

ROBINSON

633. NORTH, F.J. "'The Anatomy of the Earth'--A Seventeenth
Century Cosmogony." *Geological Magazine*, 71 (1934),
541-547.

Explores Thomas Robinson's conception of the Earth
as a living organism, analogous to the body of a man.

ROGERS

634. GERSTNER, Patsy A. "Henry Darwin Rogers and William
Barton Rogers on the Nomenclature of the American
Paleozoic Rocks." Pp. 175-186 in SCHNEER, C.J., ed.
*Two Hundred Years of Geology in America. Proceedings
of the New Hampshire Bicentennial Conference on the
History of Geology.* Hanover, N.H.: University Press
of New England, 1979, pp. xvi+385.

Biographical Studies

The Rogers brothers attempted to lay down guidelines for the naming of the Palaeozoic rocks of the Appalachian area.

635. GERSTNER, Patsy A. "A Dynamic Theory of Mountain Building: Henry Darwin Rogers, 1842." *Isis*, 66 (1975), 26-37.

Shows how Rogers's theory--one of the earliest American contributions to geological theory--arose out of his Appalachian fieldwork.

ROSENBUSCH

636. RAMDOHR, Paul. "Harry Rosenbusch 1836-1914." Pp. 343-348 in FREUND, Hugo, and BERG, Alexander, eds. *Geschichte der Mikroskopie. Leben und Werk grosser Forscher. III. Angewandte Naturwissenschaften und Technik*. Frankfurt-am-Main: Umschau Verlag, 1966, pp. 550.

Rosenbusch was a particularly effective exponent of the study of mineral specimens by thin slicing and examining under a polarizing microscope. He did much to establish a mineralogical classification of rocks.

ROUELLE

637. RAPPAPORT, Rhoda. "G.F. Rouelle: An Eighteenth-Century Chemist and Teacher." *Chymia*, 6 (1960), 68-101.

Good brief life of the chemist and part-time geologist, emphasizing the chemical basis of his mineralogical ideas.

SAUSSURE

638. FRESHFIELD, Douglas, and MONTAGNIER, Henry F. *The Life of Horace Benedict de Saussure*. London: Edward Arnold, 1920, pp. 479.

A wide-ranging naturalist who made contributions to the understanding of many aspects of Switzerland and was the first to scale Mont Blanc, de Saussure is probably best remembered as the author of the four-volume *Voyages dans les Alpes*, which set new standards in observational geology.

SCHEUCHZER, J.J.

639. JAHN, Melvin E. "Some Notes on Dr. Scheuchzer and on *Homo diluvii testis.*" Pp. 192-213 in SCHNEER, C.J., ed. *Toward a History of Geology.* Cambridge, Mass., and London: M.I.T. Press, 1969, pp. vi+469.

Indicates Scheuchzer's importance as a natural historian and geologist of Switzerland and one of the continental popularizers of the work of John Woodward.

SCHUCHERT

640. DUNBAR, Carl O. "Memorial to Charles Schuchert (1858-1942)." *Proceedings of the Geological Society of America* (1942), 212-240.

Leading palaeogeographer of the United States, Schuchert contributed particularly to the study of fossil brachiopods. He was a highly influential teacher.

SCROPE

641. RUDWICK, Martin J.S. "Poulett Scrope on the Volcanoes of Auvergne: Lyellian Time and Political Economy." *The British Journal of the History of Science,* 7 (1974), 205-242.

Investigates the analogies between the idea of an indefinitely large money supply and the actualistic insistence on a long time-scale in the geology of the political economist G.P. Scrope. His work on the volcanoes of the Auvergne is analyzed.

SEDGWICK

642. CLARK, John W., and HUGHES, T. McKenny. *The Life and Letters of the Reverend Adam Sedgwick.* 2 vols. Cambridge: Cambridge University Press, 1890, pp. xiii+539.

Reveals the complexity of Sedgwick's life as a minister of religion and Cambridge don as well as geologist, and prints much of his more controversial correspondence, including his hostility to Darwinism, though not his more polemical correspondence about Murchison on the Cambrian controversy.

643A. RUDWICK, Martin J.S. "Levels of Disagreement in the Sedgwick-Murchison Controversy." *Journal of the Geological Society of London*, 132, pt. 4 (1976), 373-375.

Argues that the violent disagreement between Sedgwick and Murchison as to the reality of and boundaries between the Cambrian and Silurian had metaphysical, theoretical and methodological components as well as technical ones. These were aggravated by personal differences and rivalry.

643B. SPEAKMAN, Colin. *Adam Sedgwick, Geologist and Dalesman*. Heathfield, Sussex: Broadoak Press Ltd., 1982, pp. 145.

A semi-popular biography, but utilizing manuscript materials, stressing Sedgwick's Yorkshire roots and the lasting ambiguities of his residence in Cambridge.

SILLIMAN

644. FISHER, G.P. *Life of Benjamin Silliman*. 2 vols. New York: Scribner, 1866, pp. 407; 408.

Silliman used his professorship to make Yale the leading center in early nineteenth-century America for mineralogical and geological studies, training a whole generation of American geologists, and founding the American Geological Association in 1819.

SLOANE

645. SWEET, J. "Sir Hans Sloane and the Mineral Collection." *Natural History Magazine*, 5 (1935), 49-64, 97-116, 145-164.

Shows how Sloane built up his collection, some of which survives in the Natural History Museum at South Kensington.

SMITH

646. COX, L.R. "New Light on William Smith and His Work." *Proceedings of the Yorkshire Geological Society*, 25 (1942), 1-99.

Prints generous extracts from unpublished Smith manuscripts, emphasizing the many proposed publishing projects which never came to fruition.

647. EYLES, J.M. "William Smith (1769-1839): A Bibliography of the Published Writings, Maps and Geological Sections, Printed and Lithographed." *Journal of the Society for the Bibliography of Natural History*, 5 (1969), 87-109.

    The introduction also surveys recent Smith scholarship.

648. EYLES, J.M. "William Smith: Some Aspects of His Life and Work." Pp. 142-158 in SCHNEER, C.J., ed. *Toward a History of Geology*. Cambridge, Mass., and London: M.I.T. Press, 1969, pp. vi+469.

    The most useful and accurate brief biographical guide to Smith, containing evaluation of recent writings.

649. EYLES, Joan M. "William Smith (1769-1839). A Chronology of Significant Dates in His Life." *Proceedings of the Geological Society of London*, no. 1657 (1969), 173-176.

650. PHILLIPS, John. *Memoirs of William Smith, LL.D. Author of the Map of the Strata of England and Wales*. London: Murray, 1844, pp. viii+150.

    Prints generous extracts from Smith's correspondence and unpublished scientific papers.

651. SHEPPARD, T. "William Smith: His Maps and Memoirs." *Proceedings of the Yorkshire Geological Society*, no. 5 (1914-1922), 75-254.

    Includes a historical survey of geological mapping in England before Smith, accounts of Smith's maps, from his 1799 map of Bath onward, and historical notices of the importance of Smith's work from contemporaries such as Fitton, Conybeare and Phillips.

SOLANDER

652. RAUSCHENBERG, Roy A. "Daniel Carl Solander, Naturalist on the Endeavour." *Transactions of the American Philosophical Society*, n.s., 58, no. 8 (1968), 1-66.

Solander was of some importance as a geological and mineralogical collector, a pupil of Linnaeus and one of the natural history circle of Banks.

SORBY

653. HIGHAM, Norman. *A Very Scientific Gentleman: The Major Achievements of Henry Clifton Sorby*. Foreword by Cyril Stanley SMITH. Oxford, London, Paris and Frankfurt: Pergamon Press; New York: Macmillan, 1963, pp. xiv+ 160.

Founder of microscopic petrology in Britain, Sorby pioneered the art of the thin-slicing of hard minerals. Shows how Sorby's petrological interests grew out of his family's connections with the Sheffield cutlery industry.

654. JUDD, J.W. "Henry Clifton Sorby, and the Birth of Microscopical Petrology." *Geological Magazine*, 46 (1918), 222-239.

655. SMITH, Cyril S., ed. *The Sorby Centennial Symposium on the History of Metallurgy*. New York: Gordon and Breach, 1965, pp. 558.

Contains discussion of Sorby and his work together with other contributions on mineralogy and metallography over the last two centuries.

SOWERBY

656. CLEEVELY, Ron J. "The Sowerbys, the *Mineral Conchology*, and Their Fossil Collection." *Journal of the Society for the Bibliography of Natural History*, 6, pt. 6 (1974), 418-481.

A bio-bibliographical account, printing much hitherto unpublished manuscript material.

657. MacDONALD, Jessie B. "The Sowerby Collection in the British Museum (Natural History): A Brief Description of Its Holdings and a History of Its Acquisition from 1821-1971." *Journal of the Society for the Bibliography of Natural History*, 6 (1974), 380-401.

Examines the Sowerbys' activities as collectors of botanical mineralogical, zoological and palaeontological specimens.

STASZIC

658. BABICZ, Jósef. "Stanislaw Staszic (1755-1826), the Polish Neptunist, and His Land Observations." *INHIGEO Zusammenfussung, VIII. Symposium, Münster und Bonn, 12-24 September 1978*, 12-15.

STENO

659. EYLES, V.A. "The Influence of Nicolaus Steno on the Development of Geological Science in Britain." Pp. 167-188 in SCHERZ, G., ed. *Nicolaus Steno and His Indice. Acta Historica Scientiarum Naturalium et Medicinalium*, Vol. 15. Copenhagen, 1958, pp. 314.

   Examines the parallels between the work of Steno and Hooke and explores possible influences. Steno's *Prodromus* was translated into English by Henry Oldenburg.

660. SCHERZ, Gustav. *Niels Stensen*. Copenhagen: G.E.C. Cada Forlag, 1963, pp. 94.

   Demonstrates Steno's fundamental contributions to palaeontology (his emphasis on the organic nature of fossil remains) and to stratigraphy (his awareness that the crust comprised successively deposited and distinct layers), and the harmony of geological and religious ideas in his theory of the Earth.

661. SCHERZ, G. *Steno. Geological Papers*. Trans. A.J. Pollock. Odense: Odense University Press, 1969, pp. 319.

   Contains a lengthy assessment by the editor of Steno's geological work, followed by papers discussing his writings on hot-springs, the *Prodromus* on solids, letters on the grottos and his pioneer palaeontological researches.

STRACHEY

662. FULLER, J.G.C.M. "The Industrial Basis of Stratigraphy: John Strachey, 1671-1743, and William Smith, 1769-1839." *Bulletin of the American Association of Petroleum Geologists*, 53, no. 11 (1969), 2256-2273.

   Examines Strachey and Smith in the context of their interest in coal prospecting on the basis of scientific geology in the southwestern counties of England.

Biographical Studies

SWEDENBORG

663. TOKSVIG, S. *Swedenborg, Scientist and Mystic.* New Haven, Conn.: Yale University Press, 1948, pp. 389.

    Examines Swedenborg's theory of the Earth in the light of his religious beliefs and his version of the corpuscular philosophy.

SUESS

664. TERMIER, Pierre. "Sketch of the Life of Eduard Suess." *Report of the Smithsonian Institution* (1914), 709-718.

    Shows the immense range of Suess's explorations, ranging from economic geology to the palaeontology of graptolites and brachiopods, and major tectonic research on the structure of the Alps.

TEALL

665. FLETT, John S. "Sir Jethro Justinian Harris Teall, 1849-1924." *Proceedings of the Royal Society of London*, 97, series B (1925), xv-xvii.

    Discusses Teall's career, placing him among the leading petrographers of the latter part of the nineteenth century.

TOULMIN

666. DAVIES, G.L. "George Hoggart Toulmin and the Huttonian Theory of the Earth." *Bulletin of the Geological Society of America*, 78 (1967), 121-123.

    Analyzes the geological ideas of Toulmin, expressed in several books published in the 1780s, with their emphasis upon the Earth's activity, regeneration and extreme antiquity or even eternality. Suggests that Toulmin most likely plagiarized from Hutton.

667. PORTER, Roy. "George Hoggart Toulmin and James Hutton: A Fresh Look." *Geological Society of America Bulletin*, 89 (1978), 1256-1258.

    According to Gordon L. Davies (item 666), George Hoggart Toulmin (1754-1817) probably plagiarized from

James Hutton, and was not important in the history of geology. But Toulmin's views differed from Hutton's in important respects, and he was perhaps more indebted to Georges Louis Leclerc de Buffon and to John Brown. That Toulmin translated the geological writings of J.A.C. Chaptal shows that his interest in geology was a lasting one.

668. PORTER, Roy. "George Hoggart Toulmin's Theory of Man and the Earth in the Light of the Development of British Geology." *Annals of Science*, 35 (1978), 339-352.

Argues that one reason for the neglect by subsequent geologists of the Uniformitarian theories of George Hoggart Toulmin may have been his inclusion of the history of man within an eternalistic, cyclical, naturalistic theory of the Earth (something which distinguished his geology from that of James Hutton).

669. PORTER, Roy. "Philosophy and Politics of a Geologist: G.H. Toulmin (1754-1817)." *Journal of the History of Ideas*, 39 (1978), 435-450.

Argues that Toulmin saw geological science and moral and political opinions as inextricably linked. Traditional cosmogonies reflected governmental tyranny and the intellectual censorship of priestcraft. A true theory of the Earth would vindicate man's integrity and liberty.

VOGT

670. VOGT, William. *La Vie d'un homme: Carl Vogt*. Paris and Stuttgart, 1896, pp. 265.

Vogt became a leading palaeontologist in the comparative anatomy tradition of Cuvier and Agassiz. He enthusiastically adopted Darwinian natural selection.

WALKER

671. WALKER, John. *Lectures on Geology, Including Hydrography, Mineralogy and Meteorology, with an Introduction to Biology*. Edited with Notes and Introduction by Harold W. SCOTT. Chicago: University of Chicago Press, 1966, pp. xliv+280.

Walker lectured on natural history at Edinburgh University from the 1780s, forming an important link between Linnaeus and Jameson. Generous selections from his lecture notes are here printed with a valuable historical introduction.

WALLERIUS

672. ZENZEN, Nils. "Johan Gottschalk Wallerius, 1709-1785." Pp. 92-104 in LINDROTH, Sven, ed. *Swedish Men of Science, 1650-1950*. Stockholm: The Swedish Institute and Almqvist and Wiksell, 1952, pp. 296.

    Examines Wallerius's mineralogy in the context of Linnaean classification and the development of a mineralogically based geology in Sweden.

WALTHER

673. GRUMBT, Eberhard. "Johannes Walther--ein Begrunder der moderner Sedimentforschung." *Zeitschrift für geologische Wissenschaft*, 3, no. 10 (1975), 1255-1263.

    Traces the development of Walther's career from his early interest in fossil shells, fish and coral, to his later becoming a leading expert on the geology of the world's deserts.

WATSON

674. FORD, T.D. "White Watson (1760-1835) and His Geological Sections." *Proceedings of the Geologists' Association*, 71 (1960), 349-363.

    Analyzes the maps, sections and other visual representations by the Derbyshire geologist.

WEBSTER

675. CHALLINOR, J. "Thomas Webster's Observations on the Geology of the Isle of Wight, 1811-1813." *Proceedings of the Isle of Wight Natural History and Archaeological Society*, 4 (1949), 108-122.

WEGENER

676A. SCHWARZBACH, Martin. *Alfred Wegener und der Drift der Kontinente.* Stuttgart: Wissenschaftliche Verlagsgesellschaft, 1980.

A detailed picture of Wegener's life and work in astronomy, climatology, meteorology, geophysics and geology, stressing the skepticism with which his ideas on Continental Drift were received for some forty years, to be revived with the development of plate tectonics in the 1960s.

676B. WEGENER, Else. *Alfred Wegener. Tagebucher. Briefe. Erinnerungen.* Wiesbaden: Brockhaus, 1960, pp. 262.

The most complete biography, with copious extracts from Wegener's papers, focusing upon his work in pioneering Continental Drift.

WERNER

677. Item deleted.

678. COLEMAN, William. "Abraham Gottlob Werner vu par Alexander von Humboldt, avec des notes de Georges Cuvier." *Sudhoffs Archiv für Geschichte der Medizin und der Naturwissenschaften,* 47 (1963), 465-478.

Discusses Von Humboldt's relationship to Werner, his teacher, from whose views he later dissented.

679. EYLES, Victor A. "Abraham Gottlob Werner (1749-1817) and His Position in the History of the Mineralogical and Geological Sciences." *History of Science,* 3 (1964), 102-115.

Emphasizes the cardinal importance of Werner's role as a teacher.

680. GUNTAU, M. "Der Aktualismus bei A.G. Werner." *Bergakademie,* 5 (1967), 294-297.

Shows that Werner was sympathetic to actualistic explanation, documenting this with extracts from Werner manuscripts.

681. GUNTAU, Martin, and MÜHLFRIEDEL, Wolfgang. "Die Bedeutung von Abraham Gottlob Werner für die Mineralogie und

die Geologie." *Geologie*, 17, pt. 9 (1968), 1096-1115.

Discusses Werner's education and his political and philosophical outlooks, and examines his output in mineralogy and geology in the light of the unity of theory and practice.

682. OSPOVAT, Alexander M. "The Place of the *Kurze Klassifikation* in the Work of A.G. Werner." *Isis*, 58 (1967), 90-95.

Shows that Werner's mineralogical classification was both highly practical for the purposes of mining technology and also related to the development of his geological ideas.

683. OSPOVAT, Alexander M. "The Work and Influence of Abraham Gottlob Werner: A Reevaluation." *Actes du XIIIe Congrès International d'Histoire des Sciences* [1971], 8 (1974), 123-130.

Argues for the considerable constructive achievement of Werner as a geologist, not least his advocacy of the uniform deposition of the strata and his sense of the history of the Earth.

684. OSPOVAT, A.M. "The Distortion of Werner in Lyell's *Principles of Geology*." *The British Journal for the History of Science*, 9 (1976), 190-198.

Argues that Lyell gave a misleading view of Werner's geology, by characterizing it as dogmatic and oversimplifying his ideas about an original universal ocean and universal rock formations. Much English-language scholarship has continued to accept Lyell's caricatures.

685. WAGENBRETH, O. "Die Geologie A.G. Werners in ihrer Wirkung von der Aufklärung bis Heute." *Zeitschrift für geologische Wissenschaften*, 8 (1980), 79-86.

Argues that Werner was a "progressive geologist" in his development of geological and mineralogical classification and in his encouragement of geological mapping and the study of raw material.

686. WAGENBRETH, Otfried. "Die Paläontologie in Abraham Gottlob Werners Geologischen System." *Bergakademie* (1968), 32-36.

687. WERNER, A.G. *On the External Characters of Minerals.* Trans. from German by Albert V. CAROZZI. Urbana: University of Illinois Press, 1962, pp. xxxi+118.

   An edition of Werner's *Von der Äusserlichen Kennzeichen der Fossilien*, a work which emphasizes the value of identification by external character.

688. WERNER, Abraham Gottlob. *Short Classification and Description of the Various Rocks.* Trans. with an introduction and notes by Alexander M. OSPOVAT. Translation and facsimile of original text (1786) in juxtaposition. New York: Hafner, 1971, pp. x+194.

   Contains a learned and sympathetic introduction dispelling many of the myths that still surround Wernerian geology in the English-speaking world. The distinction between Wernerian Neptunism and scriptural geology is particularly emphasized.

688A. Werner, Abraham Gottlob. *Gedenkschrift aus Anlass der Wiederkehr seines Todestages nach 150 Jahren am 30 Juni 1967.* Leipzig: VEB Deutscher Verlag für Grundstoffindustrie, 1967, pp. 317.

   Fifteen wide-ranging essays in commemoration of Werner which help to dispel the impression still current in the Anglo-Saxon world that Werner was little versed in empirical fieldwork and dogmatic in his Neptunist theories.

WHITEHURST

689. FORD, Trevor D. "Biographical Notes on Derbyshire Authors. John Whitehurst F.R.S., 1713-1788." *Bulletin of the Peak District Mines History Society*, 5, pt. 6 (1974), 362-369.

   Account of the pioneer stratigrapher of Derbyshire and friend of the Lunar Society circle of scientists, paying particular attention to his diagrammatic visual sections.

WOODWARD

690. EYLES, Victor A. "John Woodward, F.R.S., F.R.C.P., M.D. (1665-1728): A Bio-Bibliographical Account of His Life and Work." *Journal of the Society for the*

Biographical Studies 145

Bibliography of Natural History, 5, no. 6 (1971), 399-427.

Scholarly account of Woodward's life and publications.

691. EYLES, Victor A. "John Woodward, F.R.S. (1665-1728), Physician and Geologist." *Nature*, 206, no. 4987 (1965), 868-870.

Shows that despite the shortcomings of his theory of the Earth, Woodward possessed extensive knowledge of the strata and fossils of Britain.

692. JAHN, M.E. "A Bibliographical History of John Woodward: An Essay Towards a Natural History of the Earth." *Journal of the Society for the Bibliography of Natural History*, 6 (1972), 181-213.

693. PORTER, Roy. "John Woodward. 'A Droll Sort of Philosopher.'" *Geological Magazine*, 116 (1979), 335-343.

Biographical account of the founder of the Woodwardian Chair at Cambridge.

ZIRKEL

694. BRAUNS, R. "Ferdinand Zirkel." *Zentralblatt für Mineralogie, Geologie und Paläontologie* (1912), 513-521.

695. MOSEBACH, Rudolf. "Ferdinand Zirkel 1838-1912." Pp. 515-524 in FREUND, Hugo, and BERG, Alexander, eds. *Geschichte der Mikroskopie. Leben und Werk grosser Forscher. III. Angewandte Naturwissenschaften und Technik*. Frankfurt-am-Main: Umschau Verlag, 1966.

Trained as a mining engineer, Zirkel early developed an interest in the microscopic study of rocks in thin section. With Rosenbusch he became a leading exponent of descriptive petrography.

7. INSTITUTIONAL HISTORIES

See also 5. Studies by Area

696. AGNEW, Allen F. *The U.S. Geological Survey*. Prepared for the Committee on Interior and Insular Affairs, United States Senate, Henry M. Jackson, Chairman. 94th Congress, 1st Session, Washington, D.C.: G.P.O., 1975, pp. xi+139.

697. AGUILLON, L. "L'Ecole des Mines: Notice historique." *Annales des Mines*, 83 série, 15 (1889), 433-686.

    Examines the school from its roots under the *ancien régime*, stressing its connections with state patronage and its nineteenth-century role in the development of the mapping of France.

698. ALDRICH, Michele L. "American State Geological Surveys, 1820-1845." Pp. 133-144 in SCHNEER, C.J., ed. *Two Hundred Years of Geology in America. Proceedings of the New Hampshire Bicentennial Conference on the History of Geology*. Hanover, N.H.: University Press of New England, 1979, pp. xvi+385.

    Shows the complex mixture of utilitarian and scientific interests involved in the Surveys.

699. ALLAN, D.A. "The Royal Scottish Museum: General Survey." Pp. 5-24 in ALLAN, D.A., ed. *The Royal Scottish Museum: Art and Ethnography; Natural History; Technology; Geology*. Edinburgh: Oliver & Boyd, 1954.

700. ANDRÉE, Karl. "Aus der Geschichte der Deutschen Geologische Gesellschaft." *Deutsche Geologische Gesellschaft Zeitschrift*, 100 (1950), 1-24.

    Outline of the Society since its foundation in 1848.

701. [ANON.]. "The Completion of Fifty Years of the *Geological Magazine*." *Geological Magazine*, 51, no. 6 (1914), 241-244.

702. BACK, William. "Emergence of Geology as a Public Function, 1800-1879." *Journal of the Washington Academy of Science*, 49 (1959), 205-209.

   Shows presidential hostility to federal aid for scientific projects from Jefferson to Jackson, and explains why the U.S. Geological Survey was not founded until 1879. Geological surveying developed at a state level.

703. BAILEY, E.B. *Geological Survey of Great Britain.* London: Murby, 1952, pp. xii+278.

   Discusses predecessors of the Survey--eighteenth- and early nineteenth-century British geologists who contributed to the mapping and explication of the strata of the British Isles--as well as the Survey staff. Important discussions of the work of Murchison and Geikie.

704. BURTON, P. *The New Geological Survey, 1865-1965: New Zealand Geological Survey Handbook.* Information Series no. 52. Lower Hutt: New Zealand Department of Scientific and Industrial Research, 1965, pp. 147.

705. CAMPBELL SMITH, W. "History of the First Hundred Years of the Mineral Collection of the British Museum." *Bulletin of the British Museum (Natural History) Historical Series*, 3 (1969), 237-259.

   Assesses the collection left by Hans Sloane and accessions made under the aegis of curators such as Maty, and the role of Sir Joseph Banks.

706. CAMPBELL SMITH, W. "The Mineralogical Society (1876-1976)." *Mineralogical Magazine*, 40 (1976), 430-439.

   Surveys the work of the Society, particularly its journal, *The Mineralogical Magazine*, and its close associations with the International Mineralogical Association.

707. CHITNIS, A. "The University of Edinburgh's Natural History Museum and the Huttonian-Wernerian Debate." *Annals of Science*, 26 (1970), 85-94.

   Shows how Robert Jameson, Professor of Natural History at Edinburgh, had effective control of the museum and used it to promote his pro-Wernerian views.

708. COLEMAN, Laurence V. *The Museum in America: A Critical Study*. 3 vols. Washington, D.C.: American Association of Museums, 1939.

709. EDMONDS, J.M. "The First Geological Lecture Course at the University of London, 1831." *Annals of Science*, 32 (1975), 257-275.

   Shows that geology was taught at University College from 1827, though the first chair in geology was not created until 1841. Analyzes John Phillips's lecture course of 1831.

710. EDWARDS, Edward. *Lives of the Founders of the British Museum: with Notices of Its Chief Augmentors and Other Benefactors 1570-1870*. London: Triboner and Co.; New York: J.W. Bouton, 1870, pp. x+780.

   Largely biographical accounts of the benefactors and custodians of the library, useful to historians of geology for its accounts of Hans Sloane, Sir William Hamilton, Joseph Banks and Charles König.

711. FAIRCHILD, H.L. *The Geological Society of America, 1888-1930: A Chapter in Earth Science History*. New York: The Geological Society of America, 1932, pp. xvii+232.

   A history of the Society (founded 1888) with details of officials, membership, its bulletin, library and finances, together with an assessment of the Society's role in the development of American geology.

712. FOX, Reverend F.C. "By-Ways in the History of the Society." *Transactions of the Royal Geological Society of Cornwall*, 17, pt. 3 (1943-1944), 109-120.

713. FÜLÖP, Jozsef, and TASNADI-KUBACSKA, Andras, eds. *One Hundred Years of the Hungarian Geological Institute*. Budapest: Hungarian Geological Institute, 1969, pp. 253.

714. GEOLOGICAL SURVEY OF INDIA. *Centenary of the Geological Survey of India 1851-1951: A Short History of the First Hundred Years*. Calcutta: Geological Survey of India, 1951, pp. 122.

715. GUNTAU, M. "Die Entwicklung der geowissenschaftlichen Lehre an der Bergakademie Freiberg seit Gründung

der Hochschule in Jahre 1765." *Zeitschrift für geologische Wissenschaft*, 3 (1975), 1579-1594.

An account of the Freiberg Mining Academy which pays particular attention to the practical need to train technologically competent mines administrators, distinguishing the mines school from traditional universities.

716. GUNTHER, R.T. *Early Science in Oxford*, Vol. 3. Part I: *The Biological Sciences*. Part II: *The Biological Collections*. Oxford: For The Subscribers, 1925, pp. xii+564.

    Contains extended discussion of geology at Oxford from the time of Robert Plot and the foundation of the Ashmolean Museum.

717. HELLMAN, Geoffrey T. *Bankers, Bones and Beetles: The First Century of the American Museum of Natural History*. Garden City, N.Y.: Natural History Press, 1969, pp. 275.

718. HENDRICKSON, W.B. "Nineteenth Century State Geological Surveys. Early Government Support of Science." *Isis*, 52 (1961), 357-371.

    Examines the politics of obtaining state funding in the United States.

719. HOCART, Raymond. "La Société Française de Mineralogie de 1928 à 1953." *Bulletin de la Société Française de Mineralogie*, 77, nos. 1-3 (1954), 13-22.

720. HUDSON, Kenneth. *A Social History of Museums. What the Visitors Thought*. London: Macmillan Press, 1975, pp. 210.

    Examines the museum in relation to the state, the market and education, and the expansion of public museums over the last two centuries. The first chapter surveys the growth of scientific museums in the nineteenth century, Chapter 3 touches upon natural history and geological museums as instruments of education.

721. INGERSON, E. "The Geochemical Society." *Geotimes*, 6 (1962), 8-14.

722. JENSEN, M.L. "One Hundred and Fifty Years of Geology at Yale." *American Journal of Science*, 250 (1952), 625-635.

Teaching began at Yale in 1802; the department was formed much later.

723. JOHNS, R.K., ed. *History and Role of Government Geological Surveys in Australia*. Adelaide: South Australian Government Printer, 1876, pp. 111.

724. JONES, T.A. *Liverpool Geological Society (Established December 13th, 1859). A Retrospect of Thirty-five Years (1910-1944)*. Birkenhead: Woolman, for Liverpool Geological Society, 1944, pp. 13.

725. KOKEN, Ernst F. *Die Deutsche Geologische Gesellschaft in den Jahren 1848-1898 mit einem Lebensabriss von Ernst Beyrich*. Berlin: Starcke, 1901, pp. 69.

726. LAUDAN, Rachel. "Ideas and Organization in British Geology: A Case Study in Institutional History." *Isis*, 68 (1977), 527-538.

   Argues that it is a mistake to see the early nineteenth-century acceleration of geology in Britain as flowing largely from the foundation of the Geological Society of London in 1807: on the contrary, the Society itself had a sickly existence in its early years.

727. MACNAIR, Peter, and MORT, Frederick. *History of the Geological Society of Glasgow, 1858-1908 with Biographical Notices of Prominent Members*. Glasgow: Geological Society of Glasgow, 1908, pp. 304.

   A history organized partly by theme and partly through the biographies of leading members.

728. MANNING, T.G. *Government in Science: The U.S. Geological Survey, 1867-1894*. Lexington: University of Kentucky Press, 1967, pp. viii+257.

   Surveys the critical years during which federal aid to geology gradually came to supplement state subventions.

729. MARWICK, John. "Reminiscences of the New Zealand Geological Survey." *New Zealand Journal for Geology and Geophysics*, 14, no. 4: John Marwick 80th Birthday Issue (1971), 634-639.

730. MORRELL, J.B. "London Institutions and Lyell's Career: 1820-41." *The British Journal for the History of Science*, 9 (1976), 132-146.

Establishes that the career of a geologist such as Lyell in early Victorian England was intimately connected with newly formed scientific societies such as the Geological Society of London, while noting that Lyell feared that holding office in and performing other duties for such societies would cut into time for research and writing.

731. MURRAY, David. *Museums. Their History and Their Use. With a Bibliography and List of Museums of the United Kingdom.* 3 vols. History, vol. 1. Bibliography, vols. 2 and 3. Glasgow: Maclehose, 1904, pp. xiv+339; 363; 341.

Volume 1 is a history of museums from earliest times, with some discussion of the emergence of specifically scientific museums. The second and third volumes constitute an important bibliography arranged by museum, including extensive listings of geological and natural history museums.

732. PANNEKOEK, A.J. "Geological Research at the Universities of the Netherlands 1877-1962." *Geologie en Mijnbouw*, Jg. 41, no. 4: *50 Jaar K.N.G.M.G. Jubileum-Uitgave* (1962), 161-174.

Discusses the development of institutions and the establishment of specialties such as petrology, and describes leading figures such as K. Martin, C.E.A. Wichmann, G.A.F. Molengraaff and B.G. Ercher.

733. PFEIFFER, H. "Hallesche Dissertationen des frühen 18. Jahrhunderts zur Geologie." *Zeitschrift für geologische Wissenschaften*, 8 (1980), 171-179.

Discusses medical geology at the University of Halle in the eighteenth century.

734. PORTER, Roy. "The Natural Sciences Tripos and the 'Cambridge School of Geology,' 1850-1914." *History of Universities*, 2 (1982), 193-216.

Although the growing role of the universities in the science of geology in England in the latter part of the nineteenth century did not in general lead to production of much new research, Cambridge was an exception. This was due to Cambridge's superior resources, and to the fact that Cambridge's Natural Science Tripos Exams were designed to produce an intellectual elite.

735. PRICE, Paul H. "The Early History of Geology in West Virginia." *Proceedings of the West Virginia Academy of Science*, 35 (1950), 111-113.

736. RABBITT, M.C. *Minerals, Lands and Geology for the Common Defence and General Welfare*. Vol. 1: *Before 1879*. Washington, D.C.: U.S. Geological Survey, 1979.

   The first volume of a comprehensive official history of the U.S. Geological Survey, emphasizing the powerful national interests involved in promoting surveys of natural resources.

737. REEKS, Margaret. *Register of the Associates and Old Students of the Royal School of Mines and History of the Royal School of Mines*. London: Royal School of Mines (Old Students') Association, 1920, pp. xii+237+ 212.

   Discusses the development of the school from the mid-nineteenth century and lists its pupils.

738. RITCHIE, James. "Natural History and the Emergence of Geology in the Scottish Universities." *Transactions of the Edinburgh Geological Society*, 15 (1952), 297-316.

   Shows there was extensive teaching of geology in Scottish Universities--e.g., by John Walker and Robert Jameson at Edinburgh--long before there were specific geological chairs. The chair of geology at Edinburgh was not founded until 1871.

739. RITCHIE, James. "Geology in the Universities of Aberdeen. Memorial to Professor T.C. Phemister." *Aberdeen University Review*, 35, no. 111 (1954), 358-367.

740. ROYAL GEOLOGICAL SOCIETY OF CORNWALL. "The Centenary Celebration." *Transactions of the Royal Geological Society of Cornwall*, 13, pt. 1 (1914), 1-30.

   Founded in 1814, the Royal Geological Society of Cornwall helped to pioneer interest in the more utilitarian aspects of the science.

741. RUDWICK, M.J.S. "The Foundation of the Geological Society of London." *The British Journal of the History of Science*, 1 (1963), 325-355.

Examines the series of personal, institutional and political events that contributed to the founding of the Geological Society, and emphasizes its Baconian program for the development of descriptive geology in Britain. For counterviews see items 726 and 753.

742. SCHARDT, H. "La Société géologique suisse." Pp. 272-275 in SOCIETE HELVETIQUE DES SCIENCES NATURELLES. *Centenaire de la Société Helvétique des Sciences Naturelles. Jahrhundertfeier der Schweizerischen Naturforschenden Gesellschaft. Notices historiques et documents reunis par la Commission Historique institutée à l'occasion de la Session Annuelle de Genève (12-15 Septembre 1915).* Nouveaux Mémoires de la Société Helvétique des Sciences Naturelles, Vol. 50, 1915, pp. 316.

743. SHROCK, Robert T. *Geology at M.I.T. 1865-1965: A History of the First Hundred Years of Geology at Massachusetts Institute of Technology. I. The Faculty and Supporting Staff.* Cambridge, Mass., and London: M.I.T. Press, 1977, pp. xxiv+1032.

This volume sketches the evolving institutional and teaching structure and gives biographical pictures of the first fifty-three professors of geology.

744. SIMPSON, Brian. *Department of Geology, University College, Swansea. The First Fifty Years.* Swansea: University of Wales, 1970, pp. 17.

745. SMITH, George O. "A Century of Government Geological Surveys." Pp. 193-216 in DANA, Edward S., et al. *A Century of Science in America, with Special Reference to the American Journal of Science.* New Haven, Conn.: Yale University Press; London: Oxford University Press, 1918, pp. xii+458.

746. SOCIETE GEOLOGIQUE DE FRANCE. *Centenaire de la Société Géologique de France. Séances et excursions Juin-Juillet 1930.* Paris: Société Géologique de France, 1931, pp. 1161-1341.

747. STIRRUP, Mark. "The Early History of the Manchester Geological Society, with Some Remarks on Speculative Geology." *Manchester Geological and Mineralogical Society Transactions*, 5, pt. 2 (1897), 39-67.

Institutional Histories

748. SWEETING, G.S. *The Geologists' Association 1858-1958: A History of the First Hundred Years*. Colchester: Benham, 1958, pp. x+165.

   A history of the British Society of amateur geologists, including useful appendices listing officials, presidential addresses, etc.

749. THURSTON, William. "The First International Geological Congress." *Geotimes*, 13 (1968), 16-17.

750. TOPLEY, W. "Report Upon the National Geological Surveys. Part I. Europe." *Report of the British Association for the Advancement of Science for 1884* (1885), 221-237.

   Comparative accounts, focusing particularly upon achievements in mapping.

751. WÄCHTLER, E. "Die Grundung der Bergakademie Freiberg im Jahre 1765." *Zeitschrift für geologische Wissenschaften*, 8 (1980), 73-78.

   Discusses the history of the oldest technical academy for mining and metallurgy, founded in 1767.

752. WATTS, William W. "Fifty Years' Work of the Mineralogical Society." *Mineralogical Magazine*, 21 (1926), 106-124.

   Includes discussion of predecessors to the Society, such as the British Mineralogical Society (1799-1806), and the foundation of the Mineralogical Society in 1876.

753. WEINDLING, P.J. "Geological Controversy and Its Historiography: The Pre-history of the Geological Society of London." Pp. 248-272 in JORDANOVA, L.J., and PORTER, Roy, eds. *Images of the Earth*. Chalfont St Giles, Bucks: The British Society for the History of Science, 1979, pp. xx+282.

   Argues that the role of the Geological Society of London in the development of geology in early nineteenth-century England has been overrated. The British Mineralogical Society and the circle of enthusiasts surrounding Sir Joseph Banks were committed both to research and to the practical application of knowledge about the Earth.

754. WILLIAMS, Patricia M. *Museums of Natural History and the People Who Work in Them*. New York: St. Martin's Press, 1973.

755. WINCHELL, Newton H. "Review of the Formation of Geological Societies in the United States." *Bulletin of the Geological Society of America*, 25 (1914), 27-30.

756. WITTLIN, Alma S. *The Museum. Its History and Its Tasks in Education*. London: Routledge & Kegan Paul, 1949, pp. xv+297.

    Contains a concise historical section.

757. WOODWARD, H.B. *The History of the Geological Society of London*. London: Longmans, 1908, pp. xx+336.

    A chronological account containing valuable lists of officers, publications, donations, etc.

758. ZASLOW, Morris. *Reading the Rocks: The Story of the Geological Survey of Canada, 1842-1972*. Toronto: Macmillan, 1975, pp. 599.

    A definitive history of the Survey since 1842, emphasizing the complex and often difficult relations between it and organs of government. Helpful appendices show the administrative structure of the Survey and list staff.

8. THE SOCIAL DIMENSION

759. ALLEN, D.E. *The Naturalist in Britain*. London: Allen Lane, 1976, pp. xii+292.

Shows the deep fascination of natural history as an amateur pastime in England over the last three centuries. Geological fieldwork became popular in the early nineteenth century partly because of the Romantic appeal of antiquity and of the new palaeontology. Amateurs made major contributions to the science.

760. ALLEN, D.E. "The Lost Limb: Geology and Natural History." Pp. 200-214 in JORDANOVA, L.J., and PORTER, Roy, eds. *Images of the Earth*. Chalfont St Giles, Bucks: The British Society for the History of Science, 1979, pp. xx+282.

Investigates why geology came to lose its pride of place within the natural history sciences among amateurs in England in the second half of the nineteenth century. Suggests that this happened largely because of the growing technicalness of the science.

761. ALLEN, D.E. "Naturalists in Britain: Some Tasks for the Historian." *Journal of the Society for the Bibliography of Natural History*, 8 (1977), 91-107.

Emphasizes the need to study the social networks within which the natural historical sciences were largely pursued in their amateur past.

762. ALLEN, D.E. "Natural History and Social History." *Journal of the Society for the Bibliography of Natural History*, 7 (1976), 509-516.

Stresses the role of "fashion" and other strictly "non-scientific" factors in stimulating geology and other natural history sciences during their amateur past.

763. LEY, H. "Aufklärung und Naturwissenschaft in Westeuropa." *Zeitschrift für geologische Wissenschaften*, 8 (1980), 25-35.

Shows that the greater extremism of the Enlightenment in France led to French theories of the Earth, emphasizing a longer time-scale and even the eternity of the Earth.

764. MATHÉ, G. "Beitrage französischer Naturforscher des 18. Jahrhunderts zur Entwicklung der Geologie." *Zeitschrift für geologische Wissenschaften*, 8 (1980), 37-52.

Relates eighteenth-century French geology to the Enlightenment in that country, pointing out geologists' relative lack of involvement in utilitarian projects.

765. O'CONNOR, Jean G., and MEADOWS, A.J. "Specialization and Professionalization in British Geology." *Social Studies of Science*, 6 (1976), 77-89.

Investigates the relations between the professionalization of geology in nineteenth-century England, the growing specialization societies and periodicals. Some twentieth-century tensions between amateurs and professionals are explored.

766. PORTER, Roy. "Zentrum und Peripherie; einige Muster in der Entwicklung der Geologie im Britannien des 18. Jahrhunderts." *INHIGEO Zusammenfassung. VIII. Symposium Munster und Bonn. 12-24 September 1978* (1978), 234-249.

Traces the dialectic between metropolis as a center of geological theory, debate and publishing, and periphery as the location of fieldwork.

767. PORTER, R. "Die Geologie Großbritanniens im Zeitalter der Aufklärung." *Zeitschrift für geologische Wissenschaften*, 8 (1980), 53-62.

Examining the writings of Hutton and Toulmin in particular, discusses how far Enlightenment liberal religion and atheism led to an enlargement of the geological time-scale.

768. PORTER, R. "Creation and Credence: The Career of Theories of the Earth in Britain 1660-1820." Pp. 97-124 in BARNES, B., and SHAPIN, S., eds. *Natural Order*. Beverly Hills: Sage, 1979, pp. 255.

Examines the political, social and religious ideologies which informed theories of the Earth in Britain, and discusses their relations to the subsequent development of geology.

769. PORTER, Roy. "Gentlemen and Geology: The Emergence of a Scientific Career." *Historical Journal*, 21 (1978), 809-836.

Suggests that the "professionalization model" is not very helpful for understanding the emergence of geology in England, since up to at least the 1830s the most competent geologists were gentlemen amateurs. Assesses the role of the Geological Survey and of universities in providing paid geological employment.

9. GEOLOGY AND RELIGION

770. ALLEN, D.C. "The Legend of Noah. Renaissance Rationalism in Art, Science and Letters." Illinois Studies in Language and Literature, 33. Urbana: University of Illinois Press, 1949, pp. vii+221.

    Examines the attempts of writers using the methods of philology and classical scholarship to find a physically consistent and satisfactory explanation of the Genesis story. The failure of these attempts encouraged later theorists of the Earth to postulate solutions based on examination of the globe.

771. BROOKE, John Hedley. "The Natural Theology of the Geologists: Some Theological Strata." Pp. 39-64 in JORDANOVA, L.J., and PORTER, Roy S., eds. *Images of the Earth: Essays in the History of the Environmental Sciences*. Chalfont St Giles, Bucks: British Society for the History of Science, 1979, pp. xx+282.

    Emphasizes the many distinct traditions of natural theology that underpinned nineteenth-century geology, some particularly stressing the continuity of natural law, others emphasizing God's adaptation of terraqueous conditions to Man's needs.

772. CANNON, W.F. "The Problem of Miracles in the 1830's." *Victorian Studies*, 4 (1960), 5-32.

    By examination of the Bridgewater Treatises of the 1830s, particularly Charles Babbage's unofficial volume, Cannon stresses that the real issue was not the reality of miracles, but the nature and definition of a miracle and the criteria for distinguishing miracles from uncommon events which nevertheless lay within the lawful course of Nature.

773. CANTOR, G.N. "Revelation and the Cyclical Cosmos of John Hutchinson." Pp. 3-22 in JORDANOVA, L.J., and PORTER, Roy S., eds. *Images of the Earth: Essays in the History of the Environmental Sciences*. Chalfont St Giles, Bucks: British Society for the History of Science, 1979, pp. xx+282.

Examines the theory of the Earth of the early eighteenth-century anti-Newtonian natural philosopher John Hutchinson, stressing his adherence to a quasi-Cartesian version of the mechanical philosophy and his attempt to expound a theory from the Bible, using a revised transliteration from Hebrew.

774. DEAN, D.R. "James Hutton on Religion and Geology: The Unpublished Preface to His *Theory of the Earth* (1788)." *Annals of Science*, 32 (1975), 187-193.

Prints in full Hutton's important preface, together with analyses of its content and history.

775. DRAPER, John W. *History of the Conflict Between Religion and Science*. London: H.S. King and Co., 1875, pp. xxix+713.

A classic statement of the view that the emergence of modern science has involved a heroic but eventually successful struggle against religious dogma and ecclesiastical obscurantism.

776. GILLISPIE, Charles C. *Genesis and Geology: A Study in the Relations of Scientific Thought, Natural Theology, and Social Opinion in Great Britain, 1790-1850*. New York: Evanston, Ill., and London: Harper and Row, 1959, pp. xiii+306.

Explores the many-sided relations between religious belief and geological thought in the first half of the nineteenth century, showing the deep natural theological underpinnings of most ideas of geological order, and claiming that adherence to a biblically inspired view of the Earth's short time-scale and divine intervention at the Flood impeded the development of geological science.

777. GUNTAU, M. "Physikotheologie und Aufklärung in ihren Beziehungen zur geologischen Erkenntnis im 18. Jahrhundert." *Zeitschrift für geologische Wissenschaften*, 8 (1980), 87-106.

Discusses how natural theological reasoning both helped and hindered the development of geological thought.

778. GURALNICK, Stanley M. "Geology and Religion Before Darwin: The Case of Edward Hitchcock, Theologian and Geologist (1793-1864)." *Isis*, 63 (1972), 529-543.

    Explores the complicated biblically based religious cosmogony of the man who saw himself as the high priest of American geology.

779. KENDRICK, T.D. *The Lisbon Earthquake*. London: Methuen, 1956, pp. 170.

    Examines religious and philosophical reaction to the Lisbon earthquake of 1755.

780. MILLHAUSER, M. "The Scriptural Geologists: An Episode in the History of Opinion." *Osiris*, 11 (1954), 65-86.

    Shows that though geologists in early nineteenth-century England who shaped their science to be in accord with the Bible produced theories which were much criticized and soon superseded, their historical conception of the successive development of life became part of the orthodoxy of palaeontology and historical geology.

781. RAPPAPORT, Rhoda. "Geology and Orthodoxy: The Case of Noah's Flood in Eighteenth-Century Thought." *The British Journal for the History of Science*, 11 (1978), 1-18.

    Many theories of the Earth advanced in eighteenth-century France argued the crucial role of deluges in shaping the landscape in fossil deposition and strata formation, etc. However, these were not necessarily importantly influenced by religious motives connected with the Noachian Deluge.

782. ROUSSEAU, G.S. "The London Earthquakes of 1750." *Cahiers d'Histoire Mondiale*, 11 (1969), 436-451.

    Discusses moral and religious reaction to the minor earthquakes which rocked London in 1750.

783. SHERWOOD, Morgan B. "Genesis, Evolution, and Geology in America Before Darwin: The Dana-Lewis Controversy, 1856-1857." Pp. 305-316 in SCHNEER, C.J., ed. *Toward a History of Geology*. Cambridge, Mass., and London: M.I.T. Press, 1969, pp. vi+469.

Examines the relationship between geology and religion in mid-nineteenth-century America, focusing on James Dwight Dana's opposition to evolutionism.

784. STOKES, Evelyn. "The Six Days and the Deluge; Some Ideas on Earth History in the Royal Society of London 1660-1775." *Earth Science Journal* (Waikato, New Zealand), 3, no. 1 (1969), 13-39.

   A survey of theories of the Earth in their relationship to Genesis.

785. WHITE, A.D. *A History of the Warfare of Science with Theology in Christendom.* 2 vols. New York: Appleton, 1896, pp. xxiii+415; xiii+474.

   An outdated and now largely disproven view postulating head-on conflict between religious dogmatism and geological science in the eighteenth and nineteenth centuries.

10. GEOLOGY, CULTURE AND THE ARTS

786. AUBIN, R.A. *Topographical Poetry in Eighteenth Century England*. New York: Modern Language Association of America, 1936, pp. 419.

    Discusses the handling of interest in and learning about the Earth, its age, origins, landforms, destiny, etc., in eighteenth-century English poetry.

787. AUBIN, R.A. "Grottoes, Geology and the Gothic Revival." *Studies in Philology*, 31 (1934), 408-416.

    Shows how fossil and shell collecting were associated in the eighteenth century with ideas of age, ruin, mystery and the ravages of time in graveyard poets and designers.

788. BRUSH, S. *The Temperature of History*. New York: Burt Franklin, 1978, pp. 210.

    Includes an attempt to view the clash between Uniformitarian geology and its opponents (Catastrophism, Evolutionism) in terms of a wider distinction between "classical" ("rational") and "Romantic" ("irrational") styles of science. Focuses particularly on Lyell and Lord Kelvin.

789. DEAN, D.R. "'Through Science to Despair': Geology and the Victorians." Pp. 111-136 in PARADIS, James, and POSTLEWAIT, Thomas, eds. *Victorian Science and Victorian Values: Literary Perspectives*. New York: Academy of Sciences, 1981, pp. xiii+362.

    Utilizing literary evidence, this interdisciplinary essay establishes that geology was a variously received but always powerful intellectual stimulus throughout the nineteenth century.

790. DEAN, Dennis R. "The Influence of Geology on American Literature and Thought." Pp. 289-303 in SCHNEER, C.J., ed. *Two Hundred Years of Geology in America. Proceedings of the New Hampshire Bicentennial Conference on the History of Geology.* Hanover, N.H.: University Press of New England, 1979, pp. xvi+385.

   A lively survey from the largely religiously oriented literature of the eighteenth century to the vision of the Earth in contemporary science fiction.

791. DUNCAN, E.H. "The Natural History of Metals and Minerals, in the Universe of Milton's *Paradise Lost.*" *Osiris*, 11 (1954), 386-421.

   Important discussion of Milton's learning about minerals and the Earth.

792. ELLWOOD, Parry C., III. "Acts of God, Acts of Man: Geological Ideas and the Imaginary Landscapes of Thomas Cole." Pp. 53-71 in SCHNEER, C.J., ed. *Two Hundred Years of Geology in America. Proceedings of the New Hampshire Bicentennial Conference on the History of Geology.* Hanover, N.H.: University Press of New England, 1979, pp. xvi+385.

   Discusses geological implications of the works of the American landscape painter.

793. JOHNSON, E.D.H. *The Poetry of Earth: A Collection of English Nature Writings.* London: Gollancz, 1966, pp. xxii+423.

   An anthology of Nature poetry.

794. JONES, W.P. *The Rhetoric of Science.* London: Routledge, Kegan Paul, 1966, pp. xi+243.

   Shows the scientific component in eighteenth-century poetry, and discusses the extent to which aesthetic and religious elements were part of scientific thinking about the Earth.

795. JONES, W.P. "The Vogue of Natural History in England, 1750-70." *Annals of Science*, 2 (1937), 345-352.

   Examines social and cultural reasons for the growing interest among the general public in exploring Nature and collecting fossils, botanical specimens, etc.

796. LAMONT, A. "Geology in Literature. A Series of 12 Articles." *Quarry Managers' Journal*, 27 (1944), 555-560, 597; 28 (1944), 28-31, 77-79, 121-127, 194-202; 28 (1945), 287-291, 365-369, 405-407, 439-441, 495-499, 551-554; 29 (1945), 160-163.

Illustrates, with many quotations, the impact of geological ideas on literature.

797. LOWENTHAL, D., and BOWDEN, M.J., eds. *Geographies of the Mind*. New York: Oxford University Press, 1976, pp. 263.

A collection of essays reflecting on the relations between the reality of landscape and subjective human responses to it.

798. LOWENTHAL, D. "Past Time, Present Place: Landscape and Memory." *The Geographical Review*, 65 (1975), 1-36.

Investigates how the geological and geographical features and resonances of particular landscapes cause them to take on particular human associations.

799. NICOLSON, M.H. *Mountain Gloom and Mountain Glory: The Development of the Aesthetics of the Infinite*. Ithaca, N.Y.: Cornell University Press, 1959.

Argues for the mutual influence of aesthetics and Earth science. Up to the end of the seventeenth century, naturalists thought the Earth was in decay. Later naturalists saw mountain scenery as sublime and beautiful, and the constructive role of mountains in the global economy came to be understood.

800. OGDEN, H.V.S. "Burnet's *Telluris Theoria Sacra* and Mountain Scenery." *ELH*, 14 (1947), 139-150.

Examines the possible role of Burnet's vision of the Earth as a ruin in introducing an aesthetics of the sublime.

801. PASSMORE, J.A. *Man's Responsibility for Nature*. London: Duckworth, 1974, pp. x+212.

A philosophical and historical discussion of man's perception of the relationship between himself and his physical environment.

802. PIGGOTT, Stuart. *Ruins in a Landscape. Essays in Antiquarianism*. Edinburgh: University Press, 1976, pp. 212.

Interesting connections between early geology, antiquarianism and the sense of time, space and place. Chiefly concerns seventeenth- and eighteenth-century England.

803. POINTON, M. "Geology and Landscape Painting in Nineteenth Century England." Pp. 84-118 in JORDANOVA, L.J., and PORTER, Roy, eds. *Images of the Earth*. Chalfont St Giles, Bucks: The British Society for the History of Science, 1979, pp. xx+282.

The two were closely connected, for--within the aesthetics of John Ruskin and others--landscape painters were themselves frequently expert in geological science and were sensitive to geological resonances in their paintings--e.g., the contrast between human transience and the relative permanence of landforms. Many geologists were accomplished amateur painters.

804. TUAN, Yi-fu. *Topophilia*. Englewood Cliffs, N.J.: Prentice-Hall, 1974, pp. viii+260.

Studies of the similarities of and differences between scientific religious, aesthetic and humanistic perceptions of landscape, with particular focus on such aspects as the sacred and the profane, origins and antiquity, and order and disorder.

805. TUAN, Yi-fu. *Space and Place: The Perspective of Experience*. London: Arnold, 1977, pp. 235.

Investigates the components of the human sense of geological location, particularly its parameters of breadth and depth, familiarity and unfamiliarity, homeland and desert. Many examples are taken from the history of geography and geology.

806. TUAN, Yi-fu. *Landscapes of Fear*. Oxford: Blackwell, 1980, pp. 262.

Examines man's fear of his natural environment at various levels: religious, philosophical, symbolic, artistic, psychological, paying attention in particular to the interpretation of myth.

807. TUVESON, E.L. "Swift and the World-Makers." *Journal of the History of Ideas*, 11 (1950), 54-74.

Swift mocked the pretensions of theorists of the Earth such as Burnet, Woodward and Whiston.

808. VITALIANO, Dorothy B. *Legends of the Earth: Their Geologic Origins*. Bloomington and London: Indiana University Press, 1973, pp. xiii+305.

An investigation of how far cosmic myths (e.g., the story of Atlantis) have origins in geological events.

INDEX
(Personal names are given in full capitals)

Abyss (Biblical)   35, 112
Actualism   79, 82, 85-89, 475, 493, 640, 680
ADAMS, A.   290
ADAMS, Frank D.   31, 75, 372, 470, 533
AGASSIZ, L.   1, 218, 219, 223, 284, 340, 413-415, 445, 670
AGNEW, Allen F.   696
AGUILLON, L.   697
AITCHESON, L.   305
ALBRITTON, Claude C., Jr.   2, 3, 76, 77, 184A, 256
ALBURY, W.R.   199
ALDRICH, Michele L.   698
ALEXANDER, Nancy S.   521
ALLAN, D.A.   699
ALLEN, D.C.   770
ALLEN, D.E.   759-762
ALLEN, R.C.   337
Alpine geology   104, 217, 225, 419, 431, 433, 473, 617, 638, 664
ALTENGARTEN, James S.   274
ANDREE, Karl   700
ANDREWS, H.   128
ANNING, M.   134, 416, 417
Antarctica, geology in   366
Archaeology   167
ARCHIAC, Adolphe d'   32
ARDUINO, G.   392, 418
ARGAND, E.   419
ARKELL, William J.   4
ARRHENIUS, S.A.   420
AUBIN, R.A.   786, 787
Australia, geology in   367-369
AZCONA, Juan M.L.   404

BABICZ, Jósef   658
BACK, William   702
BAGROW, L.   235

171

BAILEY, E.B.   33, 421, 536, 537, 573, 703
BALK, R.   448
BALMER, H.   445
BANKS, Sir J.   422, 652, 705, 710, 753
BARBER, C.T.   423
BARLOW, N.   460
BARNES, B.   768
BARNETT, S.A.   463, 466
BARRANDE, J.   424
BARRELL, Joseph   97, 425
BARRETT, W.   247
BARROIS, C.   426
BARTH, T.F.W.   485
BARTHOLOMEW, Michael J.   78, 160, 574
Basalt   176, 261, 475, 509
BASCOM, F.   98
BASSETT, Douglas A.   5, 312, 472
BASSETT, Michael G.   99
BAUMGÄRTEL, Hans   530
BECKINSALE, Robert P.   114, 115
BEDDOES, T.   427
BEER, Sir G. de   175, 408
Belgium, geology in   370, 371
BELL, R.   569
BENTZ, Alfred   248
BERG, Alexander   636, 695
BERGMAN, T.   428, 429
BERINGER, C.   34
BERINGER, J.B.A.   430
BERTRAND, J.   483
BERTRAND, M.   431
BERZELIUS, J.J.   200, 216, 432
BESTERMAN, T.   247
Biblical geology. *See* Religion and geology; Scriptural geology
BIELEFELDT, E.   497
BISWAS, Asit K.   112
BJERKNES, V.   95A
BLACKER, C.   35
BLAKE, John F.   129
BLUNT, Wilfred   567
BONNEY, T.G.   433
BONTA, Bruce D.   353
BOTTING, Douglas   531
BOUCHER DE PERTHES, J.   166, 170, 173
BOULTON, W.S.   558
BOURDIER, Franck   161
BOWDEN, M.J.   797

Index

BOWEN, N.L. 434
BOWLER, Peter J. 130, 451
BOYLAN, P.J. 166
BRANAGAN, David F. 367, 368
BRAUNS, R. 694
BRECK, Allen D. 272
BREMNER, A. 214
BRIDSON, Gavin 6, 7
Britain, geology in 24, 25, 79, 124, 128, 312-336
BROC, Numa 275
BROCCHI, G.B. 578
BROCK, W.H. 264
BROMEHEAD, C.E.N. 36
BRONGNIART, Adolphe 128
BRONGNIART, Alexandre 364, 435
BROOKE, John Hedley 771
BROWN, Alexander C. 401
BROWN, Bahngrell W. 249
BROWN, L.A. 236
BROWNE, C.A. 553
BROWNE, Janet 489A
BRUSH, Stephen G. 268, 788
BRYAN, K. 468A
BUCH, L. von 436-439, 606
BUCKLAND, W. 82, 124, 132, 135, 172, 218, 324, 330, 440, 488
BUFFON, G. LeClerc 184A, 290, 441, 552, 667
BULMAN, Oliver M.B. 131
BÜLOW, Karl von 79
BURCHFIELD, Joe D. 184B, 185
BURKE, John G. 200, 203B, 269, 306
BURKHARDT, Richard W. 162
BURNET, Thomas 62, 65, 125, 184A, 296, 800, 807
BURSTYN, Harold L. 281
BURTON, P. 704
BYNUM, W.F. 291

CAILLEUX, André 37, 237
CAMBRENSIS, G. 58
CAMPBELL SMITH, W. 201, 213, 705, 706
Canada, geology in 372-377
CANNON, W.F. 80-82, 772
CANTOR, G.N. 773
CARLID, Göte 428
CAROBBI, Guido 390
CAROZZI, Albert V. 176, 177, 226, 474, 556, 557, 561, 627, 629

CARRINGTON DA COSTA, J. 400
CARSWELL, J.P. 628
Cartography 58, 235-246, 330, 333. *See also* Mapping
Catastrophism 29, 71, 80, 82, 88-93, 234, 296, 453, 456, 483, 506, 788
CATCOTT, A. 324, 442
Central heat 265, 268, 269, 540, 543, 545
CERMENATI, Mario 391
CHALLINOR, John 113, 313-318, 320-322, 621, 675
CHALMERS-HUNT, J.M. 150, 202
CHAMBERLIN, Rollin T. 443
CHAMBERLIN, Thomas C. 338, 443
CHAMBERS, R. 88, 444
CHARPENTIER, J. de 223, 445
CHARPENTIER, J.F.W. 446
Chemical geology 264-267, 420, 533, 563, 615, 637, 721
China, geology in 378
CHITNIS, A. 707
CHORLEY, R.J. 114, 115
CLARK, John W. 642
CLARKE, E.D. 447
CLARKE, John M. 509
CLEEVELY, Ron J. 656
CLOOS, H. 448, 449
CLOUD, Preston E. 8
CLOUGH, Robert T. 601
COLBERT, Edwin H. 132
COLEMAN, Lawrence V. 708
COLEMAN, William 456, 678
COLLIER, Katherine B. 38
COLLINGE, Walter E. 618
Comparative anatomy 91, 136, 424, 435, 456-458, 612
Conchology 292, 568, 597, 656, 787
CONDE, José A. 379
CONRY, Y. 461
Continental Drift 33, 46, 125, 226-234, 480, 505, 676A, 676B. *See also* Plate tectonics
CONYBEARE, W.D. 92, 324, 330, 450, 651
COPE, E.D. 144, 145, 149, 451, 452
Coral reefs 459, 462, 465, 466, 673
CORDIER, P.L.A. 453
CORSI, Pietro 163
Cosmogony 32, 38, 43
Cosmology 14, 35, 51. *See also* Theory of the Earth
COTTA, B. von 101, 454
COX, Leonard R. 133, 646
CRADDOCK, Campbell 366

CRAIG, G.Y. 538
Creation 35, 43. See also Scriptural geology
Cretaceous system 32
CROLL, Dr. J. 455
CROOK, Thomas 100
CROSS, Whitman 101
Crystallography 204, 210, 305-311, 363, 519
CUBA, geology in 379
CUMMING, David A. 592
CURWEN, E.C. 595
CUVIER, G. 88, 136, 156, 161, 172, 290, 294, 415, 424, 435, 456-458, 670
CZARNIECKI, St. 396

DANA, Edward S. 97, 106, 145, 203A, 355, 745
DANA, J.D. 203, 350, 459, 783
DANCE, S. Peter 292
DANIEL, Glyn 167
DARWIN, Charles 43, 78, 136, 153, 160, 164, 169, 184B, 187, 290, 296, 402, 426, 444, 459-466, 590, 670
DARWIN, Erasmus 303, 467
DAUBREE, A. 478
DAUDIN, H. 293
DAVIES, Gordon L. 116-119, 215, 323, 413, 508, 526, 666, 667
DAVIS, W.M. 113, 114, 277, 468A, 499
DAVIS, William 502
DAVISON, Charles 178, 179
DAVY, H. 303, 468B, 469
DAWSON, Sir W. 470
DEACON, Margaret B. 282, 283
DEAN, Dennis R. 75, 83, 186, 539, 575, 774, 789, 790
DECHEN, H. von 435
DeGOLYER, Everette L. 250-252
De la BECHE, H.T. 134, 330, 331, 471, 472
DELAIR, Justin B. 134, 135
DELAUNAY, P. 64
De LUC, J.A. 123, 473
De MAILLET, B. 184A, 474
Denmark, geology in 380
Denudation 116, 118, 119, 328, 799
DERBY, Alice G. 339
DESCARTES, René 62, 65, 773
DESMAREST, N. 56, 475
DESMOND, Adrian J. 136
DEWALQUE, Gustave 370
DICKENSON, R.E. 276

DICKEY, Parke A. 253
Diluvial geology 32, 124. See also Flood (Noah's)
DOLOMIEU, D. 476, 477
DONOVAN, Arthur 265
DOTT, R.H., Jr. 120, 468, 469, 540
DOUGLAS, James 534
Dowsing 247, 262
DRAPER, John W. 775
DUFRENOY, O.-P.-A. 200, 478
DUNBAR, Carl O. 640
DUNCAN, E.H. 791
DUNHAM, K.C. 525
DUNN, Anthony J. 114, 115
DUPONT, Edouard 606
DUPREE, A. Hunter 506
DUSEK, Val 616
Du TOIT, A.L. 479, 480

Earthquakes 126, 175-183, 343, 526, 529, 600, 627, 779, 782
EATON, A. 349, 350, 481
Economic geology 44, 45, 247-263, 376, 384, 571. See also
   Mining; Practical geology
EDMONDS, J.M. 709
EDWARDS, Edward 710
EDWARDS, W.N. 137
EHRENBERG, C.G. 482
EICHER, Don L. 187
EISELEY, Loren C. 164
Elevation, craters of, theory 437. See also Volcanoes
ELIE de BEAUMONT, L. 483, 484
ELIOT SMITH, Sir Grafton 168
ELLENBERGER, F. 180, 382
ELLS, Robert W. 373
ELLWOOD, Parry C. 792
EMBREY, Peter G. 201
ENGELWALD, G.-R. 446
Enlightenment 26A, 44, 95B, 96, 121, 187, 275, 396, 580,
   763, 764, 767
Environment 42, 49, 121, 803-806
Erosion 500
ESKOLA, P. 485
'ESPINASSE, M. 527
Evolution 43, 68, 88, 90, 130, 136, 145, 160-165, 184B,
   185, 188, 192, 197, 295, 296, 302, 334, 414, 415, 424,
   433, 444, 451, 454, 456, 463, 467, 506, 549, 574, 609,
   612, 625, 783
Exploration 59, 142A, 342, 402

Index

Extinction 81, 129, 132, 136, 151, 291, 293, 457
EYLES, Joan M. 488, 647-649
EYLES, Victor A. 9, 16, 39, 238, 324, 510, 537, 541, 593, 659, 679, 690, 691

FAIRBRIDGE, R.W. 154
FAIRCHILD, H. Le Roy 340, 711
FALCONER, H. 166, 486
FAREY, J. 598
FAUJAS de SAINT FOND, Barthélémy 487
FEATHERSTONHAUGH, G.W. 488
FENNEMAN, Nevin M. 277
FENTON, Carroll L. 40
FENTON, Mildred A. 40
FERGUSON, Walter K. 341
Fieldwork 39, 116, 344, 442, 472, 507, 536, 759. See also Practical geology
Finland, geology in 381
FISCHER, P. 607
FISCHER, Walther 102, 385
FISHER, G.P. 644
FITTON, William H. 325, 651
FLEMING, J. 124
FLETT, John S. 326, 496, 665
Flood (Noah's) 35, 159, 220, 221, 440, 770, 776, 781. See also Diluvial geology
FORBES, E. 284, 288, 489A, 489B
FORBES, J.D. 222, 264
FORD, Trevor D. 675, 689
FORD, William E. 203A
FORSTER, J.R. 201, 490, 491
Fossil Footprints 335
Fossils 34, 78, 92, 128-159, 291, 292, 298, 300, 335, 336, 343, 416, 417, 424, 430, 435, 464, 510, 529, 535, 552, 564, 568, 596, 597, 599, 614, 621, 630-632, 641, 656, 657, 673, 687, 691, 787, 795. See also Palaeontology
FOTHERGILL, Brian 514
FOUCAULT, M. 199, 294
FOURIER, J. 269
FOX, Rev. F.C. 712
France, geology in 55, 79, 128, 163, 175, 180, 243, 382-384, 607, 697, 763, 764, 781
FRÄNGSMYR, Tore 216, 432
FRANKEL, Henry 227, 228
FREEMAN, R.B. 10
FREEMAN, T.W. 278
FRENZEL, D. 492

FRESHFIELD, Douglas   638
FREUND, Hugo   636, 695
FREYBURG, Bruno von   563
FRITZ, H.   95A
FÜCHSEL, G.C.   95B, 493
FULLER, J.G.C.M.   662
FÜLÖP, Jozef   713
FURON, Raymond   64, 138, 383

GARBOE, Axel   380
GARWOOD, E.   216
GEIKIE, Archibald   41, 327, 328, 462, 487, 489A, 489B, 494, 495, 598, 602, 626, 703
GEIKIE, J.   496
GEOFFROY ST. HILAIRE, E.   88, 161
Geography   59, 274-280, 806
Geological cycles   547, 548
Geological Magazine   699
Geological publishing   39
Geological societies   327, 644, 700, 706, 711, 712, 719, 721, 724-727, 730, 740-742, 746-748, 752, 753, 755, 757, 765
Geological surveys   622, 696, 698, 702, 703, 723, 728, 729, 736, 745, 750, 758, 769
Geology (term)   89
Geomagnetism   271, 273, 511
Geomorphology   112-127, 255, 280, 312, 323, 503, 524, 617
Geophysics   26B, 32, 45, 46, 104, 184B, 251, 268-273, 285, 344, 346, 410, 419, 434, 501, 520, 531, 676A
Geosynclines   68, 97, 120, 459, 518
GERHARD, C.A.   497
GERMANN, D.   181
Germany, geology in   9, 74, 79, 128, 181, 207, 254, 385-389
GERSDORF, A.T. von   498
GERSTNER, Patsy A.   139, 542, 543, 634, 635
GEVERS, T.W.   479
GILBERT, G.K.   277, 499-502, 622
GILLISPIE, Charles C.   27, 776
GILLMORE, C. Stewart   270
GILMAN, Daniel C.   459
GINSBURG, Robert N.   103
Glaciation   119, 214-215, 334, 340, 348, 359, 414, 432, 440, 443, 445, 460, 496, 503, 606, 617, 642, 646. *See also* Ice Ages
GLACKEN, C.J.   42
GLASS, H.B.   295
GOETHE, J.W.   503
GOETZMANN, William H.   342

Index 179

GOLDSMITH, O.   504
GOODALL, Vanne M.   171
GOODFIELD, June   197
GORDON, Mrs.   440
GORTANI, Michele   392
GOTHAN, Walther   140
GOULD, Stephen Jay   165, 296, 414
GRABAU, A.W.   505
Granite   107, 448, 525, 541. *See also* Igneous rocks; Metamorphism; Neptunism
GRANT, J.   191
GRANT, R.   544
GRAY, A.   506
GREENE, John C.   43, 203B
GREENHOUGH, G.B.   507
GREGORY, H.E.   425
GREGORY, Joseph T.   141
GREGORY, W.K.   609
GRIFFITH, R.   240, 508
GROTH, P.   203
GRUBER, H.E.   169
GRUBER, Jacob W.   170
GRUMBT, Eberhard   673
GUETTARD, J.-E.   56, 111, 180, 237, 243, 245
GUNTAU, Martin   44, 84-87, 205, 254, 263, 386, 387, 411, 437, 438, 680, 681, 715, 777
GUNTER, G.   286
GUNTHER, R.W.T.   528, 564, 630, 716
GURALNICK, Stanley M.   778
GÜTH, D.   181
GUTTING, G.   232

HABER, Francis C.   188
HAGEN, Victor W. von   402, 403
HALL, D.H.   45
HALL, Sir J.   328, 509
HALL, James   120, 510
HALLAM, A.   60, 229, 230
HALLEY, E.   282, 511-513
HAMILTON, Sir W.   183, 514, 515, 710
HANSEN, Bert   218
HARKER, A.   516
HARLAN, R.   139
HARRADON, H.D.   271
HARRELL, Richard A.   375
HARRINGTON, Bernard J.   570
HARRIS, A.W.   219

HARVEY, Anthony P.   6, 7
HAUG, E.   517, 518
HAUGHTON, S.H.   401, 480
HAUSEN, Hans   381
HAÜY, R.-J.   200, 306, 519
HAWKES, Leonard   46
HAZEN, Margaret H.   344
HAZEN, Robert M.   343, 344
HEDBERG, Hollis D.   429
HELLMAN, Geoffrey T.   717
HENDRICKSON, Walter B.   611, 718
HERDMAN, W.A.   284
HERITSCH, Franz   104
HERON-ALLEN, Edward   608
HERRIES DAVIES, G.L.   See DAVIES, Gordon L.
HERSCHEL, Sir J.   81, 94
HERSCHEL, W.   520
HESS, H.   228
HETTNER, Alfred   279
HIGHAM, Norman   653
HILL, R.T.   521
HIND, H.Y.   522
Historical geology   184A-199, 355, 529, 780
HITCHCOCK, E.   340, 778
HOARE, M.   490, 491
HOBBS, W.   523
HOCART, Raymond   719
HOENIGER, F.D.   298
HOENIGER, J.F.M.   298
HOFF, K.E. von   87, 95B, 524
HOFFMAN, Friedrich   47
HOGART, R.   719
HÖLDER, Helmut   48
HOLLAND, Sir Thomas H.   329
HOLMES, A.   227, 525
HOME, E.   134
HOOKE, R.   133, 177, 183, 184A, 282, 526-529, 659
HOOKYAAS, Reijer   77, 88-91, 206, 308
HOPKINS, W.   268
HOWARD, Robert V.   142A
HOWE, S.R.   142B
HUDSON, Kenneth   720
HUGHES, T. McKenny   642
Human geology   166-174, 486, 624
HUMBOLDT, A. von   49, 276, 402, 530-532, 678
Hungary, geology in   713
HUNT, T.S.   249, 258, 264, 533, 534

HUNTER, J.   535
HUTCHINSON, J.   773
HUTTON, James   27, 30, 38, 56, 77, 107, 111, 114, 118, 184A, 186, 187, 199, 215, 261, 265, 326, 328, 427, 469, 507, 510, 520, 536-548, 580, 619, 620, 666-669, 767, 774. *See also* Plutonism
HUXLEY, T.H.   90, 280, 549, 612
Hydrology   112, 123, 126, 556
HYMAN, R.   262

Ice Ages   119, 216, 218, 221, 420, 445, 455, 496
IDYLL, C.P.   285
Igneous rocks   32, 97, 107, 110, 176, 261, 421, 427, 435, 543
India, geology in   714
Industrial Revolution   45, 260
INGERSON, E.   721
Instruments   112
IRELAND, H.A.   239
Italy, geology in   390-393, 578
IVERSEN, A.N.   629

JABLONSKI, D.   154
JACKSON, J. Wilfred   568
JACOB, Charles   517
JAHN, Melvin E.   565, 566, 639, 692
JAMESON, R.   201, 550, 551, 671, 707, 738
Japan, geology in   394
JARDINE, Sir William   2
JAUBERT, Compe   453
JEFFERSON, T.   552
JEFFREY, F.   619
JENSEN, M.L.   722
JILLSON, Willard H.   345
JOHNS, R.K.   369, 723
JOHNSON, E.D.H.   793
JONES, F. Wood   535
JONES, T.A.   724
JONES, W.P.   794, 795
JORDAN, William M.   255
JORDANOVA, Ludmilla J.   11, 121, 166, 264, 544, 586, 753, 760, 771, 773, 803
JUBITZ, K.B.   613
JUDD, John W.   240, 654
JUKES, J.B.   323, 553
Jurassic system   32, 148
JUST, Theodor K.   143

KANT, I. 554
KEFERSTEIN, Christian 50
KELLY, Sister Suzanne 51
KENDRICK, T.D. 779
KING, C. 340, 555
KING, Cuchlaine A. 122
KING-HELE, Desmond G. 467
KIRWAN, R. 201, 323, 551
KITTS, David B. 231, 232
KNIGHT, D. 614
KOBELL, Franz von 207A
KOKEN, Ernst F. 725
KUNZ, George P. 519

LACROIX, Alfred 476
LADD, H.S. 286
LAMARCK, J.-B. 88, 162, 451, 556, 557, 580, 582
LAMONT, A. 796
Landforms. See Geomorphology
LANG, W.D. 416, 417
LANGWILL, C.R. 434
LANHAM, Url 144
LANKESTER, E.R. 631
LAPWORTH, C. 99, 558, 559
La ROCQUE, Aurele 12
LATROBE, B.H. 560
LAUDAN, Rachel 232, 545, 726
LAUNAY, Louis A.A. de 52, 435
LAURENT, G. 625
LAVOISIER, A.-L. 210, 243, 561, 562
LAWRENCE, Philip 272
LEAKEY, Louis S.B. 171
LEGGET, R.F. 256
LEHMANN, J.G. 95B, 563
LEIGHTON, Henry 241
LEMPER, E.-H. 498
LENOBLE, Robert 53
LEPENIES, W. 299
LERICHE, Maurice 371
LESLEY, J. Peter 346, 347
LEVENE, C.M. 596
LEVERE, Trevor H. 375
LEY, H. 763
LHWYD, E. 564-566, 630
Lias 134
LINDROTH, Sven 406, 672
LINNAEUS, C. 206, 406, 567, 652, 671, 672

Index

LINTNER, Stephen F.   560
LISTER, M.   242, 333, 568, 631
LOCKER, S.   482
LOEWE, M.   35
LOEWINSON-LESSING, F.Y.   105
LOGAN, W.   331, 377, 533, 569, 570
LOMONOSOV, M.   411, 412B, 571, 572
LOTZE, Franz   388
LOVEJOY, A.O.   291, 300
LOWENTHAL, D.   797, 798
LUBBOCK, Constance A.   520
LUCIUS, Michel   395
LUGEON, Maurice   409, 410, 419
LULL, Richard S.   145
LURIE, Edward   415
Luxembourg, geology in   395
LYELL, Charles   27, 30, 46, 54, 61, 67, 71, 76, 78, 80-82, 86, 87, 92-94, 153, 156, 160, 163, 193, 196, 197, 216, 218, 269, 290, 460, 462, 465, 472, 489, 573-591, 625, 684, 730, 788
LYELL, Katherine M.   576
LYON, John   172
LYTE, C.   422

MacCULLOCH, J.   240, 592, 593
MacDONALD, Jessie B.   657
MACGREGOR, A.G.   421, 537
MACKENZIE, William M.   599
MACLURE, William   245, 246, 349, 594
MACNAIR, Peter   727
MANNING, T.G.   728
MANTELL, G.   132, 135, 593
MANTEN, A.A.   266
Mapping   58, 235-246, 383, 426, 446, 471, 478, 483, 493, 508, 593, 594, 651, 674, 685
MARGERIE, Emmanuel de   55, 518
Marine geology   281-289
MARSH, O.C.   144, 145, 148, 149, 596
MARTIN, Edwin T.   552
MARTIN, Helen M.   337
MARVIN, Ursula B.   233
MARWICK, John   729
MATHÉ, Gerhard   439, 764
MATHER, Kirtley F.   13
McALLISTER, Ethel M.   481
McINTOSH, John S.   148
McCARTNEY, Paul J.   471, 577

MEADOWS, A.J. 765
MEISEL, Max 14
MENARD, William H. 287
MENDENHALL, W.C. 347, 500
MENDES da COSTA, E. 201, 597
MERRILL, George P. 348, 349
Metallography 305-311, 654
Metamorphism 97, 109, 421, 424, 425, 485, 516
Meteorology 123, 229, 455, 511, 579, 622
METZGER, H. 309
MEYER, H. 189
MEYER-ABICH, A. 532
MICHELL, J. 179, 598
Microscopic geology 68, 101, 118, 131, 311, 482, 528, 636, 653, 694
MIDDLETON, W.E. Knowles 123
MILLER, H. 599
MILLHAUSER, Milton 444, 780
MILLS, E.L. 288
MILNE, J. 179, 600
MILNE-EDWARDS, H. 289
Mineralogy 39, 74, 199-213, 238, 243, 300, 307, 343, 360, 363, 370, 385, 427, 447, 478, 519, 563, 636, 637, 644, 653, 654, 672, 679, 681, 687, 752
Mining 10, 44, 259, 418, 498, 521, 601, 682, 715, 719
Mining schools 39, 697, 715, 737, 751
MITCHELL, A.C. 273
MOLLAN, R.C. 508
MOLLER, R. 493
MOLYNEUX, Gary Anderson 274
MONNET, A.G. 243, 562, 601
MONTACNIER, Henry F. 638
MOORE, R. 56
MORELLO, Nicolette 57
MORNET, D. 301
MORRELL, J.B. 730
MORRIS, W. 115
MORT, Frederick 727
MORTON, S.G. 594
MORTON, W.L. 522
MOSEBACH, Rudolf 695
Mountain building. See Geophysics
MÜHLFRIEDEL, Wolfgang 681
MULTHAUF, Robert P. 207B
MURCHISON, Charles 468
MURCHISON, R.I. 78, 326, 579, 602-605, 642, 643, 703
MURRAY, David 731
MURRAY, John 282, 284

Natural history 4, 8, 28, 44, 133, 290-304, 357, 639, 671,
    738, 759, 760, 776, 795
Natural theology 42, 43, 630, 771, 777
Naturphilosophie 302
NEALE, E.R.W. 376
Nebular hypothesis 272, 443
NEEDHAM, Joseph 378
NELSON, Clifford R. 146
Neptunism 97, 107, 124, 437, 474, 477, 507, 658, 677, 688,
    688A
Netherlands, geology in 157
NEVE, Michael 442
NEWBIGGIN, Marion I. 496
New Zealand, geology in 704
NICOLSON, M.H. 799
NORDENSKIÖLD, Erik 302
NORDSTRÖM, Johan 428
NORTH, F.J. 58, 220, 242, 330, 331, 450, 633

OAKLEY, Kenneth P. 147
Oceanography 14, 33, 55, 112, 125, 236, 281-289, 354, 474
O'CONNOR, Jean G. 765
OGDEN, H.V.S. 800
OLDROYD, David R. 190, 199, 208-210, 495, 529
OMALIUS d'HALLOY 370, 606
ORBIGNY, A. d' 607, 608
ORCEL, Jean 64, 211-213
Ordovician system 99
Ore deposits 100, 454. See also Mining
Origin of species 81, 588. See also Creation
O'ROURKE, J.E. 546, 554
OSBORN, Henry F. 145, 452, 609, 610
OSPOVAT, Alexander M. 350, 351, 682-684
OSPOVAT, D. 578
OSTROM, John H. 148
OTTER, William 447
OUTRAM, D. 457
OWEN, D. 611
OWEN, Edgar W. 257, 258
OWEN, Richard 612

PAGE, Leroy E. 124, 579
Palaeobotany 128, 140, 143, 435, 461, 470
Palaeoecology 286
Palaeontology 48, 68, 74, 91, 128-159, 161, 163, 294, 377,
    407, 418, 451, 464, 482, 486, 527, 549, 607, 609, 610, 612,
    615, 660, 661, 670, 686, 759, 780

PALLAS, P.S.   412B, 613
PANNEKOEK, A.J.   732
PANTIN, C.F.A.   28
PARACELSUS   51
PARADIS, J.C.   549, 789
PARDO, José M.Y.   404
PARKINSON, J.   614, 615
PARKS, W.A.   377
PARRY, Albert   571
PARSONS, A.B.   259
PASSMORE, J.A.   801
PATTEN, Donald W.   221
PEIRCE, C.S.   616
PENCK, A.   276, 277, 617
PESCHEL, Oscar   59
PESTANA, Harold R.   352, 353, 394
Petrography   69, 98, 101, 213, 665, 695
Petroleum geology   249-253, 257, 258, 376, 423, 521
Petrology   69, 74, 97-111, 334, 433, 485, 516, 525, 653
PFEIFFER, H.   733
PHILLIPS, John   618, 650, 651, 709
Philosophy of geology   18, 19, 77, 81, 94, 95A, 547, 616
Physiography   112, 235, 277, 280, 500, 524
PIGGOTT, Stuart   802
PIRSSON, Louis V.   106
PITMAN, J.H.   504
PLATE, Robert   149
Plate tectonics   230, 287, 354, 676A. See also Continental Drift
PLAYFAIR, J.C.   215, 225, 328, 539, 619, 620
PLINY   36
PLOT, R.   133, 621, 631, 716
Plutonism   41, 97, 175, 261, 469, 475, 507
POINTON, M.   803
Poland, geology in   369-399
PORTER, Roy S.   11, 15-17, 60, 121, 166, 191, 260, 263, 264, 332, 442, 523, 544, 561, 580, 581, 586, 667-669, 693, 734, 753, 760, 766, 767-769, 771, 773, 803
Portugal, geology in   400
POSTLEWAIT, Thomas   789
POULTON, K.   16, 17
POWELL, J.W.   342, 500, 622, 623
Practical geology   39, 44, 247-263, 364, 469, 498, 764
PRESTWICH, G.   624
PREVOST, C.   625
PRICE, Paul H.   735
Progress   78, 92, 93, 130, 590

Prospecting   44, 252, 262, 336, 423
PROSSER, Mary W.   339
PRUVOST, P.   426
PYNE, S.J.   354, 501, 502

Quarrying   10
Quaternary geology   32, 381, 617

RABBITT, M.C.   736
Radioactive dating   184A, 188, 525
Rain   123
RAISTRICK, Arthur   333
RAMDOHR, Paul   636
RAMSAY, Andrew C.   61, 331, 626
RAPPAPORT, Rhoda   16, 18, 242, 562, 637, 781
RASPE, R.E.   176, 177, 627-629
RAUSCHENBERG, Roy A.   652
RAVEN, Charles E.   632
RAY, J.   65, 133, 564, 630-632
READ, Herbert Harold   107
REEKS, Margaret   737
REGNELL, G.   407
REICH, Otto   524
REINGOLD, Nathan   354
Religion and geology   38, 41, 54, 71, 89, 90, 93, 124, 160, 198, 433, 442, 469, 473, 495, 506, 513, 544, 599, 642, 659, 663, 669, 688, 767, 768, 770-785, 803, 804
RIOS, M.   405
RITCHIE, James   738, 739
RITTERBUSH, P.   303
Rivers. See Hydrology; Physiography
ROBERTS, G.   19
ROBINSON, T.   65, 633
RODELICO, F.   393
ROGER, J.   62, 441
ROGERS, H.D.   634, 635
ROGERS, J.   434
ROGERS, W.B.   634
ROLFE, W.D. Ian   150
ROLLER, D.   93
ROMER, A.S.   463
RONAN, Colin A.   511, 512
ROSENBUSCH, K.H.F.   101, 105, 695
ROSENBUSCH, P.   636
ROSLER, H.J.   350
ROSSI, P.   192
ROUELLE, G.F.   637

ROUSSEAU, G.S.   26A, 782
ROWLINSON, J.S.   222
Royal Geological Society of Cornwall   740
RUDEL, A.   384
RUDLER, F.W.   334
RUDWICK, Martin J.S.   92, 93, 151-154, 193, 223, 244, 464, 472, 507, 582-586, 641, 643A, 741
RUPKE, Nicolaas A.   234
RUSE, M.   94

SACHS, Julius von   304
SAINTE CLAIRE DEVILLE, Charles   484
SAMPELAVO, H.   405
SANTUCCI, A.   581
SARJEANT, W.A.S.   20, 135, 335
SARTON, George   63
SAUSSURE, H.B. de   638
SCHAFFER, S.   513
SCHARDT, H.   742
SCHERZ, Gustav   659-661
SCHEUCHZER, J.J.   639
Schist   109
SCHLEE, Susan B.   281
SCHMIDT, Peter   21, 182, 389
SCHNEER, Cecil J.   22, 39, 51, 66, 120, 124, 127, 141, 161, 193, 194, 200, 228, 237, 243, 255, 265, 281, 287, 310, 355, 358, 412B, 414, 429, 501, 530, 540, 560, 591, 616, 634, 639, 648, 698, 783, 790, 792
SCHOLL, D.W.   195
SCHRÖDER, W.   23, 95A
SCHUCHERT, Charles   356, 596, 640
SCHULZ, Werner   224
SCHWARZBACH, M.   676A
Scotland, geology in   328, 329, 592
Scriptural geology   54, 599, 688, 768, 770, 773, 776, 778, 780, 784
SCROPE, G.P.   641
Sea level   126, 460
SECORD, James A.   603
SEDGWICK, A.   326, 642, 643A, 643B
Sedimentary rocks   109, 563
Sedimentology   103, 109, 425, 431, 505
Seismology   45, 178, 181, 182, 600. See also Volcanoes
SENET, André   173
SEWARD, Albert C.   516
SEYLAZ, L.   225
SHAPIN, Steven   768

Index

SHARPE, T. 142B
SHEPPARD, T. 651
SHERWOOD, Morgan B. 783
SHROCK, Robert T. 743
SIEGFRIED, R. 468B, 469
SIGSBY, Robert J. 108
SILLIMAN, B. 203A, 203B, 350, 356, 644
Silurian system 603
SIMPSON, Brian 744
SIMPSON, George G. 142A, 155
SLANKER, Barbara O. 361
SLEEP, Mark C.W. 515
SLOANE, H. 645, 705, 710
SMITH, Cyril S. 261, 311, 655
SMITH, George O. 745
SMITH, W. 156, 184A, 325, 331, 333, 336, 618, 646-651, 662
SNIDER, A. 226
Société Géologique de France 746
Société Helvétique des Sciences Naturelles 742
SOLANDER, D. 652
SÖLCH, J. 617
SORBY, H.C. 311, 653-655
South Africa, geology in 401
South America, geology in 402-403, 607
SOWERBY, J. 656, 657
Spain, geology in 55, 404, 405
SPEAKMAN, Colin 643B
STANBURY, Peter 367
STAPLETON, Darwin H. 560
STASZIC, S. 658
STEARNS, R.P. 357
STEERE, W.G. 143
STEGNANO, Giuseppe 418
STELZNER, J. 181
STENO, N. 111, 659-661
STIRRUP, Mark 747
STOCK, J.E. 427
STODDART, D.R. 280, 465
STOKES, Evelyn 183, 784
STRACHEY, J. 111, 662
STRAHAN, Aubrey 600
Stratigraphy 39, 74, 97-111, 156, 195, 336, 428, 450, 493, 558, 571, 598, 602, 660, 662, 689, 691
STRAUS, W.L. 295
STRICKLAND, H.E. 2
Structural geology 97-111
STUBBLEFIELD, Sir James 155

SUESS, E. 63, 664
SUN, Y.C. 505
Surveying 256, 342. See also Mapping
Sweden, geology in 406, 407
SWEDENBORG, E. 663
SWEET, Jessie M. 550, 551, 645
SWEETING, G.S. 748
Switzerland, geology in 55, 408-410. See also Alpine geology

Taconic system 356
TARDI, P. 64
TASCH, Paul 196
TASNADI-KUBACSKA, Andras 713
TATON, R. 64
TAYLOR, E.G.R. 65, 125
TAYLOR, Kenneth L. 66, 475, 477
TEALL, J.J. Harris 105, 109, 665
Tectonics 104, 419, 421, 449, 483
TEICH, M. 174, 260
TELLINI, Achille 391
TEMKIN, O. 295
TERMIER, Pierre 431, 664
TERRELL, John U. 623
Tertiary geology 32
THACKRAY, J.C. 604, 605, 615
THAMS, J.C. 410
THEODORIDES, J. 289
Theory of the Earth 57, 62, 125, 474, 509, 539, 541, 542, 633, 663, 768, 773, 781, 784, 807
THOMAS, H.H. 67
THOMSON, W., Lord Kelvin 184B, 268, 269, 788
THURSTON, William 749
TIKHOMIROV, Vladimir V. 68, 412A, 412B, 572
TILLEY, Cecil E. 516
Time-scale 71, 162, 167, 184A-198, 457, 513, 525, 529, 535, 547, 556, 590, 641, 666-669, 763, 767, 776
TOKSVIG, S. 663
TOMKEIEFF, Sergei I. 4, 110, 111, 537, 547, 548
TOPLEY, W. 750
TORRENS, Hugh 142B, 336
TOULMIN, G.H. 666-669, 767
TOULMIN, Stephen 77, 197
TOWNLEY, K.A. 368, 369
Triassic system 32
TUAN, Yi-fu 126, 804-806
TUNBRIDGE, Paul A. 473
TUVESON, E.L. 198, 807

Index

TYNDALL, J. 222
TYRRELL, G.W. 537

Unconformity 111
Uniformitarianism 27, 29, 30, 41, 46, 49, 54, 68, 71, 76, 80, 81, 89-93, 114, 160, 185, 193, 216, 223, 269, 296, 462, 463, 469, 472, 475, 540, 574, 576, 580, 581, 587-589, 591, 606, 625, 627, 668
Uniformity of Nature 49, 76, 89, 92, 93, 111
United States of America, geology in 97, 103, 120, 128, 141, 144, 155, 237, 241, 245, 246, 258, 259, 337-365, 552, 622
URBAN, G. 492
USSR, geology in 128, 411-412B

Veins, mineral 387
VIENOT, John P. 458
VINOGRADOV, A.P. 267, 411
VISSER, R.P.W. 157
VITALLIANO, Dorothy B. 808
VOGELSANG, H. 69
VOGT, C. 670
VOGT, E.Z. 262
VOGT, William 670
Volcanoes 47, 126, 175-183, 193, 382, 384, 425, 433, 436, 487, 495, 514, 515, 526, 575, 606, 629, 640. See also Seismology
Vulcanism 47, 175, 176, 437, 475, 477, 514, 515

WÄCHTLER, E. 263, 751
WAGENBRETH, Otfried 70, 454, 685, 686
Wales, geology in 58, 242, 312, 321, 330
WALKER, John 420, 551, 671, 738
WALLERIUS, J.G. 672
WALTHER, J. 109, 673
WATERSTON, Charles D. 551
WATSON, W. 674
WATTS, William W. 432, 559
WATZNAUER, A. 95B
WEAVER, C.E. 158
WEBSTER, T. 675
WEGENER, A. 95A, 227, 229, 230, 233, 480, 505, 676A
WEGENER, Else 676B
WEGMAN, E. 127
WEINDLING, P.J. 753
WELLS, George A. 503
WELLS, J.W. 24, 245

WENDLAND, F. 613
WENDT, H. 159
WERNER, Abraham Gottlob 38, 54, 107, 190, 199, 205, 326, 350, 351, 387, 436, 481, 503, 507, 550, 551, 606, 678-688A. See also Neptunism
WHERRY, Edgar T. 519
WHEWELL, Rev. William 29, 30, 80, 94
WHITE, A.D. 785
WHITE, George W. 24, 25, 246, 358-362, 620
WHITE, I.C. 249
WHITE, James F. 26
WHITEHEAD, Peter J.P. 597
WHITEHURST, J. 689
WHITLOCK, Herbert P. 519
WIECHERT, E. 95A
WILKINS, Thurman 555
WILLIAMS, Patricia M. 754
WILLIS, Bailey 363
WILSON, George 449, 489B
WILSON, Leonard G. 71, 364, 587-591
WINCHELL, Newton H. 258, 365, 755
WISNIOWSKI, Tadeusz 397, 398
WITTLIN, Alma S. 756
WOJCIK, Zbigniew 399
WOLLGAST, S. 96
WOOD, D.N. 3
WOODWARD, Henry 424
WOODWARD, Horace B. 72, 757
WOODWARD, J. 201, 639, 690-694, 807

YONGE, C.M. 466
YOUNG, R. 174, 260
YOURGRAU, Wolfgang 272

ZASLOW, Morris 758
ZENZEN, Nils 672
ZIGNO, Achille de 73
ZIRKEL, F. 101, 105, 694, 695
ZITTEL, Karl A. 74

For Product Safety Concerns and Information please contact our EU representative GPSR@taylorandfrancis.com
Taylor & Francis Verlag GmbH, Kaufingerstraße 24, 80331 München, Germany

www.ingramcontent.com/pod-product-compliance
Lightning Source LLC
Chambersburg PA
CBHW052107300426

44116CB00010B/1564